The Early Violin and Viola: A Practical Guide

This practical guide is intended for all violinists and viola players who wish to give – or merely to understand and appreciate – historically aware performances of early music for their instruments. It comprises discussion of the literature, history and repertory of the violin and viola, the myriad relevant primary sources and their interpretation, and the various aspects of style and technique that combine to make up well-grounded, period performances. It also considers various related instruments, contains practical advice on the acquisition of appropriate instruments, and offers suggestions for further reading and investigation. Many of the principles outlined are put into practice in case studies of six works composed from about 1700 to 1900, the core period which forms this series' principal (though not exclusive) focus. Music by Corelli, Bach, Haydn, Beethoven, Mendelssohn and Brahms is examined with a view to recreating performances as faithful as possible to the composer's original intention.

ROBIN STOWELL is a Professor of Music at Cardiff University of Wales and a professional violinist who has written extensively on stringed instruments and the conventions of performing early music. He is author of *Violin Technique and Performance Practice in the Late Eighteenth and Early Nineteenth Centuries* (Cambridge, 1985) and *Beethoven: Violin Concerto* (Cambridge, 1988) in the series Cambridge Music Handbooks. He is also editor of *Performing Beethoven* (Cambridge, 1994), *The Cambridge Companion to the Violin* (Cambridge, 1992), *The Cambridge Companion to the Cello* (Cambridge, 1999) and co-author of *The Historical Performance of Music: An Introduction* (Cambridge, 1999).

Cambridge Handbooks to the Historical Performance of Music

GENERAL EDITORS: Colin Lawson and Robin Stowell

During the last three decades historical performance has become part of mainstream musical life. However, there is as yet no one source from which performers and students can find an overview of the significant issues or glean practical information pertinent to a particular instrument. This series of handbooks guides the modern performer towards the investigation and interpretation of evidence found both in early performance treatises and in the mainstream repertory. Books on individual instruments contain chapters on historical background, equipment, technique and musical style and are illustrated by case studies of significant works in the repertoire. An introductory book provides a more general survey of issues common to all areas of historical performance and will also inform a wide range of students and music lovers.

Published titles

COLIN LAWSON AND ROBIN STOWELL *The Historical Performance of Music: An Introduction*

COLIN LAWSON *The Early Clarinet: A Practical Guide*

JOHN HUMPHRIES *The Early Horn: A Practical Guide*

DAVID ROWLAND *Early Keyboard Instruments: A Practical Guide*

ROBIN STOWELL *The Early Violin and Viola: A Practical Guide*

Forthcoming

RACHEL BROWN *The Early Flute: A Practical Guide*

The Early Violin and Viola
A Practical Guide

ROBIN STOWELL
Professor of Music, Cardiff University

CAMBRIDGE
UNIVERSITY PRESS

PUBLISHED BY THE PRESS SYNDICATE OF THE UNIVERSITY OF CAMBRIDGE
The Pitt Building, Trumpington Street, Cambridge, United Kingdom

CAMBRIDGE UNIVERSITY PRESS
The Edinburgh Building, Cambridge CB2 2RU, UK
40 West 20th Street, New York, NY 10011-4211, USA
10 Stamford Road, Oakleigh, VIC 3166, Australia
Ruiz de Alarcón 13, 28014 Madrid, Spain
Dock House, The Waterfront, Cape Town 8001, South Africa

http://www.cambridge.org

© Robin Stowell 2001

First published 2001

Printed in the United Kingdom at the University Press, Cambridge

Typeface Adobe Minion 10.25/14 pt.   *System* QuarkXPress™   [SE]

A catalogue record for this book is available from the British Library

Library of Congress Cataloguing in Publication data

Stowell, Robin.
  The early violin and viola: a practical guide/Robin Stowell.
    p.   cm. (Cambridge handbooks to the historical performance of music)
  Includes bibliographical references (p. 213) and index.
  ISBN 0 521 62380 4 (hardback) – ISBN 0 521 62555 6 (paperback)
    1. Violin – Performance. 2. Viola – Performance. 3. Instrumental music –
  18th century – Interpretation (Phrasing, dynamics, etc.) 4. Instrumental
  music – 19th century – Interpretation (Phrasing, dynamics, etc.)
  5. Performance practice (Music) – 18th century. 6. Performance practice
  (Music) – 19th century. I. Title. II. Series.

  ML855.S79 2001
  787.2′143′09033 – dc21   00-065086

ISBN 0 521 62380 4 hardback
ISBN 0 521 62555 6 paperback

Contents

Illustrations

Acknowledgements for kind permission to reproduce illustrations are due
to the Ashmolean Museum, Oxford (Figs. 3.2 and 3.4) and America's
Shrine to Music Museum, University of South Dakota, Vermillion (Fig. 8.1)

Preface

This handbook is intended for all devotees of the violin and viola who are interested in historical performance, whether as period-instrument players or performers on modern instruments, as professional musicians, students or enthusiastic amateurs, as discerning concert-goers, or as avid listeners to recordings. It aims to survey and offer some solutions to the numerous problems posed by the performer's desire to recreate a performance as close and as faithful as possible to the composer's original conception. This desire is by no means of recent origin; Johann Mattheson, for example, wrote (1739):

> The greatest difficulty associated with the performance of someone else's work is probably the fact that keen discernment is necessary in order to understand the real sense and meaning of unfamiliar thoughts. For those who have never discovered how the composer himself wished to have the work performed will hardly be able to play it well. Indeed, he will often rob the thing of its true vigour and grace, so much so, in fact, that the composer, should he himself be among the listeners, would find it difficult to recognise his own work.[1]

This handbook thus aims to introduce readers to the principal issues that require comprehension and 'keen discernment' in contemplating historical performance on the violin and viola. It surveys the most significant source materials, examines the issues of performance practice, technique and style which combine to forge well-grounded period interpretations and demonstrates how these may be applied to six case studies from a cross-section of the repertory. Recommendations for further reading and investigation form an important part of the volume's purpose, and guidance is also offered on many other relevant aspects, ranging from details of organology and repertory to advice on the acquisition of appropriate instruments, bows and other accessories.

One particular desire is to encourage readers to give due consideration to the specific aspects that make period performance different; for this involves much more than merely employing original or reproduction instruments and bows and following rules defined in treatises. Geminiani exhorted 'the Performer, who is ambitious to inspire his Audience, to be first inspired himself; which he cannot fail to be if he chuses [sic] a Work of Genius, if he makes himself thoroughly acquainted with all its Beauties; and if while his Imagination is warm and glowing he pours the same exalted Spirit into his own Performance'.[2] Then, as now, performers were admired for what they as individuals brought to the music by giving 'life' to the notes through artistry, taste, intelligence and musical imagination and by understanding and applying the largely unwritten conventions through which musical communication was realised. While historical performance will always involve conjecture and inspiration and, above all, instinct and imagination, we can go some way towards achieving its goals through systematic experiment, research and educated guesswork based on artistic intuition and experience gained within parameters defined by historical study.

This practical guide is part of a series, of which the parent volume *The Historical Performance of Music: An Introduction* (Cambridge, 1999), co-authored by the present writer with Colin Lawson, has already explored the more general, large-scale musical and practical issues. In keeping with the historical scope of the series, the period *c*.1700–*c*.1900 has provided the main focus for the textual discussion and case studies. But the seventeenth-century violin and viola repertory will not be neglected, for this provided the seedbed for the development of playing techniques well into the nineteenth century.

A book of this nature perforce has benefited from the work and influence of many others, most of whom are acknowledged in the endnotes and select bibliography. Perhaps the predominant influence in my academic career has been the late Peter le Huray, who stimulated my interest in performance practice, while my practical experience in period performance has benefited from the inspiration of musicians such as Sigiswald Kuijken, Jaap Schröder, Christopher Hogwood and many colleagues in the Academy of Ancient Music. Various travel grants from the Department of Music, Cardiff University facilitated my research, but I am also indebted to Clive Brown, Adrian Eales and Nicholas Maxted Jones for the loan of various source materials in their possession and to the staff of numerous libraries, especially Mrs. Gill Jones and her staff at Cardiff University Music Library, for their generous and ever-willing assistance. I am grateful, too, to Ian Cheverton and Howard Cheetham, who dealt respectively with the reproduction of the musical examples and photographic illustrations, and to Colin Lawson, who read the text at various stages and offered many valuable suggestions. Finally, I owe debts of gratitude to my knowledgeable copy editor, to my wife Jane, for her tireless support and encouragement over many years, and to Penny Souster and her staff at Cambridge University Press for their patience and expertise in piloting this book into print.

Pitch registers are indicated as follows:

middle C just below the treble stave appears as c^1, with each successive octave higher indicated as c^2, c^3, c^4 etc. and the octave below as c.

Fingerings are indicated in the usual manner, with o denoting an open string, 1 the index finger, 2 the middle finger and so on.

Reference is made to individual movements and specific bars of cited works thus: i/23–6 indicates first movement, bars 23–6; iv/91 denotes fourth movement, bar 91. In cases where the movement under discussion is clearly evident, bar numbers are indicated b. or bb. as appropriate.

1   Historical performance in context

The seeds of growth

Historical performance in theory and practice has truly established itself as part of everyday musical life. Period instruments are routinely encountered in the concert hall and are virtually obligatory in substantial areas of the repertory. Throughout the world there has developed an immense interest in discovering the original expectations of composers in terms of sound and musical style and in acquiring appropriate instrumental techniques for their faithful realisation. This has involved not only finding and experimenting with relevant instruments and equipment, but also exploring earlier styles of performance through the examination of a wide range of primary source materials; for, as Roger Norrington has observed: 'a relationship with the past needs to be founded on truth as well as sympathy, concern as well as exploitation, information as well as guesswork'.[1]

This notion that works of the past should be stylishly interpreted with the musical means its composer had at his disposal has a fascinating history.[2] But it was not until the late nineteenth century that musicians began purposefully to contemplate using instruments and performing styles that were contemporary with and appropriate to Baroque or Classical music. The violinist Joseph Joachim directed a Bach festival at Eisenach in 1884, where Bach's B minor Mass was performed with some care taken towards the recreation of the composer's original instruments. Joachim and his associate, Andreas Moser, also signalled a conscious change in performing attitudes with some far-sighted advice in their *Violinschule* of 1905:

> In order to do justice to the piece which he is about to perform, the
> player must first acquaint himself with the conditions under which
> it originated. For a work by Bach or Tartini demands a different
> style of delivery from one by Mendelssohn or Spohr. The space of a
> century that divides the two first mentioned from the last two

1

means in the historical development of our art not only a great difference in regard to form, but even a greater with respect to musical expression.[3]

Such observations appear to have inspired the likes of Arnold Dolmetsch to set out his philosophy of historical performance in *The Interpretation of the Music of the XVII and XVIII Centuries* (London, 1915) and put it into practice at his centre in Haslemere for the study and recreation of the traditions of performance of early music.[4]

Dolmetsch's crusade was continued by, among others, the German scholars Robert Haas and Joachim-pupil Arnold Schering[5] and his own pupil Robert Donington. Donington's *The Interpretation of Early Music* and various complementary publications based on theoretical sources have become indispensable reference works, particularly for players of stringed instruments.[6] Much of Donington's most significant work involved the decoding and clarification of notational conventions and ambiguities within established musical, idiomatic and historical contexts. These conventions will always remain for us a foreign language, but such source studies have furnished us with the necessary grammar, vocabulary and knowledge to communicate freely and expressively within it as musicians.

Thurston Dart, Denis Stevens and others also gave early music a renewed impetus in Britain through their inspirational teaching, performances and scholarship, firing the likes of David Munrow and especially Christopher Hogwood to put theory into practice and challenge string players and other musicians to take up the cause of historical performance. Similar currents elsewhere in Europe encouraged a growing corpus of string players to experiment with period instruments: the Swiss cellist and gamba player August Wenzinger in Basle; members of the Leonhardt family, whose Leonhardt Consort (est. 1955) has been enormously influential, especially in the Netherlands; Nikolaus Harnoncourt and his Concentus Musicus (est. 1953) in Vienna; or violinist Franzjosef Maier's The Collegium Aureum (est. 1964), which pioneered the recording of the early Classical repertory on original instruments, some years before major British ensembles such as Hogwood's The Academy of Ancient Music or Norrington's London Classical Players.

Indeed, the espousal of period performance by record companies has provided the major commercial impetus to the early music movement from as long ago as the 1930s; but the explosion in the recording industry in the 1960s and 1970s, together with its inviting financial rewards, attracted an ever-increasing number of converts to historical performance. Decca's (L'oiseau-lyre) complete cycle of Mozart's symphonies by Hogwood, Jaap Schröder and the Academy of Ancient Music and prepared under the scholarly eye of Neal Zaslaw in the late 1970s and early 1980s proved a significant turning-point, after which performers and scholars began to work in harness on various performance projects. Both factions recognised the irrationality of Bach being played as if it were Beethoven, and Mozart as if it were Wagner, and the 'performance practice' movement began truly to blossom.

Public acceptance of period performance has not been won easily. Early standards of performance, particularly in the concert hall, were not beyond reproach and provided ready ammunition for the movement's detractors. Equally, the vast majority of twentieth-century listeners were not fully attuned to the aims and objectives of period performers and simply failed to understand the complexities of, for example, pitch, tuning, temperament and intonation. However, Hans Keller's assertion (1984) that 'most of the authentic boys just aren't good enough as players to make their way without musicological crutches'[7] has surely been disproved in the last decade, if not before, while market forces continue to negate violinist Pinchas Zukerman's well-publicised view that historical performance is 'asinine stuff . . . a complete and absolute farce . . . nobody wants to hear that stuff'.[8]

The violin and viola literature

The upper members of the modern violin family have been the subject of lively discussion in print for countless decades, whether in musical journals, dictionaries or individual books.[9] In addition to extravagantly illustrated 'coffee-table' volumes and museum catalogues on the work and products of various illustrious luthiers, there have been various attempts at placing the violin, its technique and its executants into some kind of historical perspective, notably by Dubourg (1836), Wasielewski (1869), Moser (1923), and Bonaventura (1925).[10] However, the major influential publications on period string performance have been penned in more recent times, by David Boyden, whose monumental *The History of*

Violin Playing from its Origins to 1761 (London, 1965) was the first book to deal with the history of violin playing against the vast panorama of the violin's evolution and repertory, and the present author, whose *Violin Technique and Performance Practice in the Late Eighteenth and Early Nineteenth Centuries* (Cambridge, 1985) takes Boyden's work as a starting-point for further investigation into the nineteenth century. As already noted, Robert Donington supplemented his invaluable research into early music interpretation with *String Playing in Baroque Music* (London, 1977), and Peter Holman has also weighed in with *Four and Twenty Fiddlers* (Oxford, 1993), an historical study of the violin at the English Court 1540–1690 which incorporates an updated account of the violin's origins.

Most significant books about the instrument since Boyden's study have devoted at least a chapter (or equivalent) to aspects of technique and histori-cal performance, notably Sheila Nelson's *The Violin and Viola* (London, 1972), Walter Kolneder's *Das Buch der Violine* (Zurich, 1972),[11] *The Book of the Violin* (Oxford, 1984), *The Cambridge Companion to the Violin* (Cambridge, 1992) and *The Violin Book* (London and San Francisco, 1998). The viola has not fared quite so well, Maurice W. Riley's interesting, yet incon-sistent *The History of the Viola* (2 vols., I, Ypsilanti, Michigan, 1980; II, Ann Arbor, Michigan, 1991) being the only study of note to be devoted exclusively to the instrument, but Yehudi Menuhin's book *Violin and Viola* (London, 1976; with William Primrose and Denis Stevens) includes valuable historical and other information for the general reader. Biographical and critical per-spectives on earlier performers are incorporated in many of the above volumes as well as in Boris Schwarz's *Great Masters of the Violin* (London, 1984), Margaret Campbell's *The Great Violinists* (London, 1980) and Henry Roth's *Violin Virtuosos from Paganini to the 21st Century* (Los Angeles, 1997).

Among books on performance issues there are a number of chapters devoted to string playing, notably those in *Performance Practice: Music after 1600*, edited by Howard Mayer Brown and Stanley Sadie (London, 1989), and in some of the volumes in the series entitled 'Cambridge Studies in Performance Practice'.[12] Meanwhile, Duncan Druce has contributed a stim-ulating essay on Classical violin playing and Robert Philip's detailed study of early recordings has important implications in our attempts to recreate the performing styles of the nineteenth and early twentieth centuries.[13] Clive Brown's *Classical and Romantic Performing Practice* (Oxford, 1999) looks further back in time, incorporating much material for string players to con-template, especially in respect of accentuation, articulation, bowing gener-ally, portamento and vibrato.

While *Grove's Dictionary of Music and Musicians*, its numerous editions and its various off-shoots have been mainstays amongst musical dictionaries for entries on string performance, countless journals have provided vehicles for the dissemination of research data and other information, ranging from 'historical' ones such as the *Allgemeine musikalische Zeitung* and *Allgemeine Wiener Musik-Zeitung* to more recent examples such as *Performance Practice Review*, the organologically slanted *Galpin Society Journal* and especially *Early Music*. The latter has continued to be an important forum for practical concerns of a wide readership – scholars, players, instrument-makers, CD collectors and concert-goers – since its first issue in 1973, with significant contributions on string playing from, among others, Clive Brown, David Boyden, Roger Hickman, Robert Philip, Robin Stowell and Peter Walls.[14]

Period violinists and violists

Thanks largely to the nature and function of the instrument, few period viola players have achieved particular prominence in the early music movement. Among the many violinists who have devoted their energies to historically aware performance is the Israeli violinist of Romanian birth Sergiu Luca, who benefited from collaboration with the American scholar and violin historian David Boyden. Sonya Monosoff has also carved a niche in the field, but not exclusively, and Austrian Eduard Melkus has gained a formidable reputation as a soloist and as founder of the Vienna Capella Academica (est. 1965), even if his style and technique occasionally espoused elements that are, strictly speaking, unauthentic. Alice Harnoncourt, Marie Leonhardt, Jaap Schröder, Reinhard Goebel and Sigiswald Kuijken have also advanced the cause of historical performance; Goebel's Musica Antiqua Köln and Kuijken's La Petite Bande have each amassed a wide-ranging reper-tory and discography, while a newer generation of violinists sparked by the recording and broadcasting opportunities of the 1970s and 1980s includes Catherine Mackintosh, Monica Huggett, Priscilla Palmer, John Holloway, Simon Standage, Micaela Comberti, Pavlo Beznosiuk, Elizabeth Wallfisch, Ingrid Seifert and Alison Bury.

Andrew Manze, Lucy van Dael, Fabio Biondi, Maya Homburger, Rachel Podger and Benjamin Hudson have come to prominence in more recent times, and many more violinists who have benefited from specialist study of historical performance at various progressive conservatoires and universities world-wide are waiting eagerly in the wings. Even established soloists on the 'modern' violin such as Christian Tetzlaff and Thomas Zehetmair have been attracted by the challenges of Baroque violin playing and, into the new millennium, the Siberian virtuoso Maxim Vengerov has succumbed to his 'fascination with the past' and 'the lure of gut', demonstrating a far more liberal and intellectual attitude to performance than many of his predecessors. He confesses, 'the Baroque violin has changed me, not only my technique. It changed my mind about how to play Mozart, and Beethoven, and everything!'[15] Thus, an understanding of historical performance issues can be extremely influential in practice, whether or not the player opts to play on a period instrument.

Interpreting the evidence

Much of the philosophy and most of the aims of historical performance have already been aired in this handbook's parent volume as well as in a wide variety of books and journals on music and aesthetics.[16] Meanwhile, period performers have continued their attempts to fulfil their goal of investigating, discovering and experimenting with the (sometimes unwritten) conventions, styles and techniques of the past, gleaned from a variety of instruction books and other primary sources, and applying them as appropriate in performance on original instruments (or faithful reproductions) relevant to the historical context in which the music was conceived. In the course of such a performing regime they will be required to make decisions. Some may be based on musicological revelations gleaned from others and some founded on informed conjecture, taste and musicianship about the imprecisions of the score; but all should be made to fall naturally within the technical and stylistic parameters established by their historical investigations.

Many general issues addressed in the parent volume have relevance to performance on the early violin and viola to a greater or lesser degree. Details about primary sources, including instruments and treatises specific to the violin and viola, will be elaborated upon in the following chapters; however, period performers should also consult treatises for other instruments such as the flute or keyboards in order to develop a general historical perspective, taking in national idioms and the various different approaches to matters such as rhythm, specific ornamentation, extempore embellishment and improvisation. Other areas for serious study include articulation, melodic inflection, accentuation, tempo, expression and various aspects generally unidentified in musical notation, notably issues of pitch and temperament, the constitution and placement of ensembles and matters of direction. Such study is vital to the process of forging well-grounded historical performances, but period performers should be warned that historical evidence is often ambiguous and may raise more questions rather than provide answers.

Standards of verity

As the 'early music movement' has developed from a radical fringe activity into a major part of international musical life, its original pioneering spirit has all too easily been eclipsed by requirements that are decidedly unhistorical, such as the high standards of technical proficiency demanded by the microphone. The search to rediscover the sounds and styles of nineteenth-century music can too easily conflict with the exigencies of the recording studio and the need to produce a neat and tidy, easily assimilable product. No one will dispute the importance of mastering an instrument, but that mastery must always be combined with a continuing stylistic awareness. However, increasingly burdensome commercial pressures have often resulted in retrograde steps in terms of compromise with instruments, technique and even taste, and some players have regrettably taken as their primary sources the well-read musical directors with whom they collaborate rather than Leopold Mozart, Spohr or Baillot. Such second- or third-hand interpretations may grossly misrepresent the music, at the same time putting at risk the standards of verity practised by succeeding generations of musicians.

Such standards are also pertinent to organological considerations. As the period before 1800 witnessed arguably the most significant developments in the history of both the violin and the viola (save perhaps for the development of the Tertis model viola in the twentieth century), there are inevitably limits to the accuracy of our knowledge of the types of instruments, bows and accessories used in certain parts of the globe at any given time. Our efforts to seek the truth may therefore only be approximate, and there are bound to be compromises, some inevitably involving improvements on the past (for example, in the modern methods of making gut strings).

However, while reviving the past and aiming for historical fidelity, performers should be cautious about making improvements that might run counter to their objectives. In this regard, the relation of reproductions to original instruments and bows remains a contentious issue. Some modern makers have certainly been guilty of beefing up their reproduction instruments to make their sound more acceptable to twentieth-century ears, while weights of bows and some of their playing characteristics are regrettably also known to have been attuned to the tastes of players in modern symphony orchestras who dabble in period performance. Nevertheless, the role of stringed instruments has been crucial to the development of the historical performance movement, since such instruments constitute the life-blood of much Baroque and Classical chamber, orchestral and choral music; and the work of scholars and luthiers has provided the impetus, sources, information and essential tools for string players to experiment with and refine.

The value of historical performance

The pros and cons of historical performance have been well rehearsed and argued.[17] There have been many objections to an openly historicist view of performing; but the value of historical performance lies in the effort to reconstitute the sound of the particular period, just as the value of history lies in trying to understand the events of a particular time. Even if an informed approximation of historical performance practice is the result, this must surely always be better than reducing music from all periods to a standard style and instrumentation, as was happening from about the 1960s. In the early 1980s, Hans Keller believed that the very art of performance was being endangered by standardisation of technique, and he warned: 'What has been an art is turning into a craft.'[18] Modern players sporting a continuous vibrato consistently ignore the small and diverse articulations so important in the performance of Baroque and Classical music; as Joseph Szigeti admitted in 1964: '[we produce] a big and somewhat undifferentiated tone;

we neglect many bowing subtleties . . . we articulate with less character than even a few decades ago'.[19]

Much work needs to be done on the interface between scholarship and practice in the field to sustain the development of historical performance. With the intervention of commercial pressures, performers have failed fully to realise in sound the radical implications of recent research into texts and early recordings, even though many appreciate the conflict between their knowledge and understanding of historical performance issues and their practical realisation of them. Recorded performances from the earlier twentieth century give a vivid sense of being projected spontaneously as if to an audience, the precision and clarity of each note less important than the shape and progress of the music as a whole. Nowadays the balance has shifted significantly, so that powerful, accurate and clear performance of the music has become the first priority and the characterisation is assumed to take care of itself. If pre-war recordings resemble live performance, many of today's concerts show a palpable influence of the recording session, with clarity and control an overriding priority.[20]

Presentation of a convincing historical performance requires of its performers all manner of historical discernment (whether technical or musicological), imagination and artistry if they are to realise anything of the music's charm and power, such as they can sense them to have been at the time of composition. The study of notation, treatises, documents and history is important, but ultimately one can rarely be certain how the music sounded. Feeling, interpretation, personality and individual taste in performance play a vital role in bringing the music to life and are essential adjuncts to the use of early instruments; however, as Peter Williams has remarked, 'the *studies* part of performance practice studies are their highest purpose'.[21]

2   The repertory and principal sources

Introduction

The adoption of a core period (*c.*1700–*c.*1900) for this series of handbooks is intended both to offer optimum accessibility for its prospective readership and to cultivate some consistency of approach and expectation in the specialist case studies that form an integral part of each volume. Such temporal parameters could cause us to undervalue the achievements of numerous seventeenth-century composer-violinists, who did much to develop the violin idiom in a variety of genres, hence the sharper focus on their repertory below. Furthermore, although the six case studies appear to neglect this significant period of the instrument's emancipation and development, the first opus to be featured, Corelli's Op. 5, was probably composed some years earlier than its publication date (1 January 1700). As noted in Chapter 6, this set of sonatas belongs to the genre of accompanied duo with alternative keyboard continuo which became popular in the last quarter of the seventeenth century, and it effectively summarises and codifies the musical, idiomatic and technical achievements of violinist-composers of the period. It 'laid the foundation for his [Corelli's] fame as *the* violin master of the seventeenth century – a fame he does not deserve exclusively but must at least share with such masters as Fontana, Neri, Legrenzi, G. M. Bononcini, Stradella, P. Degli Antonii and Torelli'.[1]

The emancipation of the violin

At the beginning of the seventeenth century the violin was rapidly transformed from a provider of popular dance music into a vehicle for the most sophisticated artistic ends. This transformation was effected initially in Italy and coincided with the development of vocal monody, articulated, for example, in Caccini's *Le nuove musiche* (Florence, 1601/2), and an important tradition of virtuoso solo instrumental writing.[2] Solo parts for the

violin appeared in the canzonas and motets of composers such as Giovanni
Gabrieli and the instrument emerged in a striking solo sonata role (especially in the *Sonata per il Violino* no. 3) in Giovanni Cima's large collection of
largely sacred vocal works entitled *Concerti ecclesiastici* (1610). Claudio
Monteverdi also made a significant contribution to the progress of the violin
idiom, whether in *Orfeo*, his *Vespers* or in dramatic madrigals such as his *Il
Combattimento di Tancredi e Clorinda*.

Fired by Monteverdi's style, Dario Castello published the first book
devoted wholly to sonatas in 1621 (a second volume dates from 1629), and
his imaginative canzona-like works are stylised as 'Sonate concertate in stil
moderno', probably because they incorporate occasional flights of solo virtuosity. Giovanni Fontana, 'one of the most singular virtuosos the age has
seen',[3] directly contrasted canzona textures with the new freer vocal idiom in
his concerto-like sonatas, published posthumously in 1641, but Biagio
Marini did most to develop a violinistic idiom, first in his *Affetti musicali* Op.
1 (1617) and his Op. 3 (1620) and, most importantly, in his varied and
experimental string collection Op. 8 (1629). On its title page Marini refers to
'curiose et moderne inventione', doubtless signalling his use of scordatura,
extensive multiple stopping and the experimental nature of his celebrated
Sonata in ecco con tre violini and *Sonata per sonar con due corde*. Carlo
Farina's five books of varied pieces (1626–9) include numerous sonatas (in
Books I, IV and V) as well as (in Book II) his eccentric *Capriccio stravagante*;
the latter's vivid imitations of other musical instruments and animals
through col legno, pizzicato, multiple stopping and other effects proved to
be another innovative milestone.

With these initial forays as their inspiration, Italian violinist-composers
advanced the technical language of their instrument with remarkable haste
to prepare the ground for Corelli. Marco Uccellini exploited an extended
range in his six sonatas Op. 4 (1645) and most notably in his Op. 5 no. 8
(1649), and he utilised scordatura in his *Tromba sordina per sonare con un
violino* of Op. 5. Giovanni Pandolfi Mealli later published some extraordi-
narily extrovert *Sonate a violino solo* Opp. 3 and 4 (Innsbruck, 1660),[4] while
Giovanni Legrenzi in Venice and Maurizio Cazzati and his pupil Giovanni
Battista Vitali in Bologna further extended the idiomatic language of the
violin. Cazzati's numerous sonatas are not technically progressive, but Vitali
demonstrates his adventurousness particularly in two five-movement solo

sonatas in his *Artificii musicali* . . . Op. 13, and Pietro Degli Antonii intro-duces expressive vocal inflections to the violin line in his solo sonatas Op. 4 (1676) and Op. 5 (1686).

In France the violin took some time to free itself from its associations with dance and outdoor music. The establishment of the *Vingt-quatre Violons du Roi* in 1626 proved to be a significant turning-point in the social acceptance of the instrument, even though its solo potential essentially remained untapped for some years thereafter. The violin's progress in England was only slightly more fluid, the instrument becoming established as an alterna-tive to the treble viol in broken consorts; however, apart from some chal-lenging diminutions in consort music by William Lawes, musical and political circumstances suggest that there was no substantial body of violin music that exploited the violin in any way comparable to the advanced prac-tices of the Italian school. These were promoted in London by the likes of Nicola Matteis, who published four books of *Ayres for the Violin* in the 1680s and, according to John Evelyn, played 'like a consort of several instru-ments'.[5] Henry Purcell followed Matteis when he 'faithfully endeavoured a just imitation of the most fam'd Italian masters' in his sonatas of 1683 and the posthumous set of ten sonatas in four parts (1697).

Italian influence spread quickly to Germany, Nicolaus Bleyer's *Est-ce Mars* variations (*c.*1650) and Johann Kindermann's eccentric trio sonatas and use of scordatura being especially noteworthy. More important, though, was the work of Austrian Johann Heinrich Schmelzer, whose colourful Italianate *Sonatae unarum fidium* (1664) were the first solo violin sonatas to be pub-lished in Austro-Germany. Johann Jakob Walther and Johann Paul von Westhoff rapidly raised German violin playing to a technical level equal to the Italians, Walther's *Hortulus chelicus* (1688) incorporating a *Serenata* in which a solo violin and continuo are required to reproduce the sounds of a range of other instruments. In other pieces Walther imitated birdsong and, like Schmelzer, wrote a sonata based on the cuckoo's call, while his twelve *Scherzi da violino solo* (1676) heralded a new virtuoso tradition, a 'peak in the history of double-, triple- and quadruple-stops, for which the seventeenth-century Germans had shown such a liking'.[6] Westhoff also used programmatic devices in his sonatas, but he is better known for his *Suite* (1683) and his six unaccompanied *Partitas* (1696), which, like Pisendel's solo Sonata (?1716), were important precursors of Bach's solo Sonatas and Partitas BWV1001–1006.

One of the most outstanding violin virtuosi of the century was the Bohemian Heinrich von Biber, whose fame rests chiefly on his violin sonatas, many of which exploited 'artifices' such as canons in unison or with the voices following one another a quaver apart, scordatura and so on. His eight *Sonatae violino solo* (1681), freely and elaborately developed, demand considerable virtuosity in their execution, two of the eight involving scordatura. By contrast, fourteen of his sixteen Mystery (or Rosary) Sonatas (*c*.1676) require altered tunings, the selected tuning assisting the extra-musical inspiration of each work by providing for special tone-colouring and sonorous multiple stopping. The final unaccompanied Passacaglia, founded upon sixty-five repetitions of the descending tetrachord, is the outstanding work of its type before Bach's D minor Chaconne in BWV1004. All but one of Biber's seven brilliant partitas for two instruments and bass, *Harmonia artificiosa-ariosa*, require scordatura, which contributed much to enlarging the violin's polyphonic potential.

The mainstream solo violin repertory (*c*.1700–*c*.1900): a brief overview

The late Baroque

Corelli's Op. 5 sonatas raise the curtain on a new musical era for the violin, influencing the sonatas of successors such as Albinoni, Vivaldi, Geminiani, Somis, F. M. Veracini, Tartini and Locatelli. Veracini's first two sets of sonatas (1716; Op. 1, 1721) are dwarfed by his twelve *Sonate accademiche* Op. 2 (1744), while Tartini's output is dominated by his 'Didone abbandonata' and 'Devil's Trill' sonatas. Somis sowed the seeds of the Corelli school in France, influencing such leading figures as Leclair and Guillemain and amalgamating elements of the church and chamber sonatas into a new abstract genre.

Brossard observed (1703) that 'all the composers of Paris are nowadays possessed by a sort of passion to compose sonatas in the Italian manner'.[7] However, a synthesis of Italian and French elements was essentially achieved in the sonatas of Jean-Féry Rebel,[8] Jean-Baptiste Senaillé, Jean-Baptiste Anet and the Italian Ghignone (known as Jean-Pierre Guignon). More interesting musically are the sonatas of Louis-Gabriel Guillemain, while the true reconciliation of the French and Italian styles was effected by Jean-Marie Leclair in his four sonata collections (Opp. 1, 2, 5, 9, 1723–38).

Italian violinists played an especially significant role in London's musical life, with Geminiani and Giardini well to the fore. Few native English composers contributed to the violin repertory, but the works of Richard Jones and the 'solos' of his pupil Michael Festing are noteworthy, along with the Eight Solos (1740) of John Stanley and the five authenticated violin sonatas of German-born George Frideric Handel.[9]

Much of Telemann's music promoted music-making in the home, notably his solo fantasias (1735) and various sonata collections of which his *Sonate methodiche* Op. 13, complete with written-out elaborations of the first slow movements, are among the best. J. S. Bach's six sonatas for violin with obbligato keyboard BWV1014–19 triggered off the gradual demise of the sonata for violin and continuo, even though that genre is well represented in his *oeuvre* and was perpetuated well into the eighteenth century by Heinichen, Pisendel, J. G. Graun, Franz Benda and others. Their overall three-part texture is largely akin to that of the trio sonata, the violinist and the harpsichordist's right hand taking the two upper parts and the harpsichordist's left hand contributing the bass line.[10]

After somewhat modest beginnings with collections such as Albinoni's Op. 2 and Torelli's *Concerti musicali* Op. 6 (1698) and [12] *Concerti grossi* Op. 8, published posthumously in 1709, the concerto soon began to replace the sonata as the vehicle for advanced violin writing. Vivaldi was the predominant figure in its development, composing almost 230 works (including some for more than one solo instrument) which explore a virtuosity and expressiveness that were quite new. His earliest set of twelve concertos, *L'estro armonico* Op. 3, remained the most influential and celebrated in his lifetime, but the experimental *La stravaganza* Op. 4 (*c.*1712–13) and the six concertos of Op. 6 (1716–17) are noteworthy, and his Op. 8 concertos have since eclipsed them all due largely to the popularity of its programmatic first quartet of concertos, known as 'The Four Seasons'. The twelve concertos *La cetra* Op. 9 (1727) maintain his high standards, but his Opp. 11 and 12 collections are less successful. Vivaldi's leadership in the genre was being challenged by Pietro Locatelli, whose *L'arte del violino* Op. 3 incorporates as cadenzas twenty-four capriccios of high technical demand, and Tartini, whose 135 or so violin concertos combined virtuosity with formal clarity and elegance.

Vivaldi's influence quickly spread to Germany, J. S. Bach making keyboard arrangements of nine Vivaldi concertos, including five from *L'estro armonico*. Bach's two original solo concertos, in A minor and E major, and his Concerto for two violins in D minor closely follow Vivaldi's structural models even though their formal outlines are somewhat less stark.

Towards Classicism

The violin's importance as a solo chamber instrument initially declined during the Classical period, due to the vogue for the keyboard sonata with accompaniment; but it was preserved by such performer-composers as Gaviniès, Guénin, Paisible and Saint-Georges in France, Nardini, Pugnani and Boccherini in Italy, Giardini, J. C. Bach and Abel in England, Dittersdorf and Wagenseil in Vienna, and Mysliveček in Bohemia, before blossoming with the sonatas of Mozart and Beethoven, in which the 'accompanist' eventually attained parity with the accompanied. This is certainly the case in Mozart's nine fully mature sonatas composed in Salzburg and Vienna 1779–87 and in the last seven of Beethoven's works in the genre. Schubert was somewhat retrospective in composing three sonatas 'for piano with accompaniment of the violin' (D384–5 and 408), identified nowadays as 'Sonatinas', but his major work in the genre is his four-movement Duo in A (D574, 1817), while his Rondo brillant D895 and Fantasy in C D934 pose technical problems resulting from unidiomatic writing.

Although the violin was superseded by the piano as the dominant concerto instrument in the second half of the eighteenth century, Haydn, Viotti, Mozart and Beethoven contributed a strong spine of mainstream works, supported by the lesser concertos of composers such as Johann, Carl and Anton Stamitz, Michael Haydn, Lolli, Giornovichi and Woldemar. Haydn's three surviving concertos (in C, A and G; Hob.VIIa: 1, 3 and 4)[11] are relatively conservative works composed for the Esterházy court, while Mozart's five concertos (1773–5) testify to his experimentation and ripening craftsmanship, culminating in K.219 in A major with its 'alla Turca' finale. However, the concertos seem relatively lightweight when compared with his

Sinfonia Concertante for violin, viola and orchestra K.364/320d (1779), whose material is developed with symphonic rigour in the outer movements, to which the emotional Andante acts as a profound contrast. Of Viotti's twenty-nine violin concertos, the products of his London sojourn, including Brahms's favourite No. 22 in A minor, represent the summit of his achievement in the genre. His imaginative fusion of Italian, French and German concerto elements undoubtedly provided the main inspiration for French composers such as Rode, Baillot and Kreutzer, for Spohr's concertos and, most importantly, for Beethoven's Violin Concerto in D Op. 61 (1806).[12]

The Romantic era

The early development of the Romantic violin concerto was modelled on the work of Beethoven and the French violin school, but was fired with more virtuoso ideals, particularly the works of Spohr (15 concertos), de Bériot (10 concertos), Vieuxtemps (7 concertos), Ernst (1844) and Paganini (?6 concertos). The genre blossomed from about the mid-nineteenth century onwards in the hands of, amongst others, Mendelssohn (1838–44), Brahms (1878; Concerto for violin and cello, 1887), Max Bruch (Op. 26, 1868; Op. 44, 1878; Op. 58, 1891; *Schottische Fantasie* Op. 46, 1880), Tchaikovsky (1878), Dvořák (Op. 53, 1879–80), Saint-Saëns (Op. 20, 1859; Op. 58, 1879; Op. 61, 1880), Wieniawski (1853, 1862) and Lalo (Op. 20, 1872; Op. 21, 1873; Op. 29, 1889).

The mid-nineteenth century also witnessed the increasing popularity of various short concert works for violin with orchestra or piano. The majority were geared to virtuoso ends with sets of variations by, for example, Bériot, Vieuxtemps, Wieniawski, Ernst and Paganini as the most common fare.[13] Some adopted a more dignified approach by writing pieces of more musical substance, notably Berlioz (*Rêverie et caprice*), Smetana (*Z domoviny*), Dvořák (*Romance; Romantic Pieces*), Saint-Saëns (*Introduction et Rondo Capriccioso* Op. 28; *Havanaise* Op. 83), Tchaikovsky (*Sérénade mélancolique*; *Souvenir d'un lieu cher*) and Chausson (*Poème* Op. 25 (1896)). Salon and character pieces (romances, élégies), national dances and ephemeral arrangements of popular themes were also the rage amongst the concert-going public, especially those fantasies, potpourris or variation sets derived from opera.

The sonata for violin and piano suffered a patchy history post Beethoven, but nevertheless profited from notable contributions by Mendelssohn (Op. 4, 1825), Schumann (Opp. 105, 121; both 1851), Lalo (1853), Brahms (Op. 78, 1878–9; Op. 100, 1886; Op. 108, 1886–8), Strauss (Op. 18, 1887), Franck (1886), Fauré (Op. 13, 1876; Op. 108, 1917) and Saint-Saëns (Op. 75, 1885; Op. 102, 1896). Of a semi-nationalist sentiment were Grieg's three sonatas (Op. 8, 1865; Op. 13, 1867; Op. 45, 1887) and Dvořák's Op. 57 (1880); Dvořák's Sonatina Op. 100 (1894) is reflective of his sojourn in America.

The mainstream solo viola repertory to c.1900: a brief overview

Baroque solo repertory for the viola is sparse. Maurice Riley believes that the first pieces for the instrument were probably borrowed or adapted from works for viola da gamba, but he also mentions the existence of viola sonatas by Massamiliano Neri (1651) and Carlo Antonio Marino, and a Sonata for violin and viola by Nicholaus à Kempis.[14] Only Bach's Brandenburg Concertos Nos. 3 and 6, Telemann's two concertos (one for two violas) and works in the genre by Dömming, Gehra and J. G. Graun provide any challenging substance for the player. But the instrument played an important role in ensemble music throughout the seventeenth century, especially in France, Germany and Italy. Two violas were occasionally employed, catering for both alto and tenor registers, and many French five-part ensembles incorporated three viola parts. These ensemble parts largely filled out the prevalent harmony, but they sometimes had greater thematic significance, notably in Rosenmüller's *Sonate da camera* (1667) or Muffat's *Armonico tributo* (1701).

Two ripieno viola parts were typical in concerti grossi before Corelli, and the instrument gained an entrance into the concertino group by c.1730; but it had no place in the trio sonata other than in Germany, where Biber, Schmelzer and others recommended its use on the second violin line and Telemann composed seven *Scherzi melodichi* (1734) for violin, viola and continuo.[15]

The viola sonatas of Carl and Anton Stamitz, J. G. Graun, Janitsch, Dittersdorf, Vanhal, Hummel and Flackton achieved some popularity, while the instrument's Classical concertante repertory was drawn largely from

Mannheim (Carl and Anton Stamitz and Holzbauer), Berlin (Georg Benda, J. G. Graun and Zelter) and Vienna (Dittersdorf, Druschetzky, Hoffstetter, Hoffmeister, Vanhal and Wranitzky); but there were also notable contributions from composers such as Johannes Amon, Ignace Pleyel, Georg Schneider and Joseph Schubert, while the three concertos and concertino of Alessandro Rolla comprise the most important corpus of work during this period. However, as mentioned earlier, Mozart's *Sinfonie Concertante* K.364/320d stands as a colossus in the repertory, affording the violist (playing in scordatura) equal status with the violinist and making considerable technical and musical demands on both soloists.

Although the viola gained increased prominence in chamber music circles in the late-eighteenth and nineteenth centuries,[16] only Berlioz's 'symphony' *Harold en Italie* and, to a certain extent, Strauss's *Don Quixote* stand out as nineteenth-century concertante pieces involving the instrument in a solo capacity. Similarly, there are few remarkable sonatas of the period originally written for viola and piano;[17] even the two by Brahms (Op. 120, 1895) were composed initially for clarinet and piano.

Primary sources

Primary sources are the historical performer's raw material, the surviving evidence of, and hence the key to, past practices. Composers' autographs, sketches and drafts apart, they range from instrumental and theoretical treatises to surviving instruments, bows and accessories such as bridges, mutes and chin-rests; iconography, historical archives, references in literature, journals, newspaper reports and even letters, diaries, catalogues and advertisements are sometimes called into the equation, while early recordings have also proved an invaluable mine of information.[18] As observed in the Bach case study in Chapter 6, source materials may also extend to include aspects of other art forms such as dance, some steps possibly holding significant implications for musical tempo. The relevance and importance of each of these source-groups inevitably varies according to the repertory to be performed, its date and its geographical locality. It is the performer's task to amass and evaluate such evidence, to establish its common elements and differences, and to interpret it in keeping with its temporal and geographical relevance.

Temporal and regional differences in performance styles are reflected in the various instrumental treatises, some of them specific to the violin and viola and others of more general interest. Many of these publications are brief, of elementary nature and of comparatively little significance; however, the substantial and more advanced treatises discussed below offer the most direct access to fundamental technical instruction, interpretation and more general matters such as notation, music history, expression, taste and aesthetics. Invaluable as they are, they have numerous shortcomings. They are rarely comprehensive and often confirm the inability of words adequately to express aural sensations; their intended role is also often difficult to assess. Are they, for example, describing or prescribing contemporary practice? To whom are their principles being addressed? These are questions for which anwers should be sought before interpretations with any firm foundation can be forged.

Principal violin treatises

It was not until the end of the seventeenth century that instruction books devoted exclusively to violin technique were published, John Lenton's *The Gentleman's Diversion, or The Violin Explained* (London, 1693) being recognised as the first extant tutor specifically for the violin.[19] Like most of its immediate successors, it was intended for educated amateur musicians.[20] Its elementary content was no substitute for oral instruction by a teacher, on whom many depended in order to learn techniques 'which may be knowne but not described'.[21] Earlier in the century some treatises had begun to reflect both the liberation of instruments from their subordination to the voice and the improved social position of the violin itself by incorporating descriptions of contemporary instruments, sometimes with some basic technical information.[22] But these were publications addressed to musicians as a whole, dealing with a wide range of instruments, and were not specialist violin texts. Among the most significant of these 'multi-purpose' volumes were Praetorius's *Syntagma Musicum* (Wolfenbüttel, 1618–20), Mersenne's *Harmonie Universelle* (Paris, 1636–7), Zannetti's *Il scolaro di Gasparo Zannetti per imparar a suonare di violino, et altri stromenti* (Milan, 1645), Prinner's *Musicalisch Schlissel* (*c.*1670), Speer's *Gründ-richtiger kurtz leicht und nöthiger Unterricht der musicalischen Kunst* (Ulm, 1687) and Falck's *Idea* *boni Cantoris* (1688). John Playford's *A Brief Introduction to the Skill of Musick* demonstrates the increasing popularity of the violin in amateur circles, a complete section 'Playing on the Treble Violin' being added in a second revised edition (1658) published four years after the first.

The steady stream of unenterprising 'do-it-yourself' instruction books for the amateur continued well into the eighteenth century, whether in the form of instrumental compendia (e.g. Merck's *Compendium musicae instrumentalis chelicae*, 1695; Majer's *Museum Musicum*, 1732; Eisel's *Musicus Autodidaktos*, 1738; Tessarini's *Grammatica di musica*, 1741?) or tailored to specific instruments (e.g. *Nolens Volens or You shall learn to Play on the Violin whether you will or no*, 1695; *The Self-Instructor on the Violin, or the Art of Playing that Instrument*, 1695; the modest French tutors by Montéclair, Dupont and Corrette).[23] Plagiarism was rife – for example, Majer's treatise of 1732 includes a section drawn almost entirely from Falck's of 1688; and Prelleur's section on the violin in his *The Modern Musick-Master* (1730–1) was pirated from *Nolens Volens* (1695). Furthermore, much of the technical advice provided was extremely suspect; and few publications included much more than a guide book to the fingerboard and a few simple pieces for the student to master. Nevertheless, these works helped the violin rapidly to gain social respectability and appropriate most of the musical prerogatives of the viol.

Although still intended for use with a teacher, the first books to reflect more advanced 'professional' practice appeared from about the middle of the eighteenth century. London was again the pioneering publishing venue, but the first significant author was an Italian, Geminiani, who disseminated the technique and style of his mentor, Corelli, through his compositions, teaching, performance and violin treatise. His *The Art of Playing on the Violin* (London, 1751) provides a concise survey of technical principles and incorporates several examples and complete compositions for their mastery. Its influence was such that plagiarised versions continued to be published well into the nineteenth century,[24] and many treatises were based firmly on its principles.[25]

Curiously, four invaluable Italian sources concerning technique and performance practice essentially postdate the period of greatest Italian influence. Tartini's 'Letter' (1760) to his pupil Maddalena Lombardini is a significant document about selected technical issues, comprising a brief violin lesson in written form. His important treatise on ornaments, first printed posthumously in French as *Traité des agréments de la musique* (1771), was doubtless prepared for his violin pupils at the School of Nations in Padua. It may have been written soon after the School's foundation in 1728, but its manuscript was certainly in circulation by *c.*1750, as Leopold Mozart incorporated extracts from it into his *Versuch einer gründlichen Violinschule.*

Galeazzi's *Elementi teorico-pratici di musica* was published in two volumes (1791; 1796), each divided into two parts. The second part of the first volume provides a detailed, methodical survey of the main technical principles of violin playing and general performance practice, its sections on ornaments and expression constituting probably the most important source of information on improvisation published in Italy in the late eighteenth century. There are also detailed observations on orchestral playing, the duties of the concertmaster, solo playing and interesting insights into Galeazzi's own pedagogical approach. Campagnoli's *Metodo* (1797?),[26] strongly influenced by the theories of his teacher Nardini, appeared in many editions and was widely translated. Subdivided into five parts with an introduction devoted to general technical matters, the first four sections provide detailed systematic instruction regarding the application of the 250 progressive exercises incorporated in Part Five.

Quantz's *Versuch einer Anweisung die Flöte traversiere zu spielen* has been described as 'an omnibus of eighteenth-century information' and includes some invaluable instruction (mostly about bowing) directed principally at orchestral violinists. However, the most important and influential eighteenth-century German violin treatise was Leopold Mozart's *Versuch*, which achieved four German editions by 1800, as well as versions in Dutch (1766) and French (*c.*1770). Intended to lay 'the foundation of good style',[27] its parameters far exceed those of any previous publication, its 264 pages incorporating copious examples and constituting a detailed, systematic survey of violin playing. Although inspired by Leopold Mozart's work, other late-eighteenth-century German violin treatises were generally of a much simpler level, designed more for the instruction of orchestral violinists (*Ripienisten*) than soloists. The works of Kürzinger (1763), Petri (1767), Löhlein (1774), Reichardt (1776), Hiller (1792), Schweigl (1786 and 1795) and Fenkner (1803) thus offer a sound but somewhat limited technical foundation for their readership.

L'abbé *le fils*'s *Principes du violon* (1761) confirms the ascendancy of a French violin school in the second half of the eighteenth century. It amalgamates the old French dance tradition (as manifested in the various Menuets, Airs and Rondeaux and in the two suites of *Airs d'opéra*, which also include dances, in the form of advanced duets for two violins), the 'new' Italian sonata tradition (as represented by the numerous lessons 'in the manner of sonatas'), and a progressive attitude towards certain aspects of technique. Particularly remarkable is its instruction regarding the violin and bow holds, bow management, half position, extensions, ornamentation, double stopping and harmonics; its limited text is supplemented by numerous examples and complete compositions for the instrument.

Corrette's *L'art de se perfectionner dans le violon* (1782) and Cartier's *L'art du violon* (1798) are significant principally for their musical content. Cartier's treatise incorporates in its third part an anthology of some 154 compositions by seventeenth- and eighteenth-century French, German and Italian composers. The first two parts are of less value, the text of Part 1 comprising an amalgamation of extracts from the treatises of Geminiani, Leopold Mozart, Tarade and L'abbé *le fils*, but they confirm the advent of a more uniform approach to violin playing. Michel Woldemar's *Grande méthode* . . . (*c.*1800) is also extensively endowed with musical content, including an exhaustive study of scales, a large collection of study material, examples of cadenzas in various keys and suggestions as to varying degrees of ornamentation of a given melody.

The establishment of the Paris Conservatoire (1795) prompted a new development: the production of faculty-based treatises offering systematic courses of technical and interpretative instruction for aspiring professionals. Among the first was Baillot, Rode and Kreutzer's *Méthode de violon* (1803), which remained unchallenged as the standard French violin text for advanced performers for at least thirty years. Widely read and imitated – Fauré (*c.*1820) and Mazas (1830) include extracts verbatim in their own methods – it covers artistic, technical (though not exhaustively) and aesthetic matters (Part 2 deals exclusively with the philosophy of expression) as well as including study material. But Baillot's own *L'art du violon: nouvelle méthode* (1835), a conscious attempt to remedy the omissions of the *Méthode* initially adopted by the Paris Conservatoire, easily surpasses it in content and detail. Supported by numerous musical examples, studies and compositions, Part 1 is devoted to the mechanics of violin playing and deals with most technical and stylistic matters in unprecedented detail. Part 2 concentrates on expression and is essentially a reprint of the relevant section of the *Méthode* with a short introduction by Baillot.

Baillot's teachings had a profound influence on technical and musical development in an age in which virtuosity was openly encouraged. They were continued by his pupils Habeneck (*Méthode théorique et pratique de violon*, c.1835), Alard (*Ecole du violon*, 1844) and Dancla (*Méthode élémentaire et progressive du violon* Op. 52, Paris, 1855; *Ecole de mécanisme* Op. 74, c.1882), Habeneck's treatise acknowledging the French debt to Viotti by incorporating facsimiles of extracts from the Italian's unfinished elementary method. The Belgian school's debt to Viotti is evident in the contents of Bériot's (1858) and Léonard's (1877) instruction books, both committed to 'imitating the accents of the human voice' as opposed to cultivating virtuosity for its own sake.[28]

Such virtuosity is described by Guhr in his *Ueber Paganinis Kunst die Violine zu spielen* (1829), an informative account of Paganini's performing style. Intended not as a comprehensive violin method but 'merely as an appendix to such as already exist',[29] it focuses in particular on Paganini's tuning of the instrument, bow strokes, combination of left-hand pizzicato with bowing, use of harmonics in single and double stopping, *una corda* playing and the extraordinary *tours de force* for which he was renowned. By contrast, Spohr's conservative *Violinschule* (1832) is a more characteristic German product, restricted somewhat by the technical and stylistic limitations that the author himself imposed. Spohr objected to many of the effects employed by Paganini and other virtuosi, notably 'thrown' bowings, artificial harmonics and suchlike, preferring to cultivate a more 'Classical' on-the-string bowing technique and singing tone. Nevertheless, his principles were widely influential, many being quoted verbatim more than seventy years later by Joachim and Moser.

Spohr's pupil, David, who is also notable for his anthology of seventeenth- and eighteenth-century violin works *Die hohe Schule des Violinspiels* (1867–72), followed suit in his *Violinschule* (1864). The three-volume *Violinschule* (1902–5) published under the name of David's pupil, Joachim, appears to have been written largely by Joachim's pupil, Andreas Moser. Joachim's contribution apparently consisted only in making performing editions of several eighteenth- and nineteenth-century works. Otherwise, the treatise itself is notable for its concentration on matters of phrasing, dynamic expression and tuning (notably the so-called 'Syntonic Comma'). Among other notable Austro-German writers of violin treatises in the second half of the nineteenth century were Zimmermann (c.1842), Dont (1850), Kayser (1867), Courvoisier (1873 and 1878) and Schradieck (1875).

Principal viola treatises

Although several all-purpose instrumental instruction books were published in Germany in the late seventeenth and early eighteenth centuries, these offered scant advice regarding viola playing. The earliest treatises devoted specifically to the instrument appeared in France towards the end of the eighteenth century and were written by Michel Corrette (1773), Michel Woldemar (c.1800) and François Cupis (1803). Of comparatively little pedagogical value, they were superseded by the more substantial and slightly more sophisticated methods of Antonio Bartolomeo Bruni (*Méthode pour l'alto viola*; Paris, c.1820), Michel Gebauer (*Méthode d'alto*; Paris, c.1800) and Jacob Martinn (*Méthode d'alto*; Paris, c.1820), Bruni's incorporating a collection of significant études. Léon Firket's *Méthode pratique* (2 vols., Brussels, 1873) and Brähmig's *Praktische Bratschenschule* (Leipzig, c.1885) are arguably the most notable advanced late-nineteenth-century publications.

Overall, viola players have had a raw deal in respect of pedagogical materials and opportunities. Quantz, for example, bemoaned the eighteenth-century musical establishment's neglect of violists, and Berlioz was especially regretful of the lack of a viola faculty at the Paris Conservatoire, claiming that the instrument, 'although related to the violin, demands individual study and constant practice if it is to be played properly. The ruinous old tradition by which the viola part is entrusted to second- or third-rate violinists . . . is obsolete where modern music is concerned.'[30] Despite Berlioz's criticism, the omission was not rectified at the Paris Conservatoire until 1894. Furthermore, Klingenfeld's significantly titled *Viola School for Violin-players* (Leipzig, 1897) reflects, even at the end of the nineteenth century, both the predominance of the violin and the dearth of specialist viola players. Nevertheless, Berthold Tours and Hans Sitt were among those who published viola treatises purposefully designed for beginners.

Other treatises

Just as string players should acquaint themselves with philosophical treatises on other instruments by, among others, C. P. E. Bach, Türk and Tromlitz,[31] they should also be aware of the various treatises on theoretical musical issues, ranging from the writings of Praetorius, Mersenne, Zacconi, and Kircher to those of, amongst others, Mattheson (1739), Avison (1752), Adlung (1758), Mosel (1813) and Lussy (1874 and 1883). Although these treatises were prepared largely for academicians and tended to explain the rules and aesthetics of composition, to provide inventories or descriptions of existing (or at least of theoretically possible) instruments, or to discuss mathematical and somewhat idealised historical aspects of music, they nonetheless offer occasional clues regarding interpretative issues or other aspects of performance practice such as tuning or pitch. Lussy's two publications specifically treat rhythm, accentuation and musical expression.[32] Treatises on orchestration[33] and conducting[34] have also proved invaluable works of reference regarding the technique and potential of orchestral instruments, orchestral placement and other performance details.

Surviving instruments, bows and accessories

Information incorporated in instrumental and theoretical treatises must always be balanced against a much wider range of evidence, including experimentation with surviving instruments, bows and accessories. Such instruments provide the vital apparatus for 'laboratory' experiments in matters of technique, interpretation and style.

As will be explained in Chapter 3, most instruments made in the eighteenth century or before have undergone modification from their original condition, and few original pre-Tourte bows and other stringed-instrument accessories have survived the test of time, due either to their inherent frailty or perishability. Furthermore, violin collectors over the years have largely been less public-spirited and less concerned about their responsibility to the future than collectors of paintings and sculpture. Fortunately, though, the foresight of those who established private and public instrument collections, particularly in the late nineteenth century, has been invaluable to the progress and credibility of the historical performance movement.

One of the oldest institutional collections still prospering is that of the Gesellschaft der Musikfreunde in Vienna, whose 'Sammlung alter Musikinstrumente' originated in 1824. The acquisition of Louis Clapisson's collection by the Paris Conservatoire in 1864, the creation of the Brussels Conservatoire's museum from the private collections of François-Joseph Fétis, Victor-Charles Mahillon and others in the 1870s, and the Berlin Königliche Hochschule für Musik's procurement of Paul de Wit's first collection in 1888 was matched by private collectors such as Auguste Tolbecque in France, Carl Engel and Alfred Hipkins in Britain, and Morris Steinert in the USA. The enormous explosion in the number of specialist instrument collections established since these sparks of interest has enabled makers and players to witness at first hand the workmanship of the violin family's master craftsmen and facilitated the construction of faithful reproductions based on historical models.

Especially rich in stringed instrument treasures are private collections such as that of Mr and Mrs Laurence C. Witten II at Monroe Connecticut, USA, or Aristide Wirsta's collection of French bows at Bourg-La-Reine, France, and public collections such as The Hill Collection at the Ashmolean Museum, Oxford, England, The Ansley K. Salz Collection of String Instruments, University of California at Berkeley, and The Carel van Leeuwen Boomkamp Collection of Musical Instruments in the Gemeentemuseum in The Hague have brought excellence in the luthier's art to a wider public. The Shrine to Music Museum at The University of South Dakota, Vermillion, and The Smithsonian Institute in Washington are among many other institutions with collections of similar import, and it is gratifying to note that London's Royal Academy of Music and The Brussels Musical Instrument Musuem have negotiated new premises for displaying their ever-increasing numbers of exhibits. Photographs, descriptions, construction plans, measurements and other detailed information included in the catalogues of many of these collections have also proved immensely valuable in the dissemination of organological knowledge.[35]

The increased practice of collecting instruments has inevitably raised the controversy regarding the relative claims of preservation and investigation through use, and the potential benefits of restoration have had to be weighed continually against the possible destruction of original evidence. Most museums and institutions have taken the conservative option and preserved their instruments in stable conditions and in scientifically monitored environments, but some have attempted reconditioning and some private collectors, museums and conservatoires have taken the bolder step of allowing their instruments to be loaned to careful users. The instruments in the Smithsonian Institute, for example, are regularly played in performance by the Smithsonian Chamber Players.

Iconography

Iconographical sources have provided us with important information about performance issues, ranging from the history and construction of instruments to knowledge about composers' and performers' lives and the social and intellectual atmosphere in which they worked. Pictorial evidence from newspapers, treatises or other sources can furnish important detail about playing techniques and positions (the jacket illustration and Figs. 4.1 and 4.2 are good examples in respect of the various violin and bow holds), the numerous accessories that performers employed, the social context and conditions of their performances, or the particular groupings of instruments and their distribution. However, conclusions from such evidence may need to be corroborated from literary, archival or other sources, because pictures rarely inform us about such details of instrument construction as the materials used, the thickness of a stringed instrument's table or back, or the tension of a string.[36]

3   Equipment

The violin: origins and early history

The origins of the violin are difficult to determine. Theories connecting its evolution with instruments such as the *lira da braccio* have courted controversy.[1] Problems of terminology also blur our historical focus, as references to 'viole' could equally denote violins or viols. The first detailed description of the violin appears in Philibert Jambe de Fer's *Epitome musical* (Lyons, 1556),[2] but the instrument probably evolved in northern Italy over half a century earlier. Iconological evidence certainly suggests the existence of three-stringed, violin-like instruments in Italian frescoes of the late fifteenth century, some years or so before Gaudenzio Ferrari's famous example (1535) in the cupola of Santa Maria dei Miracoli at Saronno, which remains the earliest known illustration of the complete violin family.[3] However, the decisive step in the evolution of the violin proper was the creation (probably *c.*1505) of a consort of three sizes (soprano, alto or tenor, and bass) modelled on the viol consort, thus differentiating it from ancestors such as the *vielle* and the rebec (See Fig. 3.1). Convincing arguments have been advanced which link the spread of the 'consort principle' with that of polyphony into secular music.[4]

The violin was essentially a consort instrument until about 1600 and was used in northern Europe in consorts of four or five parts (1 or 2 violins, 2–3 violas and bass) for courtly dance music and occasionally for doubling vocal music. Evidence suggests that the violin and viola acquired their highest strings (e^2 and a^1 respectively) in the mid sixteenth century. Changes of musical style *c.*1600 and the more expressive, soloistic requirements of the time resulted in the violin's increased social esteem and artistic credibility; it began to be used in mixed or 'broken' consorts (with winds, keyboards and hand-plucked instruments) first in Italy and later in aristocratic households in England. Developments in Italy also involved the violin in contrapuntal

Fig. 3.1 Members of the violin family and related instruments as illustrated by Michael Praetorius in his *Sciagraphia* (Wolfenbüttel, 1620): 1 and 2. Small pochettes or kits, sounding an octave higher than the standard violin tuning; 3. Descant violin [violino piccolo] tuned a fourth higher than the standard violin tuning; 4. Regular descant [standard-size] violin; 5. Tenor violin; 6. A 5-string bass violin; 7. A tromba marina; 8. Psaltery.

music, and even in church music, notably in the four-part canzonas of Claudio Merulo and others and the polychoral Venetian church music of Giovanni Gabrieli. As noted in Chapter 2, Monteverdi's innovatory effects in *Il Combattimento di Tancredi e Clorinda* (1624) and the various experimental techniques in the violin's early solo repertory of sonatas for a variety of combinations by, for example, the Venetians Marini, Fontana, Castello and Legrenzi, the Bolognese Giovanni Battista Vitali, and south German and Austrian composers such as Schmelzer, Biber and Walther, further enhanced the instrument's profile in the seventeenth century.

The Renaissance violin consort proved a durable ensemble, remaining popular in England until the time of Henry Purcell, and it was essentially preserved into the eighteenth century in the practice of the French court orchestra and its German imitations. The English court violin consort reached orchestral proportions by 1612 – a total of between twenty-five and thirty is reported in 1618 – and its equivalent at the French court evidently totalled 22 in 1609, some seventeen years before its formal establishment as the *Vingt-quatre violons*. The repertory comprised essentially five-part dance music, but Jean-Baptiste Lully's use of woodwinds and trumpets with strings in his ballets and operas widened the scope of the string ensemble, and the five-part Suites of German 'Lullistes' such as Georg Muffat, Johann Kusser and Johann Fischer ensured the spread of French practices to Germany. Charles II formed his own 'Twenty-four Violins' in England (1660); their repertory, composed by Locke, Banister and others, was in four rather than five parts and often involved a string quartet arrangement with two violins.

Apart from the large mixed ensembles assembled for special events such as the Florentine intermedii or Monteverdi's *Orfeo* (1607), equivalent orchestral cultures were not apparent in Italy until the activities of Cazzati in Bologna in the late 1650s, which led in turn to that of Stradella and Corelli. The latter's twelve *Concerti grossi* Op. 6, published posthumously in 1714, finally freed the violin family from accompanying dance music or prefacing vocal music and established it as the mainstay of the orchestra.

Early centres of violin making

The first and most distinguished centre of violin making was Cremona. The tradition was established in the mid sixteenth century by the

Fig. 3.2 Violin ('Charles IX') by Andrea Amati, Cremona 1564 (Ashmolean Museum, Oxford)

Amati family, of whom Andrea (pre 1505–77) was the father figure. Many of his instruments were made for the French court of Charles IX in the 1560s and 1570s and bear the King's coat-of-arms.[5] His earliest known surviving violin (1564), preserved in Oxford's Ashmolean Museum, is a small-patterned instrument characterised by its high arching, wide purfling and elegant curves of body and scroll (Fig. 3.2). Andrea's two sons, Antonio (c.1540–?) and Giralomo (Hieronymus) (1561–1630) experimented with different forms of arching and outline, but Giralomo's son, Nicolo (1596–1684), was the dynasty's most refined maker (see Fig. 8.1, p. 173). His wider 'Grand Amati' model, designed for greater volume, proved extremely influential, and his disciples included makers such as Francesco Rugeri, Giovanni Rogeri and Andrea Guarneri.

Guarneri (c.1626–98) emulated the 'Grand Amati' pattern but never achieved the refined craftsmanship of his mentor. Two of his sons, Pietro Giovanni (1655–1720) and Giuseppe Giovanni (1666–c.1740), followed him into the trade, the latter being assisted in business for a short period by his two sons, Pietro (1695–1762) and Bartolomeo Giuseppe Guarneri (1698–1744), better known as 'del Gesù'. While his early models betray his father's influence, del Gesù's later work was strikingly individual, displaying a ruggedness of character and workmanship directed towards a massive build and powerful tone.

The Cremonese school culminated with the work of Antonio Stradivari (1644–1737), whose career is conveniently surveyed in five periods. The first, known as 'Amatisé', involved instruments modelled on Amati's 'grand pattern'; the second (1690–1700) witnessed the development of the flat, 'long pattern' violin, designed for greater sonority and probably inspired by the powerful violins of the Magginis. This model accommodated a slight increase in body length (by about 0.8cm), but with narrower upper and lower bouts. Stradivari's experiments continued first with a reversion to the shorter 'Amatisé' model, with minor variations to the outline, and later culminated in the so-called 'Golden Period' (1700–25), when he renounced the long pattern in favour of a broader, strongly-arched model of more traditional proportions, as exemplified by his 'Messiah' violin of 1716.[6] His experiments persisted into the fourth period (1725–30) – a guitar-shaped violin dates from 1727 – but imprecise cutting, disagreement in the outlines of table and back, and irregular purfling illustrate his declining powers. This decline became more apparent during the final period (1730–7), when his assistants are believed to have participated more prominently in the construction process.

Brescia was another fertile area for violin making in the mid sixteenth century, with Gasparo [Bertolotti] da Salò (c.1540–1609) as its first notable representative. Da Salò's large, highly-arched instruments, characterised by long, wide and upright f-holes and sometimes double purfling and ornamental inlay, were designed for maximum sonority. The violin maker's art spread to Venice, Florence, Rome and Bologna, Naples, Milan and Turin, and it soon flourished throughout Europe, particularly in the Tyrol, where Jacob Stainer's (c.1617–83) highly-arched early violins resembled those of Andrea Amati. Stainer's later work shows a more individual, uniquely German character and often substituted a carved lion's head for a scroll; he influenced makers not only in Austria and Germany (especially in Augsburg,

Vienna and Nuremberg) but also in France, England and even Italy. The intimate, silvery tone-quality of his violins was much in demand until the end of the eighteenth century when Stradivari's more penetrating, Classical model gained preference.

The desire for a more brilliant, powerful sound and greater agility prompted late-eighteenth-century makers to lengthen the neck (by 0.64–1.27cm to the present standard of 12.86–13.02cm) and set it at a 4–5° angle from the body of the instrument. These changes offered an increase in the playing length of string and normally required a slightly higher, thinner and more steeply curved bridge. This longer, narrower neck in turn affected the shape and dimensions of the fingerboard, which was narrowed at the peg-box end to allow the player greater left-hand agility and broadened somewhat towards the bridge. The fingerboard was also lengthened (by 5.08–6.35cm) to *c.* 26.7cm, thus facilitating high passage-work. The consequent increased pressures on the instrument led to the neck being mortised into the top-block for greater strength and the introduction of a longer, thicker bass bar. The thicker, more substantial soundpost also played its part in realising the late-eighteenth-century sound ideal.

These modifications in violin construction were implemented gradually over a substantial period of transition between *c.*1760 and *c.*1830 and most instruments were adapted to comply with late-eighteenth-century musical ideals. The new neck-setting was probably introduced by French makers, Vincetto Lancetti remarking (1823) that 'about 1800 the Brothers Mantegazza . . . were often entrusted by French and Italian artistes to lengthen the necks of their violins after the Paris fashion, an example which was followed by amateurs and professors all over North Italy'.[7] German makers were also implementing similar changes at about the same time.[8] However, some Gagliano violins made as early as the 1780s combine original necks of almost modern dimensions with fittings of eighteenth-century lightness, and the necks of some English violins *c.*1760 were already of approximately modern length .

Despite the changes in the various violin fittings, the main body of the instrument remained unaltered throughout this period of transition. Its basic design has been unsurpassed to this day despite many attempts, some apparently quite ludicrous, at 'improvement'.[9]

The viola: origins and early history

The viola seems to have originated in northern Italy at around the same time as the violin. However, the various meanings of the term 'viola' in the early sixteenth century have clouded its early history; these ranged from a general denotation of any stringed instrument, plucked or bowed, to one specifying a particular family or instrument, notably *viola da braccio* ('viola of the arm', a member of the violin family) or *viola da gamba* ('viola of the leg', a member of the viol family). The term was also qualified to distinguish between different registers within the viola range, thus explaining the occasional use of 'Alto Viola' and 'Tenor Viola' parts (e.g. in Handel's Concerto Op. 3 no. 1, Walsh edition of 1734) or the common incorporation of three viola lines exploiting different registers in seventeenth-century French five-part ensembles. Such differentiation also explains the availability of instruments of varying size.[10] Some 'tenor violas' were so large as to be almost unplayable on the arm;[11] most have been 'cut down' for ease of playing.

The Amati family was also pre-eminent in viola making in sixteenth-century Italy, contributing small and large instruments. The Andrea Amati tenor viola (1574) in the Ashmolean Museum, Oxford, has a body length of 47cm. Gasparo da Salò's instruments have also been in demand for their sonorous tone, as well as those of Peregrino Zanetto de Micheli, Ventura di Francesco Linarol, Antonio Mariani and Giovanni Paolo Maggini. From *c.*1600 viola production hit a barren patch owing to musical preferences for four- as opposed to five-part ensembles and the emergence of the trio sonata as a popular medium. The Guarneri family, for example, produced very few violas, but Stainer's instruments were particularly prized.

Makers continued to produce large and small violas throughout the seventeenth and early eighteenth centuries, but smaller models predominated thereafter until the early twentieth century, suggesting makers' response to technical advances and demands.[12] In the interim, instruments underwent similar (but proportionate) modifications of the neck, fingerboard and internal fittings to the violin to increase string tension, tonal brilliance and left-hand facility. Further experiments at acoustical improvement in the nineteenth century turned the instrument's evolution full circle and involved lengthening or enlarging the body,[13] culminating in the 'Tertis' model (with an average body length of 42.5cm) developed by Lionel Tertis and Arthur Richardson in the 1930s.

Accessories

Strings

Silk, steel, brass and copper strings were available during the seventeenth century but do not appear to have been widely used by violinists or violists. From its inception until well into the eighteenth century, the violin was normally equipped with a plain-gut e^2, a plain-gut or high-twist a^1, a high-twist or catline d^1 and a catline g string.[14] By the early eighteenth century, gut (or silk) strings wound with silver (or copper) gained preference in many countries for their superior tonal potential for the violin's g and the viola's c and g strings, allowing for an increase in mass without an increase in diameter and a consequent loss of flexibility. Emanating from Bologna, they are mentioned by Playford as sounding 'much better and lowder than common Gut Strings, either under the Bow or Finger'.[15] Their gradual adoption led to the eventual demise of the tenor-size viola.

There were distinct national preferences in stringing in the eighteenth century. Speer (1697) implies that gut strings were used on violins and records that the silver- and copper-wound viola strings available from button makers rattled when played such that they were often called bassoon-violas (*Violae di Fagotto*).[16] Gut strings continued to be used in Italy and Germany well into the eighteenth century – Leopold Mozart refers to gut strings, while Majer mentions a wound lowest string;[17] but in England the catline g was gradually replaced by an open-wound g. Early in that century, the French replaced the gut d^1 by an open-wound string and the g by a close-wound string.[18] David Boyden quotes Sébastien de Brossard's reference to a g string wound with silver and a d^1 string 'almost always partially wound [i.e. open wound] with silver', which is indicative of the future trend.[19] By the middle of the century the Italians replaced the catline g with a close-wound string, on account of its greater tonal brilliance and reliability of response, and the rest of Europe followed suit from c.1775. But despite the increased reference to overspun d^1 strings and the well-publicised disadvantages of gut – notably the need to keep them moist, their tendency to unravel, their sensitivity to variation in atmospheric temperature, the common incidence of knots and other imperfections – the combination of plain-gut e^2 and a^1, high-twist d^1 and a g with copper, silver-plated copper or silver round wire close-wound on a gut core was the norm throughout the nineteenth century.[20] Nevertheless, Gunzelheimer was still a strong advocate of all-gut violin stringing in 1855, while Alberto Bachmann recorded (1925): 'The fourth or G string is the only covered string used on the violin.'[21] A few performers, most notably Fritz Kreisler, persevered with a gut e^2 until at least c.1950; however, gut was gradually replaced by a steel (so-called 'piano-wire') variety, championed in particular by Willy Burmester and Anton Witek, which was accompanied by its metal adjuster for greater facility in fine tuning.

Available evidence regarding pitch, string tensions and string thicknesses is so conflicting, and circumstances were so variable, that it is impossible to draw definitive conclusions.[22] Some scholars believe, for example, that eighteenth-century violin strings were generally thinner than their modern counterparts, in keeping with the lower string tension and generally lower playing pitch of that period;[23] others disagree, some quoting Brossard's statement that the contemporary silver-wound d^1 and g strings were thinner than their counterparts made simply of gut.[24] Clearly, string thicknesses differed considerably according to considerations of pitch (thicker strings were employed for the lower pitch standards), the size of the instrument employed, the situation, national or individual tastes regarding string materials, and many other variables. Italian and German violinists generally used thicker strings, strung at greater tension, than the French, presumably with greater brilliance and volume in mind. However, Quantz acknowledges the use of thick and thin strings and Leopold Mozart recommends, for optimum tonal results and reliability of intonation, the use of thick strings for 'flat pitch' and large-model violins and thin strings for 'sharp pitch' and small models.[25] Paganini evidently used very thin strings, whereas Spohr claims that optimum string thicknesses for any instrument can be determined only by experiment, with equal strength and fullness of tone from each string as the ultimate goal.[26] Spohr employed the thickest strings his violin could bear, so long as their response was quick and easy and their tone bright, and he employed a string gauge to ensure the uniformity of his string thicknesses. This device comprised a metal plate of silver or brass with a graduated slit, lettered for each string, and with regular markings from 0 to 60 (See Fig. 3.3c). The scale unit of Spohr's gauge is not stated, but the thickness of each string was ascertained at the point where it became lightly wedged in the gauge (e^1=18; a^1=23; d^1=31; g=25).[27]

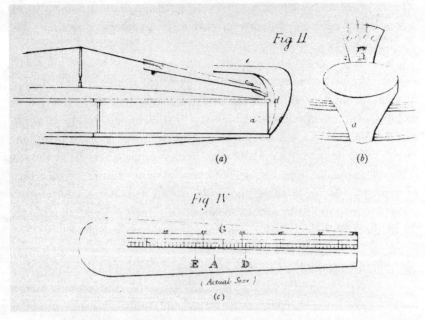

Fig. 3.3 (a) and (b) the chin-rest and its position on the instrument; and (c) the string gauge, as illustrated in Louis Spohr's *Violinschule* (Vienna, 1832)

As gut naturally wears more quickly than other materials, oiled and varnished varieties have been developed with longevity in mind. Such treatments often affect the sound quality, varnished gut strings tending to sound somewhat harsher. The life of a string may also be prolonged by regular 'grooming', by eliminating sharp edges on the bridge or tailpiece, and possibly by tuning down the string slightly after playing; most gut string varieties settle fairly quickly when re-tuned.

Chin-rest

The chin-rest (*Geigenhalter*: literally, 'violin holder') was invented by Spohr *c.*1820 to ensure the greater stability required for increased mobility of the left hand and greater freedom in bowing.[28] Spohr's model was made of ebony and was placed directly over the tailpiece, not to the left side as is usual today (Fig. 3.3a and b). It only gradually achieved general approbation, but it was probably fairly widely used, together with the various models it inspired (e.g. the low, ebony ridge employed by Sarasate and others), by the mid nineteenth century. Nevertheless, many leading players, among them Wilhelmj, evidently rejected utilising such equipment.

Mute

Use of the mute was gradually extended from ensemble to solo playing during the eighteenth century. This device, generally of wood or metal (Quantz states wood, lead, brass, tin or steel, but dislikes the growling tone produced by the wood and brass varieties)[29] underwent no fundamental change in design until the mid nineteenth century, when the inconvenience of manually applying or removing a mute during performance prompted Vuillaume to invent his *sourdine pédale*. However, this latter, enabling players to apply the mute by means of gentle pressure with the chin on the tailpiece, gained, like Bellon's invention,[30] only ephemeral success.

Shoulder pad

Pierre Baillot (1835) was one of the first writers to recommend the use of a shoulder pad to facilitate the correct and comfortable support of the instrument. He suggests that 'a thick handkerchief or a kind of cushion' might be used to fill in any gap between the player's left shoulder and the instrument, particularly in the cases of children, youths and women.[31] However, dress codes during most of our core period were such that shoulder pads were not regularly employed.

The bow: history and development

The use of a bow to draw sound from a stringed instrument has been traced back almost six centuries before the violin family's evolution; not surprisingly, violinists and violists at first adopted the types of bow employed by players of other stringed instruments such as the rebec and viol. These bows were unstandardised as regards weight, length, form and wood-type but had certain general characteristics in common. Many early-seventeenth-century models were probably quite short (*c.* 36cm), but evidence points to an increase to at least 61cm by the end of the century.[32] They were usually convex and the narrow skein of horsehair was strung at fixed tension between the pointed head (in some cases there was no distinct head, the hair merely meeting the stick in a point) and the immovable horn-shaped nut at the lower end of the stick.

Few examples of seventeenth-century bows have survived, but icono-graphical evidence suggests that fashions in bow-types related directly to musical tastes and requirements. Short, light and fairly straight bows were ideal for dance musicians and were especially popular in France, while the increased cultivation of the sonata and concerto in Italy encouraged the use of longer, straighter (but sometimes slightly convex) models capable of pro-ducing a more singing style with a greater dynamic range. Solid, convex bows of intermediate length tended to be favoured by German players, prob-ably because they offered greater facility in the execution of the German polyphonic style.[33]

The gradual interaction of national styles during the eighteenth century and the demand for increased tonal volume, cantabile and a wider dynamic range (met also by developments in instrument construction), prompted the production of longer and straighter bow-sticks. Straightening of the stick required modifications in the height and curvature of the so-called pike's (or swan's) head, in order to allow sufficient separation of the hair and the stick; and when, towards the mid eighteenth century, makers began to anticipate the concave camber of the 'modern' stick, further changes in the head-design were required for optimum hair/stick separation at the middle. Fig. 3.4 clearly illustrates these developments, ranging from the pike's head of bow A to the modified pike's head and concave camber of bow B, the tran-sitional bows C (with its raised pike's head), E, and G (with their varying degrees of concave camber and different dimensions of the pike's head), the hatchet head of bows D and F and finally the 'modern' head of bows H and I which closely resemble the model standardised by François Tourte during the 1780s.

Bow lengths varied considerably, but the eighteenth-century trend was towards bows with a greater playing length of hair, especially in Italy. Sir John Hawkins confirms (1776): 'The bow of the violin has been gradually increasing in length for the last seventy years; it is now about twenty-eight inches [i.e. 71.12cm overall length]. In the year 1720, a bow of twenty-four inches [60.96cm] was, on account of its length, called a sonata bow; the common bow was shorter; and . . . the French bow must have been shorter

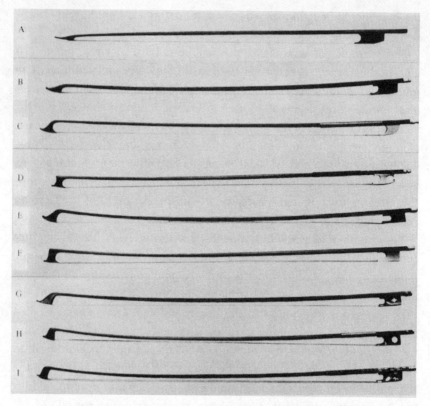

Fig. 3.4 Violin bows *c.*1700–*c.*1820 (Ashmolean Museum, Oxford)

still.'[34] By *c.*1750 the average playing length of bows measured approximately 61cm, although Tourte *père* produced some longer models – bow E (Fig. 3.4) is 74.08cm long overall with a playing length of 63.92cm. Table 3.1 provides a general overview of weights and measurements of extant violin bows *c.*1700–*c.*1780 and concurs for the most part with the statistics of the bows illustrated in Fig. 3.4. The weights and measurements of many contemporary viola bows will also have complied with those in Table 3.1, with a predominant trend towards the slightly shorter and heavier models.

Many early-eighteenth-century bows were fluted in all or part of their length. They were generally lighter than modern models, but were nevertheless strong, if somewhat inflexible, and their point of balance was generally nearer the frog, due to the lightness of the head. Most types tapered to a fine

Table 3.1 *Weights (in g) and measurements (in cm) of violin bows (c.1700–c.1780)*[35]

	minimum	medium	maximum
Overall length	70.5	72.5	73.9
Diameter of stick at frog	0.85	0.88	0.91
Diameter of stick at head	0.51	0.57	0.70
Hair to stick at frog	1.55	1.77	1.90
Width of hair in frog	0.62	0.82	1.05
Bowing length	60.1	62.5	64.2
Weight	47	51.5	58

point at the pike's head and were commonly of snakewood ('specklewood'), but pernambuco, brazil wood and plum wood were certainly known and pernambuco was increasingly used as the century progressed.

The type of nut employed for regulating the hair tension varied from a fixed nut to the *crémaillère* device (comprising a movable nut, whose position was adjusted and secured by a metal loop locked into one of several notches on the top of the stick) and, generally by *c*.1750, the 'modern' screw-nut attachment. This latter device was probably invented in the late seventeenth century, David Boyden citing a bow in the Hill collection (London), in original condition and date-stamped 1694 on its movable frog, which is adjusted by a screw.[36] The frogs of this period were completely unmounted and were of ebony, rosewood or ivory.

Few seventeenth- or early-eighteenth-century makers stamped their names on their bows. Instead, bow-types became associated with distinguished performers. Both Fétis (Fig. 3.5) and Woldemar (Fig. 3.6) illustrate four eighteenth-century bow-types, named respectively after Corelli, Tartini, Cramer and Viotti,[37] while Baillot (Fig. 3.7) illustrates six varieties (Corelli, Pugnani, two unnamed transitional types, Viotti and Tourte).

The term 'Corelli bow' appears to have designated the common early eighteenth-century Italian sonata bow with its straight or slightly convex bow and pike's head, while the 'Tartini bow' (Baillot's 'Pugnani bow' looks very similar) seems to have referred to a straight, apparently longer bow of more streamlined design, which, according to Fétis, was constructed from

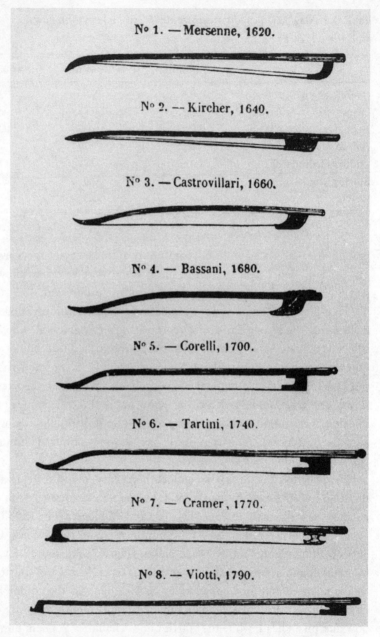

No 1. — Mersenne, 1620.

No 2. — Kircher, 1640.

No 3. — Castrovillari, 1660.

No 4. — Bassani, 1680.

No 5. — Corelli, 1700.

No 6. — Tartini, 1740.

No 7. — Cramer, 1770.

No 8. — Viotti, 1790.

Fig. 3.5 Violin bows *c.*1620–*c.*1790: Fétis, *Antoine Stradivari, Luthier célèbre* (Paris, 1856)

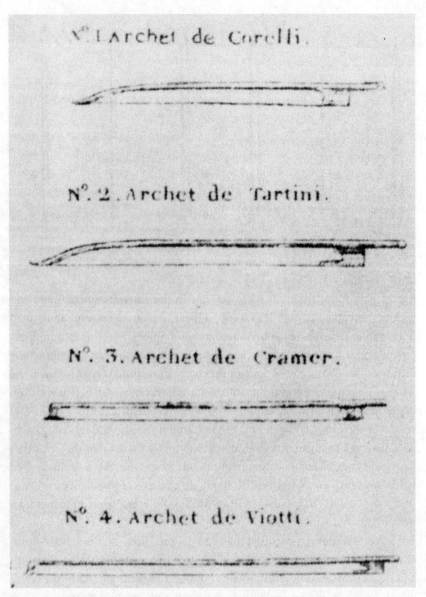

Fig. 3.6 Violin bows of the seventeenth and eighteenth centuries: Woldemar, *Grande méthode ou étude élémentaire pour le violon* (Paris, *c.*1800)

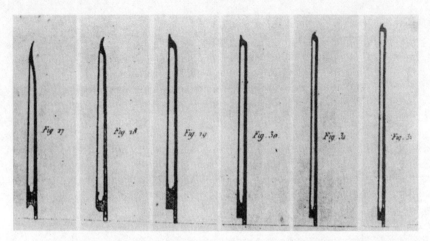

Fig. 3.7 Violin bows of the seventeenth, eighteenth and early nineteenth centuries: Baillot, *L'art du violon: nouvelle méthode* (Paris, 1835)

lighter wood and fluted at its lower end in the interests of lightness and greater manual control.[38] This would appear to be the bow-type illustrated in the violin treatises of Leopold Mozart and Löhlein as well as in numerous iconographical sources of the period up to roughly the last quarter of the century. The 'Cramer bow', one of the many transitional types between the various Italian models and the Tourte design, was in vogue between *c.*1760 and *c.*1785, especially in Mannheim, where Wilhelm Cramer (1746?–99) spent the early part of his career, and in London after he had settled there in 1772. Longer than most Italian models but slightly shorter than Tourte's eventual synthesis, it was also distinguished by its characteristically shaped ivory frog (cut away at both ends), the slight concave camber of its stick, and its bold, yet neat 'battle-axe' head (with a peak in the front matched by a peak in the back of the head proper).[39]

Michel Woldemar records that the 'Viotti bow' 'differs little from Cramer's in the design of the head (although this is more hatchet-like with a peak in the front only), but the nut is lower and brought nearer the screw attachment; it is longer and has more hair; it looks slightly straighter when in use and is employed almost exclusively today'.[40] It is possible that Fétis's and Woldemar's 'Viotti bow', with its fully developed hatchet head, is actually the Tourte bow in all but name. Certainly Tourte would have been influenced by those performers who frequented his workshops either to suggest ideas and improvements or simply to inspect and play examples of his work. Fétis implies that there was some collaboration between the two personalities, but Baillot's illustration of the 'Viotti' and Tourte bows as two distinct models, the 'Viotti bow' (c. 72.39cm) being slightly shorter than the Tourte (c. 74.42cm), suggests otherwise.[41]

François Tourte initially served an apprenticeship as a clock maker, only later joining the family bow-making business as his father's pupil and assistant. He experimented with various kinds of wood in order to find a variety which offered those qualities of lightness, density, strength and elasticity demanded by string players of his day. He eventually concluded that pernambuco wood (*Caesalpinia echinata*) best satisfied these requirements. According to Fétis, he further discovered that, after thoroughly heating the stick, he could bend (rather than cut) it to the desired concave camber, thus preserving the wood's natural resiliency.[42] Tourte's sticks tapered gradually to the point, the diameters of violin bow-sticks measuring about 8.6mm throughout the 11cm length of their lower ends and decreasing evenly by 3.3mm to their tips.[43] Jean-Baptiste Vuillaume (1798–1875) later proved that the unstrung stick could normally be expressed mathematically in terms of a logarithmic curve in which the ordinates increase in arithmetical progression while the abscissae increase in geometrical progression.[44]

Tourte also standardised the length and weight of bows of the violin family, determining the ideal length of the violin bow-stick to be 74–5cm (providing a playing length of approximately 65cm and a balance point about 19cm above the frog), and the optimum overall weight as about 56–60g, somewhat lightweight by modern standards. Viola bows were slightly shorter (c.74cm) and heavier. The pronounced concave camber of the Tourte bow necessitated changes in the design of the head to prevent the hair from touching the stick when pressure was applied at the tip. The head was consequently made higher and heavier than before, Tourte opting for a hatchet design and facing it with a protective plate, generally of ivory. He redressed the balance by adding the metal ferrule and inlay to the frog, and any further metal to the back-plates and the screw button.

From about the middle of the eighteenth century, the amount of hair employed in the stringing of bows was gradually increased (from about

80–100 to in excess of 150 individual strands, according to Spohr),[45] presumably with the contemporary demand for greater tonal volume in mind.
To counteract the irregular bunching of the hair, Tourte increased the width
of the ribbon of hair (to measure about 10mm at the nut and about 8mm at
the point)[46] and kept it uniformly flat and even by securing it at the frog with
a ferrule, made originally of tin and later of light-gauge silver. Louis Tourte,
among others, is often suggested as the inventor of the ferrule, but François
Tourte was undoubtedly the first maker to bring it into general use
c.1780–90. A wooden wedge was positioned between the hair and the bev-
elled portion of the frog so that the hair was pressed against the ferrule by the
wedge and the ferrule itself was prevented from sliding off. A mother-of-
pearl slide (recouvrement) was also fitted into a swallow-tail groove in the
frog in order to conceal the hair fastening and enhance the bow's appearance. The metal heel-plate on the frog is also believed to have been added by
makers during the last decade of the eighteenth century; François Tourte
was one of the first to use it with some consistency. Of variable dimensions,
its principal function was to strengthen the back of the frog, but it also
brought to the frog the additional weight desired by many players of that
time.

The Tourte-model bow enabled performers to produce a stronger tone
and was especially well suited to the sustained cantabile style dominant in
the period of its inception. Its ability to make smooth bow changes with the
minimum differentiation, where required, between slurred and separate
bowing brought the later 'seamless phrase' ideal nearer to reality. A normal
straight bow stroke, with the index-finger pressure and bow speed remaining constant, produced an even tone throughout its length because the shape
and flexibility of the stick enabled the index-finger pressure to be distributed
evenly. Variation of this pressure, bow speed, contact point, type of stroke
and other technical considerations provided the wider expressive range so
important to contemporary aesthetic ideals, in which the element of contrast, involving sudden changes of dynamic or long crescendos and diminuendos, played a significant role.

The hair of most pre-Tourte bows was generally capable of considerably
less tension than that of Tourte models. Thus, it yielded rather more when
brought into contact with the strings and produced, according to Leopold
Mozart, 'a small, even if barely audible, softness at the beginning of the

stroke'.[47] A similar 'softness' was also perceptible at the end of each stroke, thus resulting in a natural articulation of the bow itself. The concave bow-stick of the Tourte model, on the other hand, yields very little when pressed on the string and thus affords a more or less immediate attack. Furthermore, its quicker take-up of hair, greater strength (particularly at the point) and broader ribbon of hair also contributed to a considerable widening of the vocabulary of bow-strokes, as will be discussed in Chapter 4.

Universal approval of the Tourte bow was only slowly won. Michel Woldemar claims (1801) that the similar 'Viotti' model was exclusively used,[48] but many French makers continued to make bows modelled on pre-Tourte designs, and Baroque transitional and Tourte models coexisted in most orchestras and in solo spheres, as did violins with Baroque transitional and/or modern dimensions and fittings, well into the nineteenth century.[49] Nevertheless, Louis Spohr, who is known to have purchased a Tourte bow in Hamburg in 1803, records that Tourte's bows, though expensive, are 'the best and most sought after' and 'have won for themselves a European celebrity' on account of their 'trifling weight and the elasticity of the stick, the . . . graduated cambre . . . and the neat and accurate workmanship'.[50]

The full potential of the Tourte bow was probably not realised until the early years of the nineteenth century, when its inherent power and its expressive and other qualities could be implemented on an instrument modified to fulfil similar ideals. Apart from a few minor nineteenth-century additions, refinements and unsuccessful attempts by others to improve the bow, it has been imitated universally as the virtual blueprint for all subsequent bow makers of the nineteenth and twentieth centuries, particularly by Jean Grand-Adam (1823–69), Jacob Eury and J. M. Persoit. François Lupot (1774–1837) is normally credited with the addition (c.1820) of the under-slide (coulisse), a piece of metal affixed to the part of the frog that comes in sliding contact with the bow-stick and designed to prevent any wear on the nut caused by friction with the stick, while the indentation of the channel and track of the frog and the combination of rear and upper heel plates into one right-angled metal part are normally attributed to Vuillaume.[51] Otherwise, few of Vuillaume's inventions in bow-making survived the test of time.[52]

Although the inventor of the metal thumbplate is unknown, the device was championed by Etienne Pajeot, whose bows are generally more elegant in the profile of the head than those of Tourte. Dominique Peccatte developed a more robust, more heavily wooded stick, generally with a rounded cross-section and a higher frog than his predecessors,[53] while François Nicolas Voirin (1833–85) produced a lighter, slightly longer and more delicate-looking bow in his mature years. Particularly characteristic is the slimmer profile of the head (with a notable thinning of the two faces), which is also markedly less square than that of Tourte's design, and the different camber, the progression of which has been moved closer to the head for additional strength and suppleness in the stick. The balance of the bow was redressed by a reduction in the diameter of the lower end of the stick, where the frog was appropriately in proportion. A similar design also achieved some popularity with makers such as A. J. Lamy, the Thomassins and the Bazins but never seriously challenged the Tourte model's supremacy.

English bows tended to be made more with functional durability than artistic craftsmanship in mind, as is generally borne out by their square heads, roughly planed shafts and block-like ivory frogs. Nevertheless, these ungraceful bows generally possessed fine playing qualities. John Dodd (1752–1839) was probably the first English maker to adopt similar modifications to those introduced by Tourte. Whether he actually copied Tourte or arrived at a similar design quite independently has never been proven.[54] However, Dodd was less consistent than Tourte, experimenting widely with various weights, shapes of head, lengths and forms of stick and mountings on the nut. Close examination of his bows generally reveals cruder and more primitive craftsmanship. Many are slightly shorter (in both the stick and the playing length) and lighter than the average Tourte model; furthermore, his early sticks are not octagonal and the frogs lack a metal ferrule. Indeed, Dodd is believed to have produced full-length Tourte-model bows only late in life; those earlier sticks that have survived underwent later 'modernization', their plain ivory mountings being either adapted or jettisoned.[55]

Purchasing an early violin or viola

A useful first step towards playing, say, Baroque music on period instruments is to string a 'modern' instrument with gut strings, tuned down one semitone to $a^1 = 415$Hz (the most usual pitch employed for Baroque music nowadays), remove any chin-rest and shoulder pad and experiment with a Baroque bow. This will help to familiarise you with an early 'set-up' while you are seeking a period instrument.

The ideal purchase would obviously be a seventeenth- or eighteenth-century instrument in original condition; but this option is barely viable, especially if one is seeking a quality instrument. Few old instruments are still extant in their original condition and those which are available were either probably never worth converting in the first place or are priceless collectors' items or museum property. Some original instruments come up for auction at major auction houses from time to time and some become available from dealers. A more likely option nowadays is to purchase a suitable old instrument in sound condition and have it reconverted to its original state by a reputable restorer; but this can prove expensive and may not serve the best interests of the instrument, particularly instruments from Stradivari's time onwards. Most restorers agree, however, that Stainer/Amati-model instruments, with their high-arched plates, suffered by being modernised and are thus prime candidates for returning to their original condition.

The fact that violinists of the past played new instruments could be considered sufficient justification for using a reproduction copy, rather than searching out an original. Reasonably cheap German hand-finished instruments are available from various retail outlets, but there are several established makers worldwide, most of whom produce various different models;[56] some will also copy instruments on commission or even to a specific brief, especially when a performer requires a versatile instrument for playing music of different periods. If a reproduction instrument suitable for both Baroque and Classical music is desired, then some compromises of set-up will need to be made. Many 'period' performers own at least two instruments with different set-ups in order better to accommodate the pitches and other requirements of the various styles, periods and repertories embraced by their 'early music' ventures.

Purchasing a violin/viola bow for early music

A case can be made for historically-aware performers to have at their disposal at least four bow-types, including Baroque models to cater appropriately for the various national styles (especially French and Italian), a transitional/Classical variety and one modelled after Tourte's synthesis.

Few original Baroque bows have survived, but modern copies are readily available. Again, the cheaper end of the market is well served by general early music retailers, most of whom stock mass-produced German bows of pernambuco. Those who wish to make a greater investment will discover that there are many fine bow-makers who make copies of a range of different models; some will make only to commission (although customers are not usually committed to any purchase), but many make several bows in batches and usually have some stock for prospective purchasers to try out. Most makers also copy transitional or Classical bows, as well as Baroque models, though originals are sometimes available from dealers and instrument shops or the major auction houses.

The demand for early bows has centred on eighteenth-century models based on Baroque or early Classical designs. Prospective purchasers will need to make decisions on various factors relevant to personal preference and historical appropriateness for the repertory to be performed. Such decisions include the model, weight and balance of the bow, the choice of wood and other materials, whether the stick should be fluted, and whether to have a fixed or clip-in frog, or screw adjustment. While it is important for period performers to use bow types which have historical credibility (for example, the use of short, light bows with an appropriate thumb-on-hair grip for French dance music), they should avoid 'compartmentalising' history by subscribing to any rigid policy that only 'transitional' bows will suffice for late Mozart or 'Classical' bows for late Haydn. String players of that era would simply have used whatever equipment was available to them and the notion that they would have re-armed themselves with different bows for different periods/composers is totally spurious.

The weight and balance of bow is essentially a matter of personal taste within a range of historically credible possibilities. Various woods are offered by different makers, but snakewood is generally preferred by most 'period' performers. Broadly speaking, the more highly figured the snakewood the more expensive it will be; but it does not necessarily follow that more highly figured wood makes a better bow. Alternatives to snakewood may include pernambuco (which, though known in the mid seventeenth century, came into its own following Tourte's invaluable work), ironwood and ebony; very early bows were also made from native woods such as pear, plum or beech.

Fluting in all or part of its length can make a bow lighter while maintaining its strength, but very fine fluting (sometimes called 'reeding') can offer a better grip. While bows with fixed frogs would be historically most appropriate for music up to at least the end of the seventeenth century, their hair-tension is directly affected by the level of humidity – in dry conditions the bowhair may become too tight for comfort, whereas with high humidity it stretches and may become too loose. Some makers have reproduced the dentated bows which offered greater flexibility up to the early eighteenth century, allowing the frog to be slotted into the notch most appropriate for the desired hair-tension.[57] The use of a screw mechanism to tighten or loosen a movable frog is the most convenient method of regulating hair-tension, but, as mentioned earlier, this was probably not in general use until the early eighteenth century. Preferences regarding the materials for the frog and the button which turns the screw or simply finishes off the end of the stick are largely aesthetic, but will naturally affect the weight and balance of the bow; choices range from ivory to bone, ebony or other woods which either match or contrast with the stick.

When purchasing a bow, it is important to experiment with several examples of the appropriate model and weigh up the pros and cons of each before making a firm decision. Comfort is of the essence and personal preferences will not always match those of other players or relate to price.[58]

4　Technique

In Chapter 2 we considered the principal primary sources of information about historical performance on the violin and viola, including the most significant pedagogical treatises and their nature and purpose. This chapter is a digest of the details of their technical content and how the two instruments were played, the treatment of individual techniques reflecting not only the nature and priorities of the works and writers themselves but also the viola's lesser importance in the musical establishment and the predominance of violin treatises in the pedagogical material available to string players. Such a digest can pinpoint only mainstream developments across the various national idioms outlined in Chapter 5, so readers are cautioned to be selective in the implementation of technical issues and always to keep national style differences in mind.

Posture

Eighteenth-century violin and viola treatises consistently emphasised the importance of a comfortable, free and natural posture,[1] but it was not until the early nineteenth century that there was any general agreement as to the optimum playing position. Most nineteenth-century players sought a noble and relaxed bearing, with head upright, feet normally in line but slightly apart, and with body weight distributed towards the left side, somewhat in the fashion of Baillot's illustration in Fig. 4.1. Baillot's ideal seated position is also shown. This involved bending the right wrist and elbow rather more, turning the right leg slightly inwards (to avoid contact between knee and bow when bowing at the point on the upper strings) and supporting the left leg (and hence the body weight) on a footstool, thereby enabling the trunk to remain erect. Any exaggerated body movement when playing was avoided.

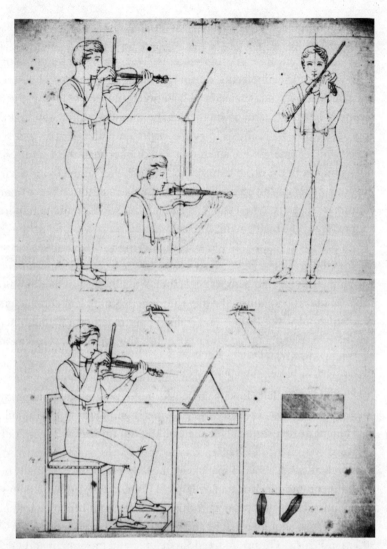

Fig. 4.1 Posture and the violin hold, as illustrated in Baillot's *L'art du violon: nouvelle méthode* (Paris, 1835), showing: (*top, left to right*) the posture in profile; how to assure oneself that the violin is stabilised properly between chin and shoulder; the posture from the front; (*middle, left to right*) a good position of the fingers; a forced and improper position of the fingers; (*bottom left to right*) the posture when playing seated; the position of the feet and their distance from the music stand.

Holding the instrument

As comparison of Fig. 4.2 and the jacket illustration will suggest, there was for some time no single accepted way of holding the violin or viola. Until well into the nineteenth century, paintings, drawings and descriptions indicate that methods varied largely between those positions at the breast, on the collar bone, and at the neck. The breast position was particularly appropriate for dance music, playing *pochettes* or small-sized violins, or for music which demanded position-work no higher than third position (with extension to e^3); the other two methods were better suited to more virtuoso music, the chin taking up a position on either side of the tailpiece to provide additional support if necessary, as in Fig. 4.2. Some theorists required the chin to steady the instrument, normally on the right (violin E-string) side of the tailpiece – arguably the more secure position. Others opted for a 'chin-off' method, as in the jacket illustration; this required the instrument to sit flat on the collar bone with its neck supported by the left hand without, as Leopold Mozart explains, allowing the violin to come into contact with 'the skin which joins the thumb and index finger together'.[2] Though perfectly adequate for playing in the lower positions, this method was less conducive to high position-work.

L'abbé *le fils* (1761) and Cupis recommended resting the chin on the instrument to the left (lowest-string side) of the tailpiece, L'abbé implying consistent use of a chin-braced grip formerly employed only to stabilise the instrument during shifts.[3] This method did not immediately gain universal approval – as noted in Chapter 3, even Spohr's chin-rest (invented *c.*1820) was originally positioned directly over the tailpiece; but it eventually became the most common. Advocated by Baillot, Habeneck and other leading theorists, it afforded firmer support for the instrument and enabled it to be held horizontally at shoulder height and directly in front of the player at almost 90°, as in Fig. 4.1. Optimum freedom of left-hand movement and flexibility of bowing were thereby gained. When seated, the player generally lowered the scroll to facilitate straight bowing (see Fig. 4.1). Cupis confirms that the viola was generally held similarly,[4] although its greater weight and size often caused the scroll to be positioned lower; it also demanded greater stretches and pressure from the fingers.

As noted in Chapter 3, Baillot was one of the first writers to recommend

Fig. 4.2 A 'comfortable method' of holding the violin and bow, as illustrated by Leopold Mozart in his *Versuch einer gründlichen Violinschule* (Augsburg, 1756)

Ex. 4.1 The 'Geminiani grip'.

the use of a shoulder pad to increase security and comfort and to avoid
raising the left shoulder.[5] During the early nineteenth century the left hand
was gradually relieved of its semi-supporting role and the common right-
arm position (closer to the player's side than formerly) required the instrument to be inclined more to the right for optimum bowing facility on the
lowest string. Baillot prescribes an angle of 45°, Spohr 25°–30°.

Placement of the left hand and fingers

Baroque and Classical violinists generally positioned the elbow well
under the middle of the instrument, closer to the body than nowadays. The
wrist was turned inwards to avoid contact between the palm and the neck of
the instrument, which, as mentioned earlier, was not allowed to sink into the
hollow between the thumb and index finger.[6] The thumb, occasionally
employed in multiple stopping, generally assumed a position 'opposite the A
natural on the G string';[7] but, for greater facility in extensions and shifting, it
was often placed 'more forward towards the second and third fingers than
backward towards the first', without projecting too far over the fingerboard.[8]

The 'Geminiani grip' (Ex. 4.1) was the most common guide to correct
elbow, hand, wrist and finger placement (in first position) on the violin until
well into the twentieth century, the hand and fingers generally forming a
curve with the fingers well over the strings. Each knuckle was bent so that
the top joints of the fingers could fall straight down on to the strings from
the same height (see Fig. 4.1). Significantly, Leopold Mozart introduced the
'Geminiani grip' in the second edition (1769–70) of his treatise as a method
of acquiring 'the true position of the hand' and, by lifting each finger in turn,
to achieve 'an extraordinary facility in playing double stopping in tune when
the moment arrives'.[9] During the nineteenth century players strove for easy
elbow manoeuvrability and flexibility of the hand position to cope with new
technical demands. Many opted for a more advanced position of the thumb,

Ex. 4.2 C. Guhr, *Ueber Paganinis Kunst die Violine zu spielen*, p. 43.

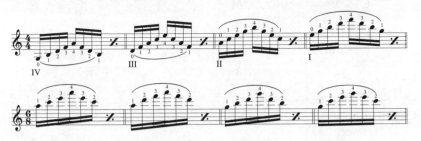

more often than not avoiding formal shifts between positions. Some of Paganini's fingerings in Ex. 4.2 render practically impossible the recognition of any definite concept of positions.

Positions and shifting

Unnecessary finger activity was avoided. Much of the Baroque repertory, particularly French dance music, required only the lower positions. This was particularly the case with the viola, which generally played a subservient role in ensemble music; but it was also true of a fair proportion of the violin repertory, the progressive technical requirements of the various seventeenth-century Italian, south German and Austrian composers mentioned in Chapter 2, as well as Vivaldi, Locatelli and others, proving exceptions rather than the rule.

Leopold Mozart claims that necessity, convenience and elegance were the only reasons for using positions other than the first.[10] Modern half and second positions assumed greater importance from *c.*1750 onwards, when most advanced violin treatises embraced at least the first seven positions. Some even extended to eleventh position and beyond in supplementary study material. However, excessively high position-work with the shorter fingerboard (pre *c.* 1800) was comparatively rare, because clarity of finger-stopping was difficult to achieve; the modifications to the fingerboard discussed in Chapter 3 encouraged exploitation of the entire range of positions.

Until at least the end of the eighteenth century, shifts were generally undertaken to conform to the music's own punctuation. They were made on the beat or on repeated notes (Ex. 4.3a), by the phrase in sequences (Ex. 4.3b),

Ex. 4.3 (a) L. Mozart, *Versuch*, p. 155.
(b) L. Mozart, *Versuch*, p. 168.
(c) L. Mozart, *Versuch*, p. 155.
(d) L. Mozart, *Versuch*, p. 156.
(e) L. Mozart, *Versuch*, p. 181.

(a)

(b) half position   * whole position   * half

(c)

(d)

(e) The third finger glides down

after an open string (Ex. 4.3c), on a rest or pause between staccato notes, or after a dotted figure played with a lifted bow-stroke (Ex. 4.3d). The unbraced methods of holding the instrument placed the onus more on the fingers than the arm to effect shifts; if possible, one position was chosen to accommodate an entire phrase, and extensions and contractions were often used (but harmonics rarely so in the eighteenth century, at least) to avoid or facilitate shifts (Ex. 4.3e). With the at first occasional, and later more consistent adoption of the more stable chin-braced grip, shifting proved less precarious. Baroque and Classical advice regarding where to shift was relaxed somewhat. Emphasis was placed rather more on the odd-numbered positions, cultivation of semitone shifts facilitated achievement of the prevalent legato ideal, and Spohr, among others, admitted the use of natural harmonics in shifting,

Ex. 4.4 An example of the kind of bold shifts employed by Geminiani.

Ex. 4.5 L'abbé *le fils, Suite de jolis airs de différents auteurs variés pour un violon seul.*

especially if one wishes 'to make one note in a passage stand out more brightly than the rest'.[11]

The mechanics of shifting are sparsely documented, but the independent role of the thumb in relation to the fingers (as opposed to the modern ideal of the hand moving more as a unit) was paramount, as Geminiani's shifting exercises clearly indicate.[12] Upward shifts tended to increase the instrument's stability against the player's neck, but downward shifts, particularly when playing 'chin-off', were less easily realised. They generally required the left hand to crawl back 'caterpillar fashion' from the high positions, the thumb moving independently of the rest of the left hand.

Like Leopold Mozart, most eighteenth-century writers advocated small upward shifts, using adjacent fingers (23–23 or 12–12), rather than the bold leaps prescribed by Geminiani, Tessarini and Corrette (Ex. 4.4), though this naturally depended on tempo and speed. Galeazzi excepted, large leaps (4321–4321) were generally favoured in descending passages, irrespective of speed.

There is conflicting evidence regarding the incidence of portamento in shifting. Some eighteenth-century writers rejected it outright,[13] but other contemporary sources, supported by certain notated fingerings (see Exx. 4.5 and 6.14), suggest that portamento was employed by some players, especially in solo contexts, either as part of the shift mechanism or as an expressive device.[14] Burney, for example, observed that 'beautiful expressions and

Ex. 4.6 (a) L. Spohr, Violin Concerto no. 10 in A, Op. 62, 2nd movement.
(b) P. Rode, Violin Concerto no. 7, 2nd movement, quoted in L. Spohr, *Violinschule*, p. 209.
(c) P. Rode, Violin Concerto no. 7, 2nd movement, quoted in L. Spohr, *Violinschule*, p. 209.

effects are produced by great players, in shifting, suddenly, from a low note to a high, with the same finger on the same string'. The use of portamento doubtless increased in the following century as shifting became more of an expressive resource. Baillot, acknowledging the interrelationship between fingering, the player's hand position and musical intentions, distinguishes between sure fingering, fingering for small hands and expressive fingering relevant to selected composers. The last category includes evidence of Kreutzer's frequent shifts on all strings for brilliance of effect, and Rode's more uniform tonal characteristics, incorporating *ports de voix*.[15]

Baillot's discussion of *ports de voix* and expressive fingering provides clues to the mechanics of shifting in the nineteenth century. Anticipatory notes (unsounded) indicate the method of shifting, the stopped finger sliding forwards (or backwards) in order to be substituted by another finger. Spohr endorses this method,[16] especially for rapid shifts involving leaps from a low to a high position in slurred bowing (Ex. 4.6a) (without glissando effect),

Ex. 4.7 (a) *vif* (lively). Employed for notes drawn with grace or pushed with energy (C. A. de Bériot, *Méthode*, Eng. trans., p. 237).
(b) *doux* (sweet). Employed for affectionate expression (C. A. de Bériot, *Méthode*, Eng. trans., p. 237).
(c) *traîné* (drawn out). Plaintive or sorrowful expression (C. A. de Bériot, *Méthode*, Eng. trans., p. 237 – extracted from Halévy's *La Juive*).

and gives a further example of a fast shift (Ex. 4.6b) in which the highest note is an harmonic. Stopping the bow momentarily during the shift also helped to make shifting inaudible (Ex. 4.6c), as many writers desired. Nevertheless, Spohr, Baillot and Habeneck allow tasteful introduction of portamento,[17] especially in slow movements and sustained melodies when a passage ascends or descends by step, accompanied respectively by a crescendo or diminuendo. Bériot uses signs to indicate three types of *port de voix: vif, doux* and *traîné* (Exx. 4.7a, b, and c), and he provides musical examples illustrating their expressive use in a variety of appropriate contexts dictated by character and mood and with emulation of the human voice as the principal goal.[18]

Paganini, among others, regularly employed glissando with striking effect, both for showmanship and for cantabile execution of double stopping. Exploitation of the glissando and portamento as an 'emotional connection of two tones'[19] (invariably in slurred bowing and with upward shifts) to articulate melodic shape, preserve uniformity of timbre or emphasise structurally important notes became so prevalent in the late nineteenth century that succeeding generations reacted strongly against it.

Ex. 4.8 (a) slide finger
(b) the 'B-portamento'
(c) the 'L-portamento'

(a)

(b)

(c)

Flesch criticises the excessive use of portamento by late-nineteenth- and early-twentieth-century violinists, the false accents it creates and the fact that it was invariably employed too slowly and merely for the player's convenience in shifting rather than for expressive ends.[20] He considers Joachim's crescendo during a portamento 'offensive'[21] and distinguishes between three portamento types: a straightforward slide on one and the same finger (Ex. 4.8a); the 'B-portamento' in which the beginning finger slides to an intermediary note (Ex. 4.8b); the 'L-portamento' in which the last finger slides from an intermediate note (Ex. 4.8c). Flesch reports that the straightforward slide and the B-portamento were commonly employed in the early years of the twentieth century, but the L-portamento was rarely used until the 1930s, when, however, it was still the least common of the three.[22] Broadly speaking, the execution of portamentos became 'generally faster, less frequent and less prominent'.[23]

Diatonic and chromatic scale fingerings

Only from c.1750 were the benefits of scale practice fully acknowledged for the cultivation of accurate intonation, finger independence, elasticity and agility, tonal clarity and many bowing disciplines. Notable nineteenth-century developments included: Spohr's fingering system for

Ex. 4.9 Habeneck *l'aîné's Fantaisie Pastorale*, quoted in P. Baillot, *L'art du violon*, p. 152.

Ex. 4.10 (a) and (b) L. Mozart, *Versuch*, pp. 66–7.

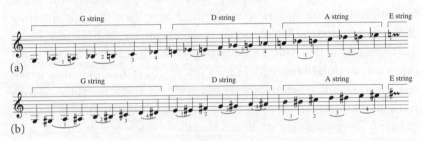

three-octave diatonic scales, in which the root position of a four-note chord of the key of a scale effectively determined the starting finger-position for most scales; and the introduction of the violin fingered-octave technique (first discussed by Baillot), which gradually found favour because of its greater clarity, accuracy and less-frequent displacements of the hand (Ex. 4.9).[24]

The two principal chromatic scale fingerings comprised Geminiani's one-finger-per-note method (with open strings where necessary) and a 'slide-fingering' of the type advocated by Leopold Mozart. Leopold's recommendation (Ex. 4.10a and b), adopted by many of his immediate successors, involved different fingerings for chromatic scales in sharps and those notated in flats. This flags up the concept of unequal semitones in Baroque and Classical string playing and the various tuning systems then in vogue (see below).

Geminiani's chromatic fingering was largely ignored in formal scale contexts by his contemporaries and his successors in the nineteenth century – the 'slide' fingering was preferred – but its principle was acknowledged in isolated passage-work, and it achieved more positive recognition in the twentieth century, notably by Carl Flesch, on account of its greater evenness, articulation and clarity.

Timbre

Although open strings were sometimes necessarily employed in the execution of shifts, *bariolage*, double and multiple stopping, and scordatura, they were invariably avoided (at least from the early eighteenth century onwards) when stopped notes were viable. Peter Walls confirms that 'the indication of fourth fingers seems often to have been the only fingering choice that composers felt any need to make themselves'.[25] Such was particularly the case in descending scale passages involving more than one string (especially in slurred bowing), in trills (except, of course, in double trills), appoggiaturas and other ornaments and in most melodic or expressive contexts, particularly in the eighteenth century, when intonation systems required some flexibility of finger-placement. Such limitations in open string usage also appear to have become more desirable as plain gut was gradually displaced by other materials in string making, and as performers began (particularly from *c.*1750 onwards) more seriously to cultivate uniformity of tone colour within the phrase. Sequences were played wherever possible with matching fingerings, bowing articulations and string changes, and the higher positions were increasingly exploited for timbral and expressive objectives. Baillot demonstrates how the timbre of each of the four violin strings can be modified in imitation of other instruments. Differences in string timbre were veiled wherever appropriate, and *una corda* playing was particularly encouraged by the late-eighteenth- and early-nineteenth-century French violin school.[26] Likewise, Galeazzi cites a Minuet for violin to be played entirely on the G string, demanding up to ninth position, and Spohr advocates exploitation of the higher positions for expressive and tonal purposes.[27] *Una corda* playing reached its zenith with Paganini's sul-G violin extravaganzas.

Vibrato

Vibrato,[28] discussed as early as the sixteenth century by theorists such as Ganassi and Agricola, has passed in and out of fashion in string playing, Thomas Mace (1676) referring to it as a 'very Neat and Pritty Grace, (But not Modish in these Days)'. Geminiani informs us that 'To perform it, you must press the finger strongly upon the string of the instrument, and move the wrist in and out slowly and equally, when it is long continued swelling the sound by degrees, drawing the bow nearer to the bridge, and ending it very strong may express majesty, dignity etc. But making it shorter, lower and softer, it may denote affliction, fear etc. and when it is made on short notes, it only contributes to make their sound more agreeable and for this reason it should be made use of as often as possible.'[29] Robert Bremner reports that many players complied with such advice; however, despite Geminiani's exceptional recommendations, which were suppressed in later editions of his treatise,[30] vibrato was generally used selectively up to the late nineteenth century as an expressive ornament linked inextricably with the inflections of the bow.[31]

Sometimes indicated by various forms of wavy line but generally freely added by the performer, vibrato was employed particularly on long sustained or final notes in a phrase, at a speed and intensity appropriate to the music's dynamic, tempo and character; it also served to emphasise certain notes for expressive purposes,[32] to articulate melodic shape or to assist in the cultivation of cantabile playing. For technical reasons, it was generally applied fairly discreetly on most instruments during the Baroque and Classical periods, although players appear to have used a range of oscillation speeds to good effect. It was doubtless more striking than the continuous variety practised today, even though the vibrato movement of Baroque and Classical players, executed with the fingers and wrist but not with the lower arm, was necessarily somewhat narrower, tighter and less intense, due to the types of violin hold then in vogue.[33] The gradual adoption of the chin-braced grip towards the end of the eighteenth century freed the left hand to cultivate a more fluid vibrato movement. Viola vibrato tended generally to be slower and less intense than that for the violin.

Leopold Mozart distinguishes three types of violin vibrato: slow, accelerating and fast. Spohr writes of four kinds: fast, for sharply accentuated notes; slow, for sustained notes in impassioned melodies; accelerating, for crescendos; decelerating, for decrescendos. He demonstrates their selective application (Ex. 4.11a) and, like Baillot, emphasises that the vibrato movement should be slight and that deviation from the true pitch of the note should be

Ex. 4.11 (a) L. Spohr, *Violinschule*, pp. 175–6. (b) G. B. Viotti's Violin Concerto no. 19, quoted in P. Baillot, *L'art du violon*, p. 138.

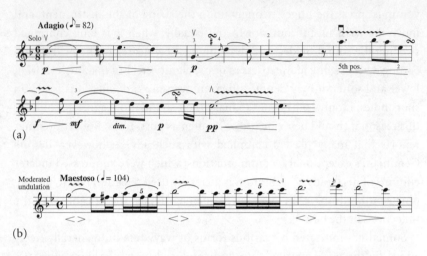

scarcely perceptible to the ear.[34] Interestingly, Spohr advocates a vibrato oscillation slightly above or below the actual note, while Baillot specifically illustrates one above the note only.

Baillot expands the vibrato concept to include three types of 'undulated sounds': a wavering effect caused by variation of pressure on the stick, the normal left-hand vibrato, and a combination of the two. He recommends that, for accuracy of intonation, notes should be begun and terminated without vibrato and provides examples of Viotti's vibrato usage, some of which link it with the 'swell' effect (Ex. 4.11b).[35] Bériot refers to 'soft', 'medium' and 'loud' vibrato, relating the device more to dynamic level than speed of oscillation, while David expands upon Spohr's four vibrato types, distinguishing thirteen in all with four relating to the swell effect. Joachim and Moser and Auer, among others, recommend selective vibrato usage, recognising 'the steady tone as the ruling one',[36] while Ysaÿe's use of the device, though more perceptible, was still restricted to long notes.

Flesch's caution that 'from a purely theoretic standpoint, the vibrato, as the means for securing a heightened urge for expression should only be employed when it is musically justifiable' suggests that the device was being used more liberally in practice.[37] He attributes the reintroduction of continuous vibrato to Kreisler, though it should probably be accredited to Lambert Massart, Kreisler's teacher, or another of Massart's pupils, Henryk Wieniawski, who 'intensified the vibrato and brought it to heights never before achieved'.[38] Nevertheless, as early recordings verify, Kreisler and Heifetz (who, ironically, was a pupil of Auer) were probably its foremost advocates, using vibrato more as a constituent of a pleasing tone than as an embellishment.

Harmonics

Although natural harmonics were exploited well before the Classical period, particularly in France (e.g. by Mondonville),[39] their unanimous acceptance was slow owing to their 'inferior' tone quality.[40] L'abbé *le fils'* brief yet progressive survey incorporates a minuet for violin written entirely in harmonics (both natural and artificial),[41] but the device was more commonly considered as a novel effect rather than a core technique. One English critic opined that it is 'of no practical utility, and would scarcely ever be resorted to, but for the purpose of displaying the dexterity of the performer'; and Leopold Mozart described the 'intermingling of the so-called flageolet' as 'a really laughable kind of music . . . owing to the dissimilarity of tone'.[42]

As mentioned earlier, natural harmonics were recommended where appropriate by Spohr and others to assist in shifting. However, it required virtuosi such as Jakob Scheller and Paganini to arouse public interest in artificial harmonics and the techniques involved in their mastery. Paganini's introduction of artificial harmonics in double stopping was innovatory. Chromatic slides, single trills, trills in double stopping and double trills, all in harmonics, as well as some interesting pseudo-harmonic effects, were all included in his repertory; furthermore, by incorporating harmonics, he extended the range of the G string to cover at least three octaves.

Pizzicato

The earliest known use of right-hand pizzicato in violin music is found in Monteverdi's *Combattimento di Tancredi e Clorinda* (1624), where the player is required to 'pluck the strings with two fingers'. The use of one finger, generally the index finger, became the norm, but the right thumb was sometimes employed for a special effect, the instrument sometimes being held across the body and under the right arm, guitar-fashion. The thumb's fleshy pad proved ideal for sonorous arpeggiation of chords or for soft pizzicato passages, as in Farina's *Capriccio stravagante* (1627). Berlioz recommends plucking with the second finger and even suggests using the thumb and the first three fingers as plucking agents for variety in certain rapid pizzicato passages.[43]

Interestingly, the invention of snap pizzicato, often attributed to Bartók in the twentieth century, actually dates back to Biber, who uses the effect to represent gunshot in his *Battalia*. However, Bartók's pizzicato *sul ponticello* indication appears to have no precedent and the pizzicato effect with the fingernail is another twentieth-century innovation. Left-hand pizzicato, rarely used in the early eighteenth century, gradually became more popular and reached its zenith with Paganini and his successors, who sometimes combined it with right-hand pizzicato or used it simultaneously with bowed notes.

Pitch

Pitch has been artificially standardised in recent historical performance. The pitches most commonly adopted nowadays are: $a^1=415$Hz for Baroque music; $a^1=430$Hz for music of the Classical period and $a^1=435$ or 440Hz for the performance of music post *c*.1830. This is no more than a convenient and over-simplified response to the evidence, in order to cater for uniformity of intonation and purpose amongst period instrument ensembles, particularly with wind instruments in mind. It is comforting, nonetheless, that such artificial standardisation has some justification in history; a universal pitch standard formed part of Quantz's wish-list in the mid eighteenth century, for he considered the variety of extant pitches inconvenient for his work as a flautist and 'detrimental to music in general'.[44]

Tuning systems and scordatura

All historical performers, and particularly keyboard specialists, should attempt to understand the considerable complexities of the various tuning systems that were adopted for much of our period in order to assist in giving conviction to the intonation of instruments of fixed pitch such as harpsichords or organs.[45] As discussed in the parent volume to this series,[46] the systems (or temperaments) employed during the seventeenth, eighteenth and early nineteenth centuries were very different from the equal temperament widely adopted since by all performers other than the majority of those interested in historical practice.

The existence of these tuning systems relates to problems concerning the characteristics of musical intervals and their relationship to each other. If a complete cycle of fifths is tuned, the final note of the cycle will not be in tune with the first, and if three perfect major thirds are tuned the highest note will be slightly less than a perfect octave above the first. While many instrumentalists and singers can adjust individual notes in performance to accommodate these peculiarities, instruments of fixed pitch have to adopt tuning systems in which some, or all, of the thirds and fifths are tempered. Equal temperament, founded on a cycle of twelve identical fifths and with the octave divided into twelve equal semitones, is thus the convenient compromise that gradually gained universal acceptance during our period, all intervals being slightly mistuned (as demonstrated by the resultant 'beats'), and with thirds and sixths being tempered much more uniformly than fifths and fourths. Its only gradual acceptance was due largely to its elimination of many of the nuances of intonation and subtleties of key-colour that played a significant expressive role in most music composed before about 1850. Several writers, including Johann Kirnberger and Pietro Lichtenthal, emphasised the importance of individual key character, which Lichtenthal used as an argument against equal temperament.[47]

Up to about the middle of the eighteenth century, string players tended to use a kind of 'just' or mean-tone intonation, though Bruce Haynes rightly remarks that 'just intonation is a kind of "holy grail" that is impossible to apply continuously'.[48] Technical matters, subjective perceptions, dynamic levels and whether or not instruments of immovable pitch were involved were among the determining factors for intonation, but major thirds were generally pure and sharps were played lower than the enharmonically equivalent flats. Such a system is described by Telemann, Quantz and several other writers, Tosi providing an eloquent summary:

Every one knows not that there is a Semitone Major and Minor, because the Difference cannot be known by an Organ or Harpsichord, if the Keys of the Instrument are not split. A Tone, that gradually passes to another, is divided into nine almost imperceptible intervals, which are called Comma's[sic], five of which constitute the Semitone Major, and four the Minor . . . If one were continually to sing only to those above-mention'd Instruments, this Knowledge might be unnecessary; but since the time that Composers introduced the Custom of crowding the Opera's[sic] with a vast Number of Songs accompanied with Bow-Instruments, it becomes so necessary, that if a Soprano was to sing D-sharp, like E-flat, a nice Ear will find he is out of Tune, because this last rises. Whoever is not satisfied in this, let him read those Authors who treat of it, and let him consult the best Performers on the Violin.[49]

Geminiani's slightly different approach, like that of many seventeenth- and eighteenth-century theorists, has much common ground with Tosi's. He divided the octave into twelve semitones, 'that is, 7 of the greater and 5 of the lesser'.[50] As Haynes explains, 'since the seven "greater" or "major" semitones each contain five commas and the five "lesser" have four, the octave will consist of a total of 55 commas, or parts . . . corresponding to a temperament now known as "1/6–comma mean-tone"'.[51]

Such a differentiation between major and minor semitones according to harmonic function was a significant expressive element in Baroque and Classical performance; it also offers one further explanation why string players were often guarded about using open strings, especially if tuned in pure fifths. Roger North endorses such caution (*c*.1726), on account of the resultant tonal differences and Pythagorean intervals:

Of the first sort [of rules for studying the violin] the chief is the sounding all the notes under the touch, and none with the strings open; for those are an harder sound than when stopt, and not always in tune, which the stop (assisted by the ear) affects[sic] with utmost niceness; so that upon instruments so handled, all the semitones, whatever keys are or however they change, are in tune to the most scrupulous of the ear. And besides all this, the power of the finger in giving temper and commixture to the notes, hath a superlative effect of sweetness.[52]

Roger North's view is later endorsed by Galeazzi and other writers, especially when keyboard instruments are involved.[53] Quantz makes positive suggestions to counteract such problems, advising violinists to tune the fifths 'a little on the flat side rather than quite truly or a little sharp, as is usually the case, so that the open strings will all agree with the keyboard. For if all the fifths are tuned sharp and truly, it naturally follows that only one of the four strings will be in tune with the keyboard. If the a^1 is tuned truly with the keyboard, the e^2 a little flat in relation to the a^1, the d^1 a little sharp to the a^1, and the g likewise to the d^1, the two instruments will agree with each other'.[54]

Towards the middle of the eighteenth century sharps began to be tuned higher than their enharmonically equivalent flats. This was due to 'the new "functional" melodic and "dynamic" role that semitones had in the modern harmonic-tonal system (e.g. the pull of the tonic on the leading note and of the sixth degree on the minor 7th made – respectively – the sharps to raise and the flats to lower)'.[55] Barbieri continues:

> In this new 'Pythagorean-functional' intonation, the pitch of the notes was also conditioned by strong emotional factors and by the character traditionally attributed to the different keys, this last one linked to the mode (major or minor) and alterations in the signature (sharps or flats). In any case, even in the middle of the 19th century the struggle between syntonic and Pythagorean had not completely faded.

The increasing demands of modulation and greater tonal diversity and the consequent greater use of enharmonic transitions necessitated some tempering of the semitones, such that there was no harmonic distinction between sharps and flats. Equal temperament was no new phenomenon – it had been adopted by players of, for example, fretted Renaissance instruments and was subsequently endorsed for keyboard music by Frescobaldi in the late 1630s; but Rameau (1737) interestingly made a complete U-turn in his views of only a decade earlier and expressed a preference for equal temperament:

He who believes that the different impressions which he receives from the differences caused in each transposed mode by the temperament [now] in use heighten its character and draw greater variety from it, will permit me to tell him that he is mistaken. The sense of variety arises from the intertwining of the keys [*l'entrelacement des Modes*] and not at all from the alteration of the intervals, which can only displease the ear and consequently distract it from its functions.[56]

Mark Lindley further informs us that equal temperament continued to be identified with Rameau's name throughout the eighteenth century in France and occasionally also in Italy. In Germany, numerous theorists championed equal temperament, notably Marpurg, Türk, Hummel and other writers of keyboard treatises, such that it became the standard keyboard tuning in the nineteenth century.[57] It also became the widely cultivated norm for intonation in general, Spohr's violin method, among others, defining 'pure intonation' as 'that of equal temperament, since in modern music no other exists. The budding violinist needs only to know this one intonation. For this reason neither unequal temperament nor small and large semitones are mentioned in this method because both would serve only to confuse the doctrine of the absolutely equal size of all 12 semitones.'[58] Nevertheless, nearly a century later, Joachim's biographer J. A. Fuller Maitland defended his subject from the charge of faulty intonation in the latter part of his career by stating that the violinist's tuning was more just than that of a keyboard instrument tuned in equal temperament.[59]

'Period' string players should thus be prepared to be flexible and respond in their intonation to unequal systems of tuning, as well as different performing situations and instrumental combinations, especially those requiring instruments of fixed pitch (e.g. keyboard and, to a certain extent, wind instruments). A similar flexibility was also required in other performing situations not involving keyboard instruments. Chesnut cites an A flat or G sharp minor triad in the finale of Mozart's Symphony in E flat major, K.543 (b. 113) written enharmonically in mixed notation G sharp–B–D sharp–A flat, together with a comparable example of a B or C flat major chord, written C flat–E flat– F sharp–B, in the Adagio of Haydn's String Quartet Op. 76 no. 6 (b. 36). The use of a mixed notation in such cases pinpoints the enharmonic change and alerts the performers to modify their temperament according to the prevailing harmonic context.[60] Sound aural judgement offered the principal recourse for the most consonant results, which generally involved mean-tone temperament, equal temperament or *substantially just* intonation.

From the evidence of treatises and fingerboard charts,[61] most eighteenth-century tunings aimed to achieve fairly pure thirds and sixths, avoiding the heavily altered thirds and sixths of equal temperament by tempering fifths to a greater degree and allowing one 'wolf' (i.e. unpleasantly large) fifth at the cumulation of the circle of fifths. The other intervals were accommodated accordingly, Mattheson providing some useful guidelines:

> The most common type of temperament . . . rests on the following three statements:
> 1. Octaves, minor sixths and minor thirds must everywhere be pure.
> 2. One must raise major sixths and fourths somewhat.
> 3. One must however lower fifths and major thirds somewhat.[62]

Interestingly, Mattheson adds, 'How much or how little this somewhat should be is another question,' which clearly had to be left to the player's discretion and aural judgement.

Scordatura has been in and out of fashion with violinists and violists, but it was particularly popular in violin playing between *c.*1600 and *c.*1750. Marini's use of the device in his Op. 8 no. 2 (1629) was imitated by Biber (for example, in his 'Mystery' sonatas) and many others: Uccellini, Bononcini, Lonati, Vivaldi, Tartini, Castrucci, Lolli, Barbella, Campagnoli and Nardini in Italy; Abel, Arnold, Fischer, Kindermann, Pachelbel, Schmelzer, Strungk and Westhoff in Germany; and Corrette, Le Maire, Tremais and Berthaume in France. Walther, on the other hand, despised its use.[63] Many composers were attracted to the new colours, timbres and the increased sonority or brilliance offered by different tunings of stringed instruments and the consequent tension changes of the relevant strings. Furthermore, scordatura could provide new harmonic possibilities, extend the range of instruments (for example, by lowering the violin G string), assist in imitating other instruments, or facilitate the execution of whole compositions or certain technical passages, especially those involving wide intervals, intricate string-crossing or double stopping, which might otherwise be impossible.

The particular tuning employed was generally indicated at the beginning of each composition or movement, accompanied, in most cases, by a form of tablature indicating a key-signature for each string.[64] The violin was thus treated as a transposing instrument, the music being notated according to the disposition of the fingers and not according to the pitches produced. This notation required players to observe three fundamental rules in performance: to use first position wherever possible, to use open strings wherever possible unless otherwise indicated, and to apply accidentals only to the register indicated.

Scordatura viola tunings were rarer. Perhaps the most notable are Mozart's recommendation of raising all the viola strings a semitone in his *Sinfonia Concertante* (K.364/320d), in order to gain greater facility (through fingering in D major) and additional brilliance and clarity of tone, and Carl Stamitz's similar specification for both solo violin and viola in his *Sinfonia Concertante*. Other examples of similar semitonal scordature include Carl Stamitz's Viola Sonata in B flat major, his Second Viola Concerto in B flat major, and concertos by Sperger (in E flat major) and Amon (E major), while Vanhal's Concerto in F, Druschetsky's in D, Voigt's in C (Op. 11) and Amon's in A require all four strings of the viola to be raised by a tone. Richard Strauss's requirement of the solo violist to tune the C string down a semitone to accommodate the low B in the third variation of *Don Quixote* is a notable later orchestral example.

Scordatura gradually lost popularity during the nineteenth century, although it never became obsolete, the numerous disadvantages of the device outweighing its advantages. Mazas, Spohr, Bériot, Prume, and Winter were among those composers who employed it, but Paganini was undoubtedly its most prolific exponent, using it to simplify his violin music, to add tonal brilliance and to reproduce, on open strings, harmonics which would normally have to be stopped.

Holding the bow

Interest in the expressive potential of the bow, 'the soul of the instrument it touches',[65] increased dramatically during the eighteenth century. Vital to the fulfilment of such ideals was a natural and flexible bow hold. The close relationship between the manner of holding the instrument and bow suggests that, without the chin-braced violin/viola hold, the right elbow was positioned close to but detached from the body in a natural, unconstrained manner below the level of the bow-stick (see Fig. 4.2). Herrando claims that the elbow should be separated from the body by about the distance between the extended thumb and index finger.[66] The resultant method of applying pressure from the bow to the strings for the production of tonal and dynamic variety was very different from the modern method, in which the entire weight of the hand and arm is applied. In Baroque playing the only pressure agent was the index finger.

During the nineteenth century, the elbow took up a position closer to the body than formerly, necessitating a characteristically high, supple wrist position, especially when bowing at the heel (see Fig. 4.1). The trend in more recent times has been to strike a compromise between these two elbow positions and to 'flatten out' the wrist at the frog.

As nowadays, many factors influenced the bow grip adopted by players: national style, musical demands, personal taste, the size of the hand and fingers, and the balance (and hence the type) of the bow itself. In the early Baroque period, the thumb was placed typically on the hair near the frog. Italian violinists introduced a thumb position on the under side of the stick, but the thumb-on-hair 'French grip', with three fingers placed on top of the stick and the little finger commonly braced in the back of the stick, persisted in France into the eighteenth century and was especially suitable for heavily accented dance music.[67]

The standardisation of bow construction prompted a corresponding, if gradual, standardisation of bow holds. The prevailing cantabile ideals and the increasing popularity of the sonata and concerto in mid-eighteenth-century France led to the demise of the 'French' grip in favour of the greater freedom and subtleties of tone production offered by the Italian method (with four fingers on the top of the bow-stick and the thumb placed on its underside). Furthermore, L'abbé le fils and Cupis imply that the hand was placed at the frog and not, as Geminiani, Corrette and Leopold Mozart had advised, slightly (c.3–7cm) above it (see Fig. 4.2).[68] The normal bow grip of nineteenth-century violinists involved placing the thumb at the frog; however, some players (e.g. Mazas, Bruni, Paganini and Dancla) employed the old 'Italian' grip for optimum balance with the hand rounded naturally and the thumb a short distance from the frog, even with Tourte-model bows.

Contrary to the practice of late-nineteenth and twentieth-century players, violinists and violists of earlier times kept the thumb fairly straight on the bow. Baillot explicitly stated: 'Avoid bending the thumb',[69] seeking a secure grip without stiffness in the hand, fingers or wrist. However, such statements must inevitably have been interpreted somewhat loosely, as some degree of thumb bending would have been required to achieve the requisite flexibility of the fingers.

Opinion varied regarding thumb placement; normal practice was to position it opposite the second finger,[70] but positions between the index and second fingers, or between the second and third fingers, were also used.[71] These thumb positions naturally affected the contact-point of the index finger on the bow. The so-called 'German' grip has a contact-point at the first joint of the index finger; the 'Franco-Belgian' between the first and second joints but nearer the second, with the thumb approximately opposite the second finger or between the second and third fingers.

Up to about the end of the eighteenth century players generally separated the index finger slightly from the others for the control of volume, by applying or releasing pressure as required. The second and third fingers, naturally rounded, merely rested on the stick, while the fourth finger aided balance when bowing in the lower half. The nineteenth-century fashion was to avoid separation of the index finger from the others on the stick and to encourage a combination of thumb, index finger (on or near the middle of the second joint) and wrist-joint pressure on the bow.[72]

Corrette's, Herrando's and L'abbé *le fils*'s recommendation that the stick should be inclined slightly towards the fingerboard was endorsed by most writers, the degree of inclination being modified to suit the instrument, string thicknesses and the desired musical effect. However, some discouraged the practice; Leopold Mozart claims that such inclination of the bow has a detrimental effect on tone quality, but his illustration (Fig. 4.2) appears to contradict his text.

Bow strokes and bow management

The player's vocabulary of bow strokes and general bow management naturally depended to a great extent on the particular bow type and bow hold employed. Most pre-Tourte bows required a manner of playing adjusted more to clearly divided phrases and sub-phrases than to sweeping melodic lines; as discussed in Chapter 5, the unequal stresses of their down- and up-strokes were generally brought into line with the hierarchy of beats in the bar through the 'rule of down-bow'.

The fundamental short bow stroke of the Baroque and early-Classical periods was executed by only the wrist and forearm, but the upper arm was also brought into play for longer strokes; this upper-arm movement natu- rally was directed upwards and downwards but was never lateral. A low elbow and suppleness of the wrist and fingers were thus of paramount importance (although no mention was made of the degree that the wrist should turn in towards the body),[73] particularly in the execution of smooth bow-changes and string crossing; for, as discussed in Chapter 5, the natural stroke of most pre-Tourte bows was of an articulated, non-legato character (especially in the upper third). The player could vary the degree of articula- tion and modify the stroke by adding nuances appropriate to note-lengths and the tempo and character of the music, as well as by the regulation of bow speed, pressure and the point of contact. Leopold Mozart was the first to pinpoint the relationship between bow speed and volume.[74]

Few pre-Tourte bows were suited to accented bowings such as *martelé* or sforzando effects, which were used only rarely during the eighteenth century. Similarly, 'bounding' strokes such as *sautillé*, *spiccato* and 'flying staccato' were sparingly employed for bravura effect. True legato bowing was achieved only by slurring. The capacity of the slur was enlarged substantially and slurred bowings (whether or not so notated) were increasingly exploited during the Classical period to emulate the human voice, especially in slow movements. The execution of slurred staccato, confused somewhat by the variety and ambiguity of notation, was necessarily governed by the music's tempo and character. Dots above or under the notes in slow movements nor- mally indicated an on-the-string execution rather like a *portato*; strokes above or under the notes were more common in faster tempos and generally indicated playing in 'lifted' style, brief passages being executed in either up- or down-bow but longer passages normally being taken in the up-bow (Ex. 4.12a).

The 'Viotti' bowing (Ex. 4.12b), the slurred tremolo and the *portato* strokes are all related to the slurred staccato. However, the slurred tremolo (Ex. 4.12c), involving repeated notes on the same string under one slur, was

Ex. 4.12 (a) L'abbé *le fils*, *Principes*, p. 54. (b) M. Woldemar, *Grande méthode*, p. 48. (c) A. Bailleux, *Méthode raisonnée*, p. 11.

played either staccato (normally indicated by dots or strokes under a slur) or legato (implied by a slur alone). The expressive *portato* stroke, its articulations generally indicated by dots or lines above or under the slur, was confined mainly to slower tempos. *Bariolage*, the alternation of notes on adjacent strings (of which one is usually open) in either separate or, more usually, slurred bowing (Ex. 4.13a), and *ondeggiando* (Ex. 4.13b), similar to the slurred *bariolage* but with a potential range over more than two strings, were also part of the pre-Tourte bow's typical repertory.

These bow strokes represent merely a point of departure for the appreciation of an expanding and developing eighteenth-century technique, as some transitional bows were capable of all but matching the repertory of the Tourte model. As discussed in Chapter 3, the advent of the Tourte bow

Ex. 4.13 (a) L'abbé *le fils*, *Principes*, p. 79.
(b) P. Gaviniès, *24 Matinées*, no. 12.

(a)

(b)

shifted the emphasis away from the articulated strokes, subtle nuances and delayed attack of most mid-eighteenth-century models to a more sonorous, smoother cantabile style advocated by Viotti and his school, with the added capability of a more or less immediate attack, *sforzando* effects and accented bowings (e.g. *martelé*, *saccadé* and *fouetté*) and various 'bounding' strokes (*spiccato*, *sautillé*, *ricochet* etc.).

The full modern vocabulary of bow strokes began to emerge at the beginning of the nineteenth century; the French school again gave the lead, thanks largely to Baillot. However, many theorists suggest that on-the-string strokes in the upper part of the bow were more part of ordinary playing than off-string strokes well into the nineteenth century,[75] particularly for a light staccato effect, and the instruction *punta d'arco* was commonly used to indicate a short, detached bow stroke at or near the point.[76] This was a particular characteristic of the German playing style well into the nineteenth century and was probably further ingrained into German interpretation by Spohr's rejection of *spiccato* as a 'contemptible kind of bowing, and not in keeping with the dignity of Art'.[77] It was perpetuated in the various celebrated editions of David and Joachim, even though the latter admits the performer some latitude of interpretation. Claiming that *col punto d'arco* commonly indicated the use of the more 'serious and characterful' *martelé* bowing in moderate tempos, Joachim and Moser accede to the use of *spiccato* strokes 'produced close to the nut of the bow' only in faster passages in which *martelé* was impossible or which required a lighter interpretation, as in the coda of the finale (Presto) of Beethoven's Quartet Op.132.[78] Another

Ex. 4.14 Beethoven, Piano Trio Op.1 no.1, fourth movement, ed. F. David.

characteristic of German bowing style is illustrated by David's use of slurred staccato to realise a sharply articulated effect that would probably be achieved nowadays as an off-string stroke in the middle or lower half (Ex. 4.14).[79]

Baillot's survey, unique in the way it integrates bow speed and articulation, forms the most extensive catalogue of violin bowings from the first half of the nineteenth century and demonstrates that French violinists of the period, unlike those reared on German traditions, employed the full range of available bow strokes. Baillot classifies bow strokes in two basic categories according to speed: slow or fast (a classification few modern players would endorse). He also admits a 'composite' stroke which adopts elements of slow and fast strokes simultaneously.

The fundamental fast strokes were the *détachés*, which could be 'muted' (*mats*) – on-the-string strokes articulated by wrist and forearm (*grand détaché, martelé, staccato*); 'elastic' (*élastiques*) – mostly off-the-string strokes exploiting the resilience of the stick (*détaché léger, perlé, sautillé, staccato à ricochet,* flying staccato); or 'dragged' (*traînés*) – composite, on-the-string strokes (*détaché plus ou moins appuyé, détaché flûté*). The lifted bow stroke played a less prominent role, Ex. 4.15a being executed generally with the bow on the string, its movement checked momentarily (usually for no more than a demisemiquaver's duration) between the notes and the second note sounded through gentle wrist movement (Ex. 4.15b). *Bariolage* and the 'Viotti' and 'Kreutzer' bowings still remained in the repertory of slurred strokes, and other specialised bowings such as *tremolo, col legno, sul ponticello* and *sulla tastiera* were increasingly employed.

Bowing indications and articulations were more thoroughly annotated in the late eighteenth and the nineteenth centuries, ostensibly to avoid ambigu-

Ex. 4.15 (a) and (b) F. Habeneck, *Méthode*, p. 68.

(a)

(b)

ity of interpretation. However, as noted in Chapter 5, inconsistent use of signs, notably of the dot and wedge, imposed extra responsibility on performers to interpret the music faithfully. With the general trend towards enlarging the capacity of the slur, bow apportionment and a general appreciation of the interdependence of bow speed, pressure and contact point (together with their combined effect on tonal quality and volume) became paramount for convincing execution.

Multiple stopping

The notation of polyphony was ambiguous; it aimed to clarify both the musical progression and the melodic and harmonic functions of the voice parts rather than provide precise prescription as to note durations. It was often impossible to perform multiple stopping in the sustained manner implied. Chords were thus generally spread either upwards or downwards (usually according to the register of the main melody note to be sustained), or played as arpeggios. Rapid upward spreading using the down-bow (even successions of chords which involved retaking the bow) was the more common practice.

Most players evidently held the lowest note a little (some went as far as holding it for almost its full value), presumably to emphasise the harmonic progression; the other chord members were then sounded as appropriate, normally in a rapid cross-string movement but always according to context, tempo or the exigencies of the polyphony. However, the fact that Leblanc prescribes a series of three-note chords in his Sonata in E flat (*c*.1767) to be played in a down-bow with all three strings struck simultaneously shows that other options were open to the performer, especially in combination with the less sweeping curvature of Baroque bridges.[80]

The less yielding qualities of the Tourte bow resulted in differing approaches to multiple stopping. Three strings could be played simultaneously (by pressing on the middle string in a down-bow at the frog) but only in *forte*, or if 'broken'. Four-note chords were also 'broken', perhaps 2+2, commencing either before or on the beat, 3+1 or 2+1+1. Spohr provides the first-known evidence of the modern practice of breaking a four-note chord upwards in twos where the lower two notes (played together before the beat) are only of short duration while the upper two notes (played together on the beat) are sustained for their full length. A down-bow was normally employed, even for consecutive chords, but arpeggiation of chordal progressions was less common than formerly. Open strings were generally sounded (where possible) in multiple stopping for optimum sonority.

5   The language of musical style

Introduction

As noted in Chapter 2, we must be prepared to assimilate details from a wide variety of sources, some of which may not be directly related to our specialist instrument, in order to enter more closely the sound-world of a particular composer. Just as we need to learn the grammar and vocabulary of a foreign language in order to express ourselves freely within it, our understanding of a composer's full expressive range requires an intimate acquaintance with the musical conventions and idioms of his time, many of which will not be part of present-day practice. These may involve unwritten conventions that were simply expected to be observed and annotations in scores that may require something other than a literal realisation, as well as instrumental preferences and technical differences mentioned in Chapters 3 and 4; a knowledge of pertinent national or regional idioms, which tended to be more diverse and less homogeneous than in modern music-making, will also be essential, as the first two case studies in Chapter 6 will confirm.

National idioms and changes in style

The respective qualities of the three principal national idioms of the Baroque period – Italian, French and German[1] – have been discussed at some length in this series' parent volume.[2] Like Georg Muffat and many other writers before him,[3] Quantz directly contrasts these idioms and their implications for composition, singing and playing. He particularly stresses the Italians' unfettered, capricious, expressive and virtuoso approach to composition and performance in contrast to the formal severity, refined precision and thoroughly ordered, mannered approach of the French. His preference for a 'mixed' German style which incorporated the best features of all kinds of foreign music, led to the cultivation of an expressive, ornate 'galant' idiom and, eventually, the realisation of his vision of 'a good style that is universal'.[4]

When contemplating historical performance, we should be mindful that composers assimilated and often wrote in idioms other than their native ones. Our Bach case study is one case in point. Even with the emergence of a more cosmopolitan style in the Classical era, national characteristics are often evident; and there were countless nineteenth-century trends which distinguished the music of one country or even individual composer from another, whether through the use of folk materials, extra-musical ideas or other elements. As Baillot observes:

> Each composer gives an imprint to his works – an individual
> stamp, a style of his own – which comes from his manner of feeling
> and expressing . . . a performer may have the ability to render the
> music of one composer and not be able to play that of another; his
> fingers, his bow, his technique, everything objects, because he does
> not have within himself the flexibility necessary to take on all the
> styles, or he is not well enough prepared to grasp the different ways
> of phrasing and the different *accents* to give to the phrases.

Baillot considers taste and 'genius of performance' as the prerequisites that 'enable performers to identify the composer's intentions and interpret them with facility and precision'.[5]

Spohr distinguishes between a correct style, which comprises faithful execution of the notes, signs, and technical terms, and a 'masterly style' by which the performer 'can from his own soul interpret the composer's intentions' through expressive bow management and fingering selection, portamento, vibrato and flexibility of tempo.[6] Focusing on Rode's Seventh Violin Concerto and his own Ninth Violin Concerto, he illustrates appropriate interpretative and stylish detail through signs and technical instructions (see Ex. 4.6b and c). He also provides brief remarks about string quartet- and orchestral-playing.

Joachim and Moser describe Spohr as 'the greatest of lyrical violinists' but attribute any German characteristics in his style more to the influence of German Romantic opera than to any national school of violin playing, recognising, too, that the Italian art of singing long provided a model for string players.[7] They also observe that differences in performance have arisen 'less from national dissimilarity than from personal artistic idiosyncrasy', and conclude that 'the ability to see into the heart of a musical work of art and to perform it with purity of style does not depend upon political frontiers, nor even on the psyche of a race. It is founded on the artistic disposition of the individual, on the mental atmosphere in which he has matured, and on the training which has fallen to his lot.'[8] More importantly, they concede that 'a work by Bach or Tartini demands a different style of delivery from one by Mendelssohn or Spohr. The space of a century that divides the two first mentioned composers from the last two means in the historical development of our art not only a great difference in regard to form, but even a greater with respect to musical expression.' Nevertheless, they emphasise that artistry lies in the performer's capacity 'so to grasp the intentions of the composer, that during the rendering of the piece they seem to come from him as the expression of his own thoughts.'[9]

Specific and extempore ornamentation

Traditions of specific and extempore ornamentation varied according to national preference during the late seventeenth and early eighteenth centuries, as the broad survey in the parent volume of this series confirms.[10] In France the intended ornaments (primarily the appoggiatura, mordent, trill and turn) or, at least, the incidence of ornamentation were generally indicated by specific signs,[11] whereas Italian musicians were largely expected to court tradition and exercise their own judgement and taste, notably, for example, in inserting cadential trills. Italian freedom of interpretation also extended to the introduction of extempore ornamentation, as is verified by the Corelli case study in Chapter 6. Arbitrary elaboration played comparatively little part in French practice, although performers should not feel restrained from making tasteful extempore additions.[12] The German approach was essentially a compromise of the Italian and French, but some German composers began well before 1750 to notate precisely the interpretative details of their compositions and thus write fairly fully ornamented melodies.[13]

During the second half of the eighteenth century the three main channels of ornamental theory and practice began gradually to merge into some measure of general agreement.[14] This was mainly the work of Quantz,

Marpurg, Agricola and especially C. P. E. Bach, who, amidst the emerging homophonic *style galant*, modified and extended French practices into a more international language of ornaments governed by the *Affektenlehre*. Bach's *Versuch* became a model for numerous subsequent treatises on the subject, his successors gradually loosening his strict, somewhat inflexible instruction in keeping with the whole nature and function of ornamentation.

Nevertheless, the interpretation of such a vital component of the Classical language as the appoggiatura was never uniform. Türk particularly values this ornament for its provision of continuity, charm, vitality, lyricism and harmonic interest through dissonance. He records that long appoggiaturas normally take half the value of the succeeding note, or two-thirds (or sometimes even one-third, if the harmony so requires) if the succeeding note is dotted, and his compilation of contexts in which the appoggiatura should be short provides an invaluable check-list for its realisation in the works of Haydn, Mozart and their contemporaries.[15] The appoggiatura is always slurred to its main note and is usually stressed slightly.

A similar variety of trill interpretations coexisted, ranging from C. P. E. Bach's upper-note preparation, to the main-note trills of Adam (1804), Hummel (1828) or Spohr (1832), or even of the mechanical clocks associated with Haydn. However, when the diversity of possible trill terminations is also taken into account, it becomes apparent that no firm, all-embracing rule can be applied regarding trill interpretation; thus, performers will need to make tasteful decisions based on melodic, harmonic, technical, rhythmic and other considerations. Baillot, for example, illustrates four trill preparations and four terminations and remarks: 'Any of the four *preparations* can be used with any of the four *endings*, depending on the character of the phrase in which the trill occurs; the choice depends on taste.'[16] The additional range of interpretation achieved by varying the number, rhythm, speed and nuances of the notes comprising this ornament should also enter the equation.

By the end of the eighteenth century, the function of ornamentation had changed from one of achieving melodic continuity to one of articulating structure, trills tending to mark out the various sections of Classical concerto or sonata movements. Furthermore, the extraordinary variety of possible interpretations of ornaments and the increasing idiosyncrasy of many composers' styles resulted in a developing trend for individual ornaments to be notated more precisely, by indicating, for example, the exact value of appoggiaturas. A minimum of signs came to be used and complex ornaments tended to be written out as fully as possible (either in normal-sized notes as an integral part of the rhythmic scheme, in small notes extra-rhythmically, or in a compromise between the two), in such a way that their interpretation (apart from a certain rhythmic freedom) could not be doubted.[17]

Period performers need to exercise appropriate taste and judgement in the 'replication' of earlier approaches to ornamentation. They should consider some or all of the following questions when seeking to interpret a particular ornament: On what note should the ornament begin? Should it start before, on or after the beat? How fast should any repercussion be? What are the harmonic implications and how long should the dissonance (if any) last? How flexibly should the ornament be executed? Should nuances be added? Is the introduction of accidentals necessary? How should the ornament be terminated? Answers to these questions will inevitably vary according to the style, character and nationality of the music, the context and the type of ornament, and the views of those theorists whose treatises are deemed most relevant to its interpretation; but it is imperative that answers are sought and carefully considered in appropriate contexts if an informed performance is to evolve.

Context and character provide Türk's principal guiding lights, especially with regard to extempore ornamentation, and he recommends that 'Only those places should be varied (but only when the composition is repeated) which would otherwise not be interesting enough and consequently become tedious.' The repetition of an Allegro is one case cited, but 'longer elaborations are most frequently used in compositions of a gentle, pleasing character in slow tempo, and particularly in an Adagio'. He points out that some passages or compositions, particularly those expressing sadness, pride and seriousness, so arouse the emotions in their original forms that the performer should refrain from embellishing them and intensify the expression only through variation of tone or volume.[18]

With the advent of the high Classical style, the performer's freedom to add extensive improvised ornamentation to enhance expression was curtailed, even though Mozart and Beethoven evidently varied their ornamental figuration in performance, especially in slow movements.[19] We will also learn in Chapter 7 of Beethoven's reaction to Bridgetower's extempore additions to the violin part of the 'Kreutzer' sonata, which appears to have been very different from his rebuke for his pupil Czerny's keyboard elaborations in Beethoven's Op. 16.[20]

The function and tasteful interpretation of fermatas also changed with the musical and social climate. Interpretations could range from a straightforward prolongation, at the performer's will, of the note(s) or rest thus indicated to improvised embellishment of that note or an extended cadenza.[21] Cadenzas, passages or sections of variable length and indefinite form, were normally extemporised by performers but were sometimes written out, notably by Torelli in the passages headed 'Perfidia' in some of his concerto movements, or by Corelli in his various written-out *points d'orgue* above the *tasto solo* bass in some of his Op. 5 sonatas. Derived from the vocal aria as a natural result of ornamenting cadences, a cadenza was generally introduced near the end of a composition or movement (normally, for instrumental music, a concerto, but sometimes in sonatas) on a pause either on the dominant of the key, or, in the case of Classical concertos, somewhat inconclusively on the tonic six-four chord.[22]

Concerto cadenzas normally ended with a trill on the dominant chord prior to the orchestral re-entry; in the eighteenth century, they tended to serve as much to demonstrate the performer's musicianship and tasteful expression as his technical prowess. Quantz was the first writer to expand the largely ornamental early-eighteenth-century concept of the cadenza, comprising normally non-thematic elaborations of the final cadence, into a more meaningful part of the musical design. He recommended that cadenzas should be constructed from the main motifs of the relevant movement and his advice served as a model for Türk's and many later studies.[23] Cadenza length depended to some extent on the solo instrument, Quantz claiming that 'a string player can make them as long as he likes, if he is rich enough in inventiveness'. Robert Levin's analysis of Mozart's extant keyboard cadenzas and his calculation that they are approximately ten per cent of the length of the relevant movement seems a useful guideline for violinists and viola players to emulate.[24]

The Classical and early Romantic eras witnessed an expansion in the scope of the cadenza. It was normally of pertinent musical content and fulfilled both an architectural function, counter-balancing the orchestral exposition

in the concerto structure, and a dramatic one of allowing the soloist opportunity for unfettered display. Some cadenzas were written out by composers
either for use in performance or as models for students to imitate. Mozart's
written-out cadenzas for the first and second movements of his *Sinfonia
Concertante* K.364/320d for violin and viola provide as good examples as any
of the appropriate length, design and pertinence of the melodic content he
employed, while the attempts of Marius Flothius are among the most successful at composing stylish cadenzas for Mozart's Violin Concertos K.211,
216, 218 and 219.

Most of Türk's guidelines for cadenza construction are pertinent to
instruments other than the piano. In his view a cadenza should present a
brief summary of the most important elements of the movement, with no
undue repetition; it should be in character with the movement and should
not include additional difficulties which transcend that character; it should
not be too long; any modulation should be brief, and neither to a remote key
nor even to a key not broached in the movement; it should contain elements
of surprise, novelty, wit and a variety and abundance of ideas; and, with
regard to its execution, it should sound spontaneous and neither calculated
nor pre-composed.[25]

While Beethoven preserved the tradition of cadenza improvisation in his
Violin Concerto Op. 61, he later adapted the work for piano (as Op. 61a) and
included a written-out cadenza for piano and solo timpani.[26] Beethoven's
extant cadenzas demonstrate a wider harmonic, tonal and, in some cases,
technical vocabulary than those of his predecessors and do not conform to
the Classical model described above; and, although some nineteenth-
century violinists and singers preferred to attune their cadenzas to their own
technical prowess, the increasing trend was for composers to write out
cadenzas in full in order either to guard against the technical excesses of virtuosi or to counteract the lack of invention displayed by many contemporary performers.

Eingänge or lead-ins were indicated by fermatas and generally occur at
imperfect cadences on the dominant or dominant seventh chord and at
perfect cadences in the dominant, mediant or submediant keys. Their function was to provide a brief non-modulatory transition, generally metrical
but in an improvisatory style, into a new section of a work, such as the
refrain of a rondo movement. An *Eingang* usually terminates with a second
fermata, while a passage which interlinks with the ensuing music is normally

termed an *Übergang*. Guidance for formulating lead-ins may be found in various treatises, notably C. P. E. Bach's *Versuch* and Türk's *Clavierschule*.[27]

Rhythmic alteration

Rhythm was also directly affected by national traditions, particularly in the Baroque period when certain rhythms were not necessarily performed as written. Period performers should thus be mindful of the practice of 'overdotting' (the exaggeration of already dotted rhythms), the assimilation of 'clashing' rhythms and the French tradition of inequality (*notes inégales*) in order to achieve their goals.

Most of the evidence for overdotting emanates from mid-eighteenth-century German theorists such as Agricola, C. P. E. Bach and Leopold Mozart and is relevant largely to German and Italian music.[28] Leopold Mozart explains: 'Dotted notes must be held somewhat longer, but the time taken up by the extended value must be . . . stolen from the note standing after the dot'. Similar advice was given for the execution of the short notes in 'Lombard rhythm'.[29] Overdotting is particularly pertinent in French overtures; when two parts have simultaneous dotted figures of different note-values (e.g. two dotted quaver-semiquaver figures against one dotted crotchet-quaver), it was usual to overdot the latter to synchronise its quaver with the other part's final semiquaver.[30]

The performance of triplets in the seventeenth and eighteenth centuries seems to have varied to some extent according to national tradition,[31] but the synchronisation of clashing binary and ternary rhythms in Baroque music is generally appropriate when duplets are set against triplets and dotted figures are set against triplets or sextuplets, depending, of course, on the performer's taste, his appreciation of the harmonic and rhythmic aspects of the musical context, and the character of the piece. Although Quantz rejects the convention for its resultant 'lame and insipid, rather than brilliant and majestic' expression, duplets and dotted figures were generally modified to accommodate triplets when both appear simultaneously. Nevertheless, it is likely that, in the third movement of J. S. Bach's Violin Sonata BWV1017, the duplets were synchronised with the triplets and the semiquavers played exactly as notated.[32]

The expressive French convention of *notes inégales* is outlined in numerous French, Spanish and Italian sources of the late seventeenth and early eighteenth centuries, yet no two accounts seem in precise accord, thereby suggesting the importance of individual taste in its application.[33] Sometimes indicated by the term 'pointer' or 'inégaliser', but often not prescribed at all, the convention related most commonly to the alternate lengthening and shortening (or, less commonly, shortening and lengthening) of evenly written successions of conjunct notes. The longer notes fall in the stronger accentual positions (e.g. in a group of four notes that start on the beat, the first and third are longer than the second and fourth) and are normally half the length of the basic metric pulse. But, as is further clarified in the parent volume to this series, such a norm was not without exception.[34] The possible introduction of *notes inégales* into some movements of Bach's E major Partita will be aired in Chapter 6. Although *notes inégales* were generally applied consistently throughout a movement, they might be varied, or even abandoned entirely in accordance with the prevailing expression, which, along with considerations of tempo, generally determined the degree of inequality introduced.

Inequality was never applied when notes were slurred or dotted; when any of the instructions *notes égales, marqué*, or *croches égales* was given; when dots or strokes were placed over notes that would otherwise be played unequally (the dots signified equality, while strokes indicated equal, staccato notes); when the notes moved by leap; or with repeated notes. Although theorists ceased to discuss *notes inégales* towards the end of the eighteenth century, the convention persisted into the following century, as the evidence of barrel organs and other mechanical instruments testifies. However, the increasing trend from the late eighteenth century onwards was for composers to notate their rhythmic requirements with greater unanimity and precision.

Affect, rhetoric, and phrasing (general principles)

Baroque and earlier writers and musicians believed that 'the true aim of music is to move the feelings'.[35] Parallels were commonly drawn between musical performance and oratory. Quantz writes:

> Musical execution may be compared with the delivery of an orator.
> The orator and the musician have, at bottom, the same aim in
> regard to both the preparation and the final execution of their pro-
> ductions, namely to make themselves masters of the hearts of their
> listeners, to arouse or still their passions, and to transport them

now to this sentiment, now to that. Thus it is advantageous to
both, if each has some knowledge of the duties of the other.[36]

The study of rhetoric and oratory was part of general education during the
Baroque period and it is therefore not surprising such parallels had cre-
dence.[37]

Performers of that era were thus duty-bound to seek out and realise the
particular 'affect' of a movement or piece – an emotional or moral state
such as sorrow, valour, or tranquillity – along with symbolic 'figures' that
may have affective connotations. Quantz looks towards differentiating a
multiplicity of affects in one movement, claiming: 'You must, so to speak,
adopt a different sentiment at each bar, so that you can imagine yourself
now melancholy, now gay, now serious etc. Such dissembling is most necessary in music'.[38] Different keys were associated by many Baroque composers with different affects – generally a major key expressed gay, bold,
serious or sublime sentiments, while a minor one expressed flattery, melancholy and tenderness; and the character or dominant sentiment of the
piece was generally clarified by the word at its beginning.[39]
Instrumentation, rhythm and the ebb and flow of consonance and dissonance were also part of the language of affects, which could further be dis-
cerned by melodic intervals and articulations. Quantz explains: 'Flattery,
melancholy and tenderness are expressed by slurred and close intervals,
gaiety and boldness by brief articulated notes, or those forming distant
leaps . . . Dotted and sustained notes express the serious and the pathetic;
long notes, such as semibreves or minims, intermingled with quick ones
express the majestic and sublime'.[40]

The performer was considered to be an equal creator with the composer
during the seventeenth and eighteenth centuries (indeed, they were often
one and the same) and was expected to remain faithful to the composer's
conception of a work. Quantz repeatedly insists that the performer should
'divine the intention of the composer', to 'seek to enter into the principal
and related passions that he is to express' and to 'take on the feeling which
the composer intended in writing it'.[41] Good performance thus involved 'a
language of the feelings'; *forte* and *piano*, for example, were used 'to produce
the same effects that an orator does by raising and lowering his voice', and
the finer points of articulation, phrasing, ornamentation and expression,

including realisation of a composer's rhetorical approach to the craft of composition, were vital if the musical 'speech', as composed and performed, was to 'affect' the listener in a similar manner as its literary counterpart.[42] Schulz and Türk thus liken melodic phrase divisions to commas in speech and emphasise the importance of their clear articulation.[43]

Nineteenth-century theorists persisted with such analogies. Baillot, for example, claims that 'Notes are used in music like words in speech; they are used to construct a sentence or create an idea; consequently, one should use full stops and commas just as in writing, to distinguish its phrases and sentences and to make it easier to understand'. Joachim and Moser confirm that phrasing, as 'the systematic arrangement of musical thoughts into musical sentences', has 'the same meaning in music as articulation and punctuation have in speech', while Bériot considers such punctuation more important in music than in literature.[44]

Articulation, accentuation and melodic inflection as constituents of phrasing

Articulation signs were extremely rare before the seventeenth century and remained scarce throughout the Baroque period.[45] Performers thus held responsibility for understanding and realising intelligently this fundamental rhetorical element. Quantz explains:

> Musical ideas that belong together must not be separated; on the other hand, you must separate those ideas in which one musical thought ends and a new idea begins, even if there is no rest or caesura. This is especially true when the final note of the preceding phrase and opening note of the following one are on the same pitch.[46]

Conjunct notes were normally played smoothly unless otherwise indicated, whereas notes proceeding by leap were generally played detached.[47] Most eighteenth-century theorists seem to have cultivated three broad categories of articulation, with staccato and legato (often indicated by a slur or *ten.*) serving as the two extremes and a semi-detached 'ordinary' manner of playing in the middleground.[48] Articulation marks of the modern, more abstract type (for example, dots, horizontal and vertical strokes) became more common towards the end of the century, but their application was inconsistent and their meaning often ambiguous. The dot seems to have been used largely to indicate a lighter, less abrupt staccato than the stroke or wedge.[49]

The final choice and extent of articulation, including the interpretation of signs, depended substantially on the particular idiom, tempo and character of the movement, as well as the individual taste of the performer and the acoustics of the performing venue. Detached playing, for example, was better suited to faster, rather than slower movements and a growing reverence for a more legato 'ordinary style' of playing, brought to full fruition in the nineteenth century, is evident both in the increased incidence of slurs and in the technical and expressive literature about most instruments by the end of the eighteenth century.[50]

Bow management provided the main articulation resource for violinists and violists, but pizzicato remained a possible alternative and fingering principles were naturally closely interlinked with articulation and phrasing. The natural stroke of most pre-Tourte bows was of an articulated, non-legato character (especially in the upper third). Leopold Mozart's 'small, even if barely audible, softness'[51] at the beginning and end of each stroke is a reference to the typical delayed attack (through only gradual take-up of hair) of pre-Tourte bows, their lightness at the tip and their balance point (closer to the hand).

Unlike modern staccato, the eighteenth-century staccato stroke[52] involved a 'breath' or articulation between notes somewhat greater than the articulation of the normal separate stroke – Tartini required staccato notes to be sounded for only half their notated values.[53] It was often conveyed by lifting the bow from the string after each stroke, especially in slow tempos, and implied the use of a dry, detached stroke in the lower part of the bow, with some feeling of accent, though not comparable to the sharp attack of the modern staccato. In fast movements the bow necessarily remained on the string in the upper half, producing an effect similar to the modern *spiccato*. As noted in Chapter 4, articulation silences often afforded players the opportunity to effect shifts of the left hand; true legato bowing with most pre-Tourte bows was achieved only by slurring, due emphasis and length being given to the first note of a slur.

After *c*.1800, the slur became less a 'pronunciation mark' and more a technical instruction. Its capacity was enlarged substantially, particularly after the advent of the Tourte bow, and slurred bowings were increasingly exploited during the Classical period as a means of emulating the qualities of the human voice, especially in slow movements. Nevertheless, correspondence between Brahms and Joachim reveals that Brahms followed Classical composers in regarding the shortening of the second of a pair of slurred notes as obligatory, whereas in longer phrases it was optional.

In order to give appropriate shape and meaning to the music, period performers must seek to re-establish the surface detail of accentuation within phrases as an expressive resource. Such accentuation is normally conveyed by stress or prolongation. The latter involves both adherence to the hierarchy of the bar and emphasis of important notes within phrases (called 'agogic accents') and is one of the basic tenets of Baroque music. It could also apply to groups of bars, phrases and even to movements and whole works, offering a complex, yet clearly recognisable structure of tension and relaxation, kept alive and vivid by other hierarchies such as consonance and dissonance. A dissonance was always stressed, even if it coincided with a weak beat, and its resolution was unstressed. Furthermore, if a longer note followed a short note, the longer note was normally stressed, even if it coincided with an unstressed part of the bar, as in the popular 'La Follia' melody.

That these practices were still relevant to early twentieth-century performance is confirmed by Joachim and Moser, who write of 'imperceptible dwelling' on principal notes or 'slight lingering' on notes with vibrato on strong beats. They further remark: 'even among notes of equal value occurring in one and the same bar, there exist, for those who are sensitive, certain differences which may receive, in accordance with the character of the passage in question, more or less distinct significance in the rendering'.[54] The length of such prolongations was a matter of taste, but Türk's rule that a note should not be prolonged for more than half its written value is a significant pointer to the proportional implications of this practice.[55]

Realising the hierarchy of the bar involved giving due emphasis to the 'good notes' (*note buone*); this concept, already well developed by the end of the sixteenth century, was re-stated in many seventeenth- and eighteenth-century treatises. The *note buone* were notes of natural rhythmic stress – particularly the first note of each bar, but also other notes (such as the third crotchet beat in 4/4), depending on the tempo. They were accommodated in string playing by the rule of down-bow, which required the 'good' notes to be played with the stronger down-bow and the 'bad' notes with the weaker up stroke.[56] In bars with an uneven number of notes, players had to adjust bowings accordingly. As noted in the Bach case study in Chapter 6, the rule was especially applicable to string playing in the French style of the seventeenth century and formed the basis of Lully's bowing style, as related by Muffat.[57] Especially characteristic was the *reprise d'archet*, a method of such adjustment which became a stylistic nuance, involving re-taking a down-bow (when the tempo allowed) to preserve the hierarchy of the bar, and *craquer*, which involved taking two notes in the same up-bow.

Although the rule of down-bow provided the foundation for eighteenth-century Italian and German bowing principles, it was treated rather less systematically in those two countries; nevertheless, Spohr recommends commencing 'as often as possible every bar with a down-bow and finish with an up-bow'[58] and the rule has remained a guiding force in bowing to this day, despite its outright rejection by Geminiani and the greater equality of emphasis in the up- and down-strokes afforded by the Tourte bow. Geminiani refers to 'that wretched Rule of drawing the Bow down at the first Note of every Bar' and cautions 'the Learner against marking the Time with his Bow', a view that was also held to some extent by Quantz, Reichardt and others.[59]

The relative sparseness of dynamic markings in Baroque and much Classical music,[60] the dominance of two basic markings in surviving sources (*piano* (*doux*) and *forte* (*fort*)) and the rare use of crescendo and diminuendo prescriptions have led some musicians incorrectly to introduce the principle of terraced dynamics into their performances, contrasting large sections of music played uniformly softly and loudly. Although echo effects were common in Baroque music, such interpretations ignore the fact that dynamic markings traditionally served as a framework for the structural design of a piece or movement, with either dynamic unity or dynamic contrast between sections (although not necessarily in the extreme 'terraced' manner) as a prevailing feature.[61] Among other misleading annotations is a *p* followed closely by *f*, which may, dependent upon the music's character, indicate a crescendo (and hence *f* followed closely by *p* a diminuendo) rather than any sharp dynamic contrast. Furthermore, some indications held different meanings for different composers or theorists – Walther, for example, took *pp* to mean *più piano*, not *pianissimo*. Informed decisions based on considerations of style, good taste and musicianship should prevail.

Stylish interpretation requires supplementing the notation, however sparse or dense, with subtle, finer shadings to enhance the melodic line.[62] For example, it was natural to: play dissonant notes more loudly than consonances, since the former arouse our emotions and the latter quieten them; to add the *messa di voce*, or swell, as an expressive ornament on long notes, often with vibrato;[63] to crescendo a little to high notes, and diminuendo from them; and to follow the contours of the music through subtle shadings. Geminiani equates *forte* and *piano* with the effects that an orator achieves 'by raising and falling his voice', while Leopold Mozart provides numerous examples where subtle nuancing would normally inflect a performance, whether or not notated.[64] He recommends cultivation of the four divisions of the bow for expressive playing, nuanced bowings ($<; >; <>; <> <>$) that were widely imitated well into the nineteenth century, even by some users of Tourte-model bows. Bériot includes them in his treatise, but he emphasises that expression must embrace a whole phrase and deplores the practice of swelling the sound towards the middle of each stroke.[65]

Composers began to incorporate more detailed expressive annotations towards the end of the eighteenth century. Nevertheless, Baillot emphasises the performer's role in making good any omission of annotated nuances and ensuring an appropriate sense of proportion in their use. For the violinist 'must bear in his soul that expansive force, that warmth of feeling which spreads outwards, communicates, penetrates, burns. It is this sacred fire which an ingenious fiction made Prometheus steal in order to give life to mankind'.[66] In achieving such a goal Bériot surveys the 'prosody of the bow', remarking upon the need 'to mark all the long syllables with a down bow, and the short by an up bow'. He indicates his recommended shadings of some popular operatic arias graphically in terms of bar hierarchy and tessitura, and he also provides musical examples of extracts from Beethoven, Viotti and Mozart which demonstrate the relationship between accent and characterisation. Spohr, meanwhile, urges players to take advantage of the bow's natural weight distribution, using up-bows for crescendos and down-bows for diminuendos whenever appropriate.[67]

Tempo and tempo rubato

For the determination of tempo, more faith was placed for some time in the time signature of a piece and its amount of musical activity than in tempo descriptions. Nevertheless, written directions, usually in the form of Italian terms, were increasingly employed during our core period. They often suggested the mood, character and style of the movement in addition to tempo, and Leopold Mozart considered them 'indispensable for the purpose of indicating the pace at which the piece should be performed, and how to express the emotions conformably with the composer's intention'.[68]

This series' parent volume has already cautioned performers about the ambiguity of time-words during our period and how their significance varied by period and country. It has also outlined the various ways in which tempo was measured before the development of the metronome (c.1815);[69] of these, the most systematic, Quantz's relation of tempo to the human pulse (treated as averaging eighty beats per minute), is explored further in the Bach case study in Chapter 6, as are also the advantages and disadvantages of deducing tempos for stylised dances from practical dance reconstruction, using contemporary dance treatises as sources.[70]

The most common Italian time-words of the Baroque were, in their most usual order from slow to fast: adagio; largo; andante; allegro; vivace; and presto.[71] However, the confusion caused by inconsistencies in the description and inter-relationship of some time-words often placed the onus on the performer to infer an appropriate tempo from the music itself, whether deduced from note-lengths, the rate of harmonic change or even considerations of structure. Leopold Mozart regards this process as 'among the highest accomplishments in the art of music . . . Every melodic piece has at least one phrase from which one can clearly recognise the tempo the music demands. This phrase, if other considerations are taken into account, often compels one into its own natural speed'.[72]

Eighteenth- and early-nineteenth-century composers used a variety of simple, (mainly) Italian terms to indicate tempo, most treatises providing clear descriptions of each time-word's particular characteristics. The commonest terms in Classical scores are andante and allegro, both of which are often qualified with clear tempo implications; however, confusion seems to have existed over the meaning of andantino, some theorists (e.g. Galeazzi and Cartier) believing the term to signify a slower speed than andante, and some (e.g. Türk, Clementi and Hummel) the opposite.[73] Furthermore, Kirnberger, like many eighteenth-century theorists, records that metre played a role in determining tempo, time signatures with smaller denominators normally implying faster performance than those with larger ones; for example, he associates specific metrical indications with specific tempos: 2/2 suggests 'serious and emphatic', 6/16 is 'lighter and faster than 6/8', and 3/2 is 'ponderous and slow'.[74] The perceived need to define tempo more explicitly led to more extensive use of qualifying clauses, particularly by Beethoven, who even headed some movements with dual-purpose Italian/German terms, the Italian indicating tempo and the German the relevant character.[75]

The invention of the metronome alleviated many problems of tempo determination, but raised other issues, as metronome marks were not necessarily suitable to all conditions and circumstances. Those metronome indications for specific works by Mozart remembered by some of his younger contemporaries, for example, appear to have limited value;[76] and while Beethoven attached great significance to both the correct realisation of his tempos and his metronome markings, some of the latter have given cause for doubt.[77] As discussed in Chapter 7, Brahms, like Mendelssohn before him, questioned the value of the metronome and its associated markings and found nothing new in the notion of the so-called 'elastic tempo'.[78] At best, metronome markings serve as useful guides to a tempo that will realise the character of the music; they were sometimes even contradicted in composers' own performances of their works, as early recordings clearly demonstrate.[79]

Tempo rubato (literally 'stolen time'), an expression first coined by Tosi (1723) for a technique introduced centuries earlier during the Middle Ages and Renaissance,[80] was employed as an expressive melodic effect. Interlinked with principles of accentuation and often regarded as a species of ornament, it seems to have been applied eventually to four different

expressive techniques; the most common involved a natural flexibility of the
prescribed rhythm within a constant tempo, after which the ensemble
between melody and accompaniment was restored.[81] The term also
extended in certain cases to: the modification of dynamics and/or the dis-
placement of natural accents (resulting, for example, in unaccented 'strong'
beats of the bar);[82] the expansion of the bar(s) to incorporate more notes
than the time signature theoretically allows, and a flexible yet rhythmically
controlled performance of these passages;[83] or flexibility of tempo by introducing arbitrary, unwritten accelerandos or ritardandos over an extended
musical period.[84]

   Much expressive rhythmic freedom was allowed in static harmonic passages and sections of improvisatory character in seventeenth-century Italian
sonatas by composers such as Cima, Castello, Pandolfi and Uccellini, and
Franz Benda was later renowned for his use of expressive rubato in his concertos and sonatas.[85] Tosi claimed that 'whoever does not know how to steal
the Time in Singing . . . is destitute of the best Taste and greatest Knowledge'.
Geminiani, however, was criticised by Burney for being 'so wild and
unsteady a timist', confusing the opera orchestra in Naples with his '*tempo
rubato*, and other unexpected accelerations and relaxations of measure'.[86]
Though an advocate of strict time-keeping, Leopold Mozart concedes that
tempo rubato enters the realm of the virtuoso, warning accompanying
players accordingly;[87] and the lower three string players would do well to
heed such a warning in, for example, the second movement of Haydn's
String Quartet Op. 54 no. 2, where the first violinist's arabesque (bb. 19ff.)
comprises a written-out rubato which delays the expected melodic notes
and results in dissonance through enforced harmonic overlapping.

   Richard Hudson refers to a number of articles in the *Allgemeine musikalische Zeitung* in the early nineteenth century that condemned rubato, and
Robert Schumann is reported to have likened the playing of some virtuosi to
the progress of a drunkard.[88] Nevertheless, Czerny's systematic appreciation
of the expressive potential of rubato confirms the range and perceived value
of the device. He lists eleven situations for retarding, many of which have
structural significance, such as a melodic reprise or a transition to a different
rhythmic movement; but some are in response to Italian terms such as *ral-
lentando, ritenuto, smorzando* and *calando* and even *espressivo*, and some are

related directly to style and affect, emotions of 'sudden cheerfulness, impatience . . .' etc. occasioning some quickening of tempo, and feelings of grief or 'wavering hesitation' being matched by slowing of the pulse.[89]

Baillot, Spohr, Joachim and Moser and other writers give due attention to tempo rubato in their treatises. Baillot describes it as 'a way of altering or breaking the pulse which derives from syncopation'. Used sparingly,

> it tends to express trouble and agitation and few composers have notated or indicated it; the character of the passage is generally sufficient to prompt the performer to improvise according to the inspiration of the moment. He must only make use of it in spite of himself, as it were, when, carried away by the expression, it apparently forces him to lose all sense of pulse and to be delivered by this means from the trouble that besets him. We say that he only appears to lose the sense of pulse, that is he must preserve a sort of steadiness that will keep him within the limits of the harmony of the passage and make him return at the right moment to the exact pulse of the beat . . . *Often a beautiful disorder is an artistic effect.* This disorder . . . will become an *artistic effect* if it results from effort and inspiration and if the artist can use it without being forced to think of the means he is employing.[90]

Ex. 5.1 sheds some light on Baillot's implementation of the device, although he cautions readers that 'like all impassioned accents it will lose much of its effect if it is performed according to the book'.

Spohr distinguishes between 'correct delivery', which includes 'steadiness in regard to *Tempo*, neither hurrying nor dragging the measure', and 'consummate mastery of style', which might involve 'the occasional deviation from a strict *tempo* . . . for the purpose of producing certain effects, as, for instance, an acceleration of time in passages of a fervent or impetuous character, and a slackening or lingering in those episodes expressive of tenderness or pathos'. Regarding the execution of Ex. 5.2 Spohr remarks: 'In the second half of the 28th and 30th bars, the first notes of the ascending scale should be dwelt upon somewhat beyond their actual value, this departure from strict time being compensated for by a slight acceleration of the remaining notes'. He stresses that the acceleration must not lessen the effect

Ex. 5.1 G. B. Viotti's Violin Concerto no. 19, quoted in P. Baillot, *L'art du violon*, pp. 136–7.

of the diminuendo and suggests that the bow be proportioned accordingly.[91] He is guarded about the application of tempo rubato to his own compositions, claiming that only rarely is the device necessary for the enhancement of their expression.

In keeping with Spohr's sentiments, Joachim and Moser stress the importance of dynamic, timbral and rhythmic manipulation in giving an

Ex. 5.2 L. Spohr, *Violinschule*, p. 199.

impression of tempo modification without destroying the unity of a movement or piece through segmentation. They apply rubato in repertories past
and present to avoid 'deadly dullness. It is not sufficient to play the notes correctly', they continue; 'the living spirit of a work of art must be made apparent if its reproduction is to make any impression'.[92] They further claim that
transitions from one tempo to another of very different character should be
effected smoothly and with 'no sudden shock', citing as their example
Wagner's poetic views regarding the transition from the opening fugal
Adagio ma non troppo e molto espressivo to the ensuing interlinked Allegro
molto vivace of Beethoven's String Quartet Op. 131.

Wagner railled against unmusical conductors who sustained the same
tempo throughout a movement, arguing that each theme in a piece needed
its own tempo: 'It is essential ... that the tempo shall be imbued with a life as
delicate as the life of the thematic tissue ... in Classical music written in the
later style, modification of tempo is a *sine qua non*;'[93] his particular concept
of tempo flexibility influenced Hans von Bülow, Mahler and numerous
other early-twentieth-century musicians. Similarly, Elgar stated that his
works should be performed 'elastically and mystically' and not 'squarely and
... like a wooden box',[94] and early recordings confirm that his flexibility of
tempo went far beyond the copious annotations in his scores – witness, for
example, his recording of his Violin Concerto with the young Yehudi

Menuhin as soloist. While such flexibility of tempo is still a significant expressive tool nowadays, performances tend to be more regular and 'ironed-out' than those of about a century ago.

Taste

Taste serves as the final arbiter in the interpretation of historical evidence, whether this involves source materials, organological issues, instrumental technique or elements of musical style. Broadly speaking, Spohr's sentiments echo those of most of his predecessors and successors who have written on the subject within our core period:

> All these means of expression which go to form the finest style can only fulfil their aim when refined taste presides over their employ-ment, and when the soul of the artist guides his bow and animates his fingers. If, therefore, the scholar is in some measure master of the mechanical part of his art, he should devote himself with zeal to the cultivation of his taste, and of all that may tend to arouse and intensify his feeling. Nothing is more favourable to this devel-opment than frequent opportunities of listening to the perfor-mance of noble works by the most accomplished exponents, and a judicious directing of his attention, by the teacher, to the intrinsic beauties of various compositions, and to the means employed by the executants to produce the desired effect in their interpreta-tion.[95]

Even though interpreting appropriately a wide range of historical styles was not part of a seventeenth- or eighteenth-century performer's brief, good musical taste is consistently mentioned in sources, particularly those of the eighteenth century. It required performers to exercise discrimination and judgement concerning issues that would best serve the interests of the music and was informed by a thorough understanding of those issues – 'Nature, reason and the experience of art are our guides,' wrote Mattheson[96] – including the parameters within which the composer was operating, the consequent national or other stylistic boundaries which should be heeded and a detailed acquaintance with the (perhaps unwritten) conventions rele-vant to the music. Joachim and Moser's remark that 'all rules applied to the art of music performance are not of unbending strictness'[97] also lays greater responsibility on performers to make appropriate interpretative and technical decisions.

Period performers thus need to acquire a wide range of knowledge and technique and a wealth of experience, as well as to exercise an extraordinary degree of intelligence, musicianship and taste if they are to devise satisfactory solutions to problems for which there are no definitive or widely accepted answers. While they will have to rely substantially on their intuitive response to the expressive implications of early music, their purpose in educating themselves as musicians is to be able to play instinctively and express themselves tastefully within a given language and stylistic framework, without being misled by the styles and tastes of the intervening years. Only then will they be in a position to re-construct stylish, historical interpretations that are convincing, and at the same time individual and vivid.

6 Historical awareness in practice 1 – three eighteenth-century case studies: Corelli, Bach and Haydn

This chapter, like Chapter 7, attempts to signal the application of issues discussed in the previous chapters to three works selected from the violin and viola repertory of the series' core period. Spatial limitations mean that it is not possible to deal in detail with all aspects; to do so could also lead, in many cases, to undesirable duplication. However, taken together, these case studies demonstrate the wide range of issues that need to be addressed by period performers; they also illustrate the limits of our knowledge in some areas.

Corelli: Sonata in A major, Op. 5 no. 9

Introduction

As both composer and violinist Arcangelo Corelli's (1653–1713) reputation and influence were immense in European musical circles, and his twelve *Sonate a violino e violone o cimbalo* Op. 5 have long been considered mainstays of the violinist's repertory. Published in Rome on 1 January 1700, they were probably written much earlier, since we know that Corelli obsessively re-worked his compositions and withheld their publication until he considered them incapable of further improvement.[1] These sonatas appeared in about fifty editions by the end of the eighteenth century, published as far afield as in Amsterdam, Bologna, Florence, London, Madrid, Milan, Naples, Paris, Rome, Rouen and Venice;[2] they served as the cornerstone on which 'all good schools of the violin have been since founded', the title page of the Bolognese edition (1711) declaring their pedagogical purpose, 'all'insegna del violino'.[3]

Text

Three facsimiles of the first printed edition (Rome, 1700) are readily accessible.[4] Estienne Roger's third edition of these sonatas (1710) is also an invaluable source, as it incorporates what he claimed were Corelli's improvised embellishments ('wherein have been included the ornaments of the Adagios of this opus, composed by M. Corelli, as he plays them'). John Walsh made a similar claim in the following year when he reprinted Roger's third edition. This edition is also available in facsimile. It is not absolutely certain that the ornaments in Roger's and Walsh's editions were the work of Corelli himself, although the greater weight of evidence seems to endorse the publishers' claims for their authenticity. Doubts have centred around Roger's repeated assurances of their authenticity, which possibly indicate that many of his contemporaries were sceptical about their origin, and Roger North's remark: 'Upon the bare view of the print anyone would wonder how so much vermin could creep into the works of such a master'.[5] However, Marc Pincherle has claimed that in specifying the date of the counterfeit by Walsh and Hare, December 1711, William Smith removed the last possible doubts.[6]

Joseph Joachim and Friedrich Chrysander's edition of the Op. 5 sonatas, available in the Lea Pocket Scores series (no. 166), is also based on Roger's publication with the ornaments attributed to Corelli, while Roger's edition is identical with the fourth edition of Pierre Mortier, which serves as the basis for the edition (2 vols., Schott, Mainz, 1953) by Bernhard Paumgartner and Günter Kehr. Most nineteenth- and early-twentieth-century editions should be avoided; even one 'with marks of expression, bowing, and fingering' by one of the pioneers of the early music revival, Arnold Dolmetsch (Novello, n.d.), is astonishingly wayward.

Title and instrumentation

The title of Corelli's Op. 5, *Sonate a violino e violone o cimbalo* poses interesting questions. The most challenging word is 'o'.[7] Generations have assumed that it should be understood as meaning 'and/or'. Increasingly, however, scholars have been troubled by the lack of either linguistic support or hard historical evidence for such an interpretation. Tharald Borgir, Peter Allsop and others believe that there is more evidence for taking Corelli's title page literally than opting for the conventional keyboard-plus-cello solution.[8] Allsop writes: 'Although much of the violone part of Corelli's Op. 5 may fit perfectly well on the harpsichord, elsewhere the melodic instruments dialogue on an equal basis, and in some of the florid variations in La Follia (no. 12) it is the bass which predominates in figurations which are decidedly not idiomatic for the keyboard'.[9] He concludes that these works were intended in the first instance as unaccompanied duos for violin and violone (normally cello; see 'Instruments' (below)), a fashionable genre in the last quarter of the seventeenth century, with the *option* of *replacing* the cello with a harpsichord. Although this manner of performance is still not widely accepted, Borgir observes: 'The most persuasive argument for taking the option "violone o cimbalo" [violone or harpsichord] at face value is the fact that, in the publications employing that expression, the bass part is never referred to as the basso continuo in 17th-century sources . . . The titles avoid any possibility of misunderstanding by mentioning the names of the instrument[s] and avoiding any implication that the bass should be realized'.[10]

F. T. Arnold cites one case in which the violinist Veracini was accompanied only by a cello and claims that this must have been an exceptional occurrence.[11] However, secular instrumental music was the only Italian musical genre in which the continuo was not obligatory and in which its performance by single-line instruments was considered satisfactory. Such a performance approach is specified in numerous manuscripts and publications from the latter half of the seventeenth century. If the resultant sonority was wanting or the texture too thin, additional notes could be introduced by the cellist as a kind of partial realisation of the bass line.[12] However, there is little evidence to support David Watkin's suggestion that the cellist would have been required to provide harmonic support through the addition of chords and embellishments.[13]

Arnold and others have argued that the 'o' in the title should read 'e' (i.e. 'and'), referring to works by Vivaldi and Valentini that use 'o' in the title but 'e' in the parts. However, Corelli, in a letter of 1679, suggests the possibility (in an earlier sonata for violin and lute) of a single violone accompaniment, '. . . which will have a very good effect'. Furthermore, Borgir concludes that Arnold's argument is invalid for seventeenth-century performance because the option of using either a spinet or a violone is firmly rooted in the practice of that time. However, he does concede that Arnold's examples may be indicative of an increasing tendency to use both instruments (keyboard and cello) in music written after *c*.1700, both players performing from the same part.[14]

Instruments

The term 'violone' on the title page would appear to be used in the seventeenth-century Italian sense as the bass member of the violin family. However, as suggested earlier, the very active bass line in movements like the Fugue of Sonata no. 4, or the final section of the Follia Variations make it reasonable to regard 'violone' here as indicating the violoncello.[15]

Sonate da chiesa were commonly accompanied by organ continuo; but Corelli's stipulation of 'cimbalo' indicates that, if a keyboard instrument were to be employed, his Op. 5 was intended for the harpsichord, and hence the chamber. An Italian-style harpsichord, with its characteristically tangy sound, ample attack and clear registral timbres would be the ideal instrument.

Harpsichord continuo

If the violin and harpsichord performing option is favoured, keyboard players should make a careful study of continuo sources more or less contemporary with Corelli. These aim for fuller and richer accompaniments than our modern approach to figured bass realisation, which fosters discretion and unobtrusiveness. Heinichen, whose taste was strongly coloured by Italian influence (he lived in Italy 1710–16), writes about accompaniments 'as full-voiced with the left hand as with the right. In this manner is then created a six-, seven- or eight-part realization, depending on the technical proficiency of the player'.[16] Writers such as Muffat, Francesco Gasparini and Geminiani, and Tonelli's fairly dense written-out realisations of Corelli's Op. 5 support Heinichen's recommendations.

If these realisations represent continuo style during Corelli's lifetime, modern continuo players should contemplate a texture of between five and eight parts as the norm, with only rare departures from a chordal style and few textural embellishments such as rhythmic arpeggios or written-out trills. All consonances and some dissonances (especially in cadences) should be routinely doubled, and the left hand should be as actively engaged in chord-playing as the right, leading to frequent changes in the original bass line. No systematic attempt should be made to avoid doubling the violin part; full-voiced chords should frequently be re-struck to drive the music forward and common notes should not be tied over. The emphasis throughout should be on harmony, which may be 'modernised' with the addition of sevenths and ninths or supplemented with chords supplied above rests in the bass line.[17]

Pitch

Performers should contemplate playing at a pitch a tone below modern pitch in deference to that prevalent in Rome in the early eighteenth century.

Bowing and national style

The differences between the three principal national idioms – the Italian, French and German – during the Baroque period have been examined in the parent volume to this series, where the Italians' tendency towards virtuosity, caprice and fantasy in their performances was emphasised.[18] Italian violinists were also renowned for the volume they drew from their thick-stringed instruments, using their longer bows.[19] They were also more flexible than the French in matters of bowing, being less constrained by the rule of down-bow.

Ornamentation and national style

As noted in Chapter 5, the Italians generally cultivated a free approach to extempore ornamentation that enabled a sensitive performer to transform a simple melodic skeleton into an intricately shaped, highly expressive and often flamboyant melody.[20] Of course, such an approach fundamentally altered the status of the text as an authoritative statement of intent; indeed, in present-day performances, the editions of Corelli's Op. 5 published by Estienne Roger (1710) and pirated by Walsh (1711), with ornamented versions (supposedly by Corelli himself) of the slow movements of the first six sonatas, have almost usurped Corelli's original publication of 1700.

Several other sets of notated ornaments for Corelli's Op. 5 survive.[21] Some represent the fumblings of beginners, while some are teaching manuscripts; others reveal attempts to record the embellishments of celebrated violinists, and still others have different allegiances and purposes. The so-called Walsh Anonymous and Tenbury embellishments, for example, are clearly for harpsichord. Of the ornamentations for violin, those by Dubourg, Geminiani and Roman and the Manchester Anonymous manuscript combine 'specific ornaments' (trills and those indicated by signs) with 'free' ornaments and variations. The Tartini (not an autograph, incidentally, so the attribution is made on the assumption that it is a pupil's copy of a dictated exercise) and Festing ornamentations consist almost entirely of 'specific' ornaments, while the Dubourg appears to be a performing copy. The Roman is, according to Robert Seletsky, a player's notebook that comprises sketches of individual bars and cadences as well as longer passages and the variation fragments,[22] while the Manchester Anonymous MS seems to illustrate how Corelli's music was used as a basis for technical exercises; with few exceptions, they distort the character and shape of the music such that it is difficult to imagine any other intention.

Available sources thus demonstrate a wide range of approaches to melodic elaboration, reflecting players' tastes, technical facility, or even the nature of the occasions for which they were prepared. Broadly speaking, the overall length of the piece or movement is generally preserved; the principal notes of the melody are still readily perceptible; the ranges of the original parts are rarely exceeded; the harmonies are not significantly altered; slow movements are more elaborate than fast ones and the printed note-values often do not 'add up'; and sequential patterns and repetitions are not necessarily retained. Evidence also points to an increase in the density of the notated embellishments as the eighteenth century progressed, both Roger North and later Quantz condemning this development for intruding upon the metrical flow of the music.[23]

Period performers should be cautioned against replicating literally any of these ornamented versions; they should rather use them as models of good practice for the development of their own free fantasy, as was the declared intention of Roger's 1710 edition. Head-in-the page performances of predetermined embellishments would be completely contrary to the philosophy of extempore ornamentation, which demands freedom, spontaneity, adventurousness and a flexibility to adjust one's ornamental additions to suit different circumstances, occasions and venues.

Table 6.1 lists the extant sources for extempore ornamentation pertinent to Op. 5 no. 9,[24] while Ex. 6.1 demonstrates the sheer variety of ornamentation applied to the opening bars of the Largo. Particularly interesting are Geminiani's elaborations, published complete by Sir John Hawkins;[25] as a

Table 6.1 *Extant sets of free ornamentation for Corelli's Op. 5 no. 9*

	1	2	3	4	5	6	7	8	9
Preludio: Largo	*	*	*	*	*	*	**		
Giga: Allegro	*	*	*						
Adagio	*	*	*	*					*
Tempo di Gavotta: Allegro	*	*	*					*	

Index to the sources:
1. Ornaments by Matthew Dubourg (1703–67), a pupil of Geminiani; 2. Walsh Anon., a manuscript bound into a London re-edition of Op. 5 by Walsh and Hare (*c*.1711); 3. Ornaments by Francesco Geminiani (as published in John Hawkins, *A General History of the Science and Practice of Music* (London, 1776)); 4. Ornaments by another Geminiani pupil, Michael Festing (*d*. 1752); 5. Ornaments possibly in the hand of Giuseppe Tartini and probably used in his teaching: Padua Biblioteca Antoniana, MS 1896; 6. Cambridge University Library Add. MS 7059 (*c*.1735); 7. Manchester Public Library (Newman Flower Collection), MS 130; 8. Written into a copy of a Walsh edition of Op. 5, housed in the Biblioteca communale Aurelio Saffi, Forli; 9. Written by (or for) Anna Sophia Gipen into a copy of a Walsh edition of Op. 5 (London, 1740).

Corelli pupil, Geminiani's approach faithfully reflects the habitual practice of both his teacher and the taste of the time, offering a balance of chordal and linear decoration and even introducing embellishment in the final Gigue.[26] The embellishments of one of Geminiani's more renowned pupils, Matthew Dubourg, are more flamboyant, clearly demonstrating that the character of additional extempore ornamentation was inevitably coloured by the player's temperament and taste.[27]

Expression

Typically for the period there are less than ten dynamic annotations in Op. 5 no. 9 and these extend only to indications of *forte* and *piano*. However, this should not preclude performers from introducing a wide range of subtle shadings. Even though composers did not begin to use specific signs for crescendos and diminuendos until much later in the century, Scipione Maffei's remarks about orchestral playing in Rome (1711) during Corelli's lifetime suggest a highly expressive performing approach:

Ex. 6.1 Some surviving elaborations of the opening bars of the first movement of Corelli's Op. 5 no. 9.

It is known to everyone who delights in music that one of the principal means by which the skilful in that art derive the secret of especially delighting those who listen, is the *piano* and *forte* in the theme and its response, in the gradual diminution of tone little by little, and in the sudden return to the full power of the instrument; this is frequently practised with marvellous effect in the great concerts at Rome.[28]

Ex. 6.1 (*cont.*)

Most of Corelli's movements lack an initial dynamic marking and the first expressive indication is commonly *piano*, from which it may be concluded that *forte* was the normal level at which the relevant movement should be commenced. This is certainly the case in Op. 5 no. 9; the first dynamic given in the Preludio is *piano* (for an echo passage starting in b. 20). Similarly, the ensuing Giga includes a *piano* three bars before the end for a repeated cadential passage. The brief Adagio is devoid of dynamic markings, but the final

Tempo di Gavotta incorporates some striking contrasts, *forte* being applied consistently to one recurring two-bar cadential phrase.

Tempo

The tempo and character of each movement of these sonatas are generally indicated by one simple Italian time-word from the following range (from the slowest to the fastest): grave, adagio, largo, andante, allegro and vivace.[29] From the limited number employed, the hierarchy of these words in the set seems much clearer than in Baroque music as a whole, and the dance titles used in many of nos. 7–12 serve to qualify these words and inform other aspects of performance such as phrasing, articulation and accentuation.

Op. 5 no. 9 comprises four movements headed respectively Largo, Allegro (Giga), Adagio, and Allegro (Tempo di Gavotta). Each of these tends to describe mood and character directly and tempo indirectly, largo meaning 'broad' (hence 'slow'), adagio meaning 'at ease' ('slowly'), and allegro meaning 'cheerfully' ('fast'). Gigues were described by many theorists as pieces with a cheerful affection and a lively tempo,[30] while most Gavottes were of fairly rapid tempo and light character. Above all, the general advice is normally not to take slow movements too slowly, nor fast movements too quickly, with judgement and good taste, informed by musical knowledge, intelligence and understanding, acting as the arbiters.[31] Nevertheless, performers should bear in mind Muffat's description of the Italians' exploitation of extremes of tempo, dynamic, and articulation for dramatic purposes:

> The Italians . . . are accustomed to proceed much more slowly than we do in the directions Adagio, Grave, Largo etc. – so slowly sometimes that one can scarcely wait for them; but at the directions Vivace, Presto Più Presto, and Prestissimo much more rapidly and in a lively manner. For by exactly observing this opposition or rivalry of the slow and the fast, the loud and the soft, the fullness of the great choir and the delicacy of the little trio, the ear is ravished by a singular astonishment, as is the eye by the opposition of light and shade.[32]

J. S. Bach: Partita no.3 in E major for violin solo, BWV1006

Introduction

Bach's Sonatas and Partitas for Solo Violin BWV1001–1006 were probably written at Cöthen, although he may have begun work on them at Weimar, where he was more active as a violinist. Their actual date of composition is unknown, but it is probably about 1720, the completion year stated on the title page of the extant autograph fair copy. They represent the culmination of Baroque polyphonic writing for a string instrument, surpassing in musical interest and technical demands works by Westhoff and Biber mentioned in Chapter 2. Bach may also have been directly influenced by the playing of Johann Georg Pisendel (1687–1755), a pupil of Torelli and later of Vivaldi, who served at the court of Saxony in Dresden and met Bach in Weimar in 1709 and again in Dresden in 1717, when he performed his own solo Sonata (1716).

Bach was himself a very able violinist,[33] but it is doubtful that he ever performed these unaccompanied works. Their intended recipient is unknown – Pisendel, Volumier and Joseph Spieß have all been conjectured in this role – and their principal purpose may even have been a pedagogical one. Such a possibility is reinforced by the observations of Forkel and C. P. E. Bach, as well as Agricola's remark (1774) that they were intended as studies that 'present all possible difficulties to enable the student to acquire a firm control of them'.[34] Bach's technical demands, though thoroughly idiomatic, are formidable and exacting. Particularly significant are his lavish use of multiple stopping to sustain a complete polyphonic texture and his exploitation of 'polyphonic melody', in which a single line is made to suggest a fuller texture by constantly shifting between implied voices.

Ever since these works were rediscovered in the early nineteenth century, Bach's textural experiments have presented problems to interpreters and sometimes caused the pieces to be misunderstood. Schumann and Mendelssohn, for example, each considered the sustained passages of unaccompanied melody somewhat stark and provided piano accompaniments by way of 'improvement'. Furthermore, between the two world wars, Arnold Schering and Albert Schweitzer became convinced that Bach's multiple stopping could only be executed faithfully with a giant, steeply curved bow whose hair was capable of being slackened and tightened by the player's thumb so that all four strings could be sounded sonorously at once. They thereby unwittingly assisted in introducing the so-called 'Vega Bach bow', a prototype totally unknown to Bach and foreign to his principles.[35]

Three four-movement sonatas in the *da chiesa* scheme alternate with three multiple-movement partitas ('Partia' in the autograph) or dance suites. The partitas are of varied and unorthodox design, although the basic Allemande–Courante–Sarabande–Gigue model is discernible in the first two. No. 2 supplements that model with the monumental Chaconne and no. 1 adds a 'Double' to each movement and ends with a borea (It. for bourrée) rather than a gigue. The Third Partita in E major, however, comprises seven movements and includes only one (the gigue) of the four dances that form the nucleus of the normal suite. It incorporates instead a brilliant Preludio and some of the optional, lighter movements (*Galanterien*) sometimes used after the Sarabande. Unlike the first two partitas, which (apart from the Sarabande of no. 1), employ Italian designations, the dances in no. 3 are of French origin.

Text

Few musical works have undergone as much alteration and misrepresentation as Bach's sonatas and partitas. During the composer's lifetime and for some years after his death, they circulated in manuscript copies. Since the initial publication of the fugue from Sonata No. 2 in Cartier's *L'art du violon* (Paris, 1798) and the first issue of all six works in 1802, about fifty editions have appeared, each bearing the name of an illustrious performer or scholar and reflecting the technical and interpretative practices of their respective eras;[36] but some later twentieth-century publications, notably by Günter Hausswald (1958), Ivan Galamian (1971), Henryk Szeryng (1981) and Max Rostal (1982), have displayed more reverence towards primary sources, of which the extant autograph manuscript, housed in Berlin's Deutsche Staatsbibliothek, is one of the most impressive calligraphic examples of Bach's characteristic hand.

Most violinists will opt nowadays for the version prepared by Günter Hausswald for the *Neue Bach Ausgabe* as the clearest and most reliable study text.[37] However, they are advised to use this in conjunction with at least a facsimile of the autograph,[38] as some of Hausswald's editorial conclusions are not verified in that principal source and his critical commentary is often found wanting. At other points, ambiguities in the autograph are inter-preted without any editorial explanation.[39]

Bach and Dance Music

French Court dancing was especially in favour on all social levels in Germany in the late seventeenth century, ranging from informal social and recreational dancing to formal social dancing and elaborate theatrical pres-entations. Numerous French dancing-masters were imported to teach and choreograph in the courts in Bach's circle, including those at Celle, Cöthen and Dresden, as well as in Leipzig, and it is therefore not surprising that French dance styles, along with Italian and German, were reflected in Bach's music.[40]

Bach was reasonably faithful in preserving the character and rhythmic structure of the French dances in this Third Partita, so violinists may benefit from knowledge of these forms when attempting to recreate their essential elegance in performance. Quantz provides useful descriptions of French dances; those relevant to the Third Partita are included below, together with guidelines for an appropriate tempo for each, applying his theory of equat-ing tempo with 'the pulse beat at the hand of a healthy person'.[41]

Although dance steps can be performed correctly only within narrow margins of speed, they can never serve as sure guides to tempo. Donington points out that 'both the steps and the figures of a dance may have varied widely, sometimes almost unrecognisably, at different times and places; and with them, the tempo'.[42] Furthermore, Bach's stylised dance forms tend to differ somewhat from their original dance inspiration, often slowing down and becoming more flexible as regards rhythm and phrasing.[43] Interestingly, Neal Zaslaw failed to establish any real consistency for Baroque tempos in his survey of French sources, which rates Bourrée, Gigue and Gavotte slower, and Loure faster, than Quantz's values.[44]

As mentioned in Chapter 3, French violinists tended to use shorter bows than their Italian counterparts. In distinguishing French and Italian dance styles in performance, Quantz advocates 'a heavy yet short and sharp bow-stroke, more detached than slurred. That which is delicate and singing is rarely found in it. Dotted notes are played heavily, but the notes following them briefly and sharply. Fast pieces must be executed in a gay, hopping and springing manner with a very short bow-stroke, always marked with an interior stress'.[45]

Preludio

Since preludes were often improvised in the seventeenth and eighteenth centuries, it is not surprising that this notated Preludio, founded on the rhythmic and melodic three-note motif announced at the very beginning, is pseudo-improvisatory in character. Its Italian title, its figuration derived mainly from broken chords and its incorporation of concertante elements suggest a fairly slick tempo; but prospective performers should forgo the simple, quasi-sewing-machine style of, say, Arthur Grumiaux (for all his admirable technique and refined musical intellect), in favour of an approach which is more flexible and charismatic, with subtle nuancing and phrasing. Bach's annotated echo effects at bb. 5–16, 45–51 and 61–7 should be realised without question, while features such as the moving bass-line on the main crotchet beats of bb. 94–5 and the bass pedal in bb. 120–2 should be subtly conveyed. Any ritardando in the final bar seems inappropriate.

Loure

Unlike many of its French court models, this Loure comprises carefully balanced phrases (each strain beginning with a four-bar phrase, made up of two-bar segments), clear harmonies, and ornamented melody. Numerous French writers referred to the Loure as a 'slow [French] gigue';[46] one frequent common denominator between the two dances is the characteristic dotted rhythm of the first bar. The moderate, fluid 6/4 metre and slow tempo of the Loure, however, give it a more languid quality. Walther concurs with Mattheson's description of the Loure as 'slow and dotted' and of 'a proud and arrogant nature', and advises that 'the first note of each half bar has a dot, which is to be well prolonged'.[47] Brossard recommends marking 'the first beat of each bar more perceptibly than the second', while Quantz requires the bow to be 'detached at each crotchet, whether it is dotted or not'. He also maintains that 'the quavers that follow the dotted crotchets in the loure ... must not be played with their literal value, but must be executed in a very short and sharp manner'.[48] His approximate tempo for this dance, based on his human pulse theory, is crotchet = 80.

Gavotte en Rondeau

Originally a French peasant dance, the Gavotte's adoption in aristocratic circles during the sixteenth century led to its musical refinement. It
could express a variety of affects, ranging from 'tender' (Bacilly) and 'graceful' (Dupont) to 'joyful' (Mattheson). Freillon-Poncein described gavottes
as 'very slow and serious airs, whose expressiveness is very touching', while
Grassineau (1740) called them 'brisk and lively by nature'.[49] Rousseau
referred to this dance's qualities as 'ordinarily graceful, often gay and sometimes also tender and slow'; he noted the remarkable variety of speeds
adopted but stressed that moderate tempos were most common, insisting
that they could be 'fast or slow, but never extremely fast or excessively
slow'.[50] Quantz's recommended tempo is slightly less than semibreve = 80,
but Donington's recommendation of crotchet = $c.120$ and Kirkpatrick's of
minim = $c.120$ demonstrate the characteristic variances.[51]

Menuet I and II

Generally lighter in character than the Italian Menuetto, the
Menuet symbolises more than any other dance the elegance and nobility of
the French court. Originally a lively folk dance in the Poitu region of south-
western France, it was adopted by aristocratic society in the 1660s. Even as a
court dance it was quite fast and jolly at first, but with increasing refinement
it gradually became slower and more measured. Rousseau refers to
Brossard's description of the dance as joyful and swift but contradicts him,
describing its character as 'a noble and elegant simplicity; the movement is
moderate rather than quick. It may be said that the least gay of all the kinds
of dances used in our balls is the menuet'.[52]

Although the music of the Menuet is set in bars of 3/4, performers should
be mindful that the true metre is 6/4, where the beat is the dotted minim,
and the points of repose are on beats two and four. As Quantz remarks: 'A
menuet is played springily [hebend], the crotchets being marked with a rather
heavy, but still short, bow-stroke, with a pulse beat on two crotchets'.[53]
Phrases are normally balanced in groups of 4+4 bars (unusually, Menuet I
contains a six-bar phrase (bb. 13–18)), with frequent use of hemiola, and the
tempo is moderate. These two Menuets contrast in style and texture, the
drone effect of Menuet II giving it a musette-like, rustic quality. Quantz suggests a tempo of crotchet = 160, but Menuet II is traditionally played slightly

slower than its companion, which, despite the omission in many editions, should be reprised with repeats after Menuet II.[54]

Bourrée

Most eighteenth-century theorists describe the character of the bourrée as gay or joyful, but Mattheson writes of its qualities of 'contentment and pleasantness, as if it were somewhat untroubled or calm, a little slow, easygoing and yet not unpleasant'.[55] In duple metre with a minim beat, the characteristic rhythmic phrase is eight beats (4 bars) in length, with points of repose on beat three and the first half of four, and seven and the first half of eight. Despite Mattheson's relaxed view of the bourrée, most theorists regarded it as a faster dance than the gavotte. A reasonable tempo range would probably be minim = 112–20, but Quantz suggests a seemingly over-fast minim = 160. He comments: 'A *bourrée* and a rigaudon are executed gaily, and with a short and light bow-stroke. A pulse beat falls on each bar'.[56]

Gigue

Eighteenth-century theorists are unanimous in their description of the Gigue as a lively, spirited and joyful dance, Mattheson characterising it with 'an ardent and fleeting zeal, a passion which soon subsides'. Quantz suggests 'a short and light bow-stroke . . .' for its execution, and a speed of dotted minim = 80 would align with his theories on tempo.[57]

Rhythmic alteration

Little rhythmic alteration is required in this Partita. However, performers may wish to prolong the dotted crotchets and shorten the ensuing quavers somewhat in the Loure, and they might consider playing the quavers in b. 4 in Lombard style (short–long), certainly in the repeat. Rhythmic inequality might also come into consideration, particularly for conjunct quavers in the first Menuet.

Ornamentation

Bach prescribes only a few trills and appoggiaturas in this Partita. While there is no rule that determines the shape of individual Bach trills, Neumann makes some useful suggestions as aids to tasteful trill selection. He recommends first omitting the trill and considering whether the addition of a brief (on-beat) appoggiatura, or a (pre-beat) grace note would be desirable. If so, then starting the trill with the upper auxiliary note would seem appropriate; if not, then a main-note start will be preferable.[58] As a rough rule of thumb, a trill on the pitch of its preceding note will mostly suggest an upper-note start, as will one that follows a falling third (e.g. the Loure b. 1); a trill slurred to its preceding upper neighbour will always start on the main note. When the preceding upper note is a long written-out appoggiatura, the repercussion can often start in anticipation. Sometimes, technical considerations necessitate a main-note start, but the speed of trill repercussion should always be appropriate to its context and the overall affect.

The three appoggiaturas in the pair of Menuets also require careful consideration. That in b. 12 of Menuet I is normally most satisfactory as a short appoggiatura of approximately a quaver's length (although either a crotchet- or minim-long appoggiatura can sound well). The two appoggiaturas in Menuet II (bb. 2 and 10) are most effective as a quaver's duration, thereby aligning each to the legato, predominantly quaver movement that underlies the dominant pedal.[59]

There are, of course, conventional places at cadences where performers are expected to add a trill or similar ornament, even if none is indicated. Cadential trills should thus routinely be provided, for example, at b. 135 of the Preludio or at bb. 39 and 63 in the Gavotte en Rondeau and might also be appropriate in b. 7 and equivalent places of the Gavotte en Rondeau. As always, musical taste and intelligence must be the arbiter.

Ornamenting the repeats

All dances in this Partita are marked to be repeated. Such prescriptions should be respected unless there are strong reasons for the contrary. Repeats offer opportunities for the addition of discreet extempore ornamentation or, perhaps, for varying nuances, dynamics or articulation, while retaining the movement's character. This is certainly the case in the Loure, for the repeats of which the lute version (BWV 1006a) might provide inspiration for appropriate ornamentation (Ex. 6.2). The various reprises of the 'A' section of the Gavotte en Rondeau may also justifiably be embellished, but such elaborations should be tastefully graduated so that the final statement (from b. 92) is the culmination of the movement. Similarly, violinists should

Ex. 6.2 J. S. Bach: Partita no. 3 in E. Ornamented version of the repeat of the opening of the Loure.

graduate elaborations to the various repeated sections of Menuet I, remembering, of course, that both sections should also be repeated on the da capo following Menuet II. The faster Bourrée and Gigue are less suited to such adventurous embellishment, yet might accommodate some; in all cases, French (as opposed to Italian) taste should be emulated and the elaborations performed elegantly, spontaneously and with flexibility, as if improvised.

Articulation and other bowing issues

Although Bach occasionally used staccato dots and strokes, articulation signs in the solo violin works are confined to slurs; these are designed largely to observe the rule of down-bow, by favouring the stronger down-bow on the 'good' notes requiring most stress and thereby marking the rhythmic hierarchy of the bar. Problems occasionally arise when surmised intended bowings, particularly in polyphonic movements, are not indicated, or where the exact start or, more frequently, the end of a slur is unclear.[60] Indeed, several editors have arbitrarily changed Bach's original phrasings and articulations (some, admittedly, with the qualities and characteristics of the modern bow in mind); even the *Neue Bach-Ausgabe* includes some divergences from Bach's autograph, normally on account of perceived writing errors or imprecisions in the placement of bowings, which were sometimes clarified by other sources.[61] However, Bach's original articulations, supplemented in the case of the substantially French-styled Third Partita by Georg Muffat's observations on the Lully style of performance, best convey the subtle melodic inflections of his phrasing, which often disregards the bar-line.

Muffat's observations are expounded in his *Florilegium Secundum* and offer unique insights into late-seventeenth-century French style as well as evidence of its increasing vogue in Germany.[62] He focuses on five principal considerations: purity of intonation, bowing, tempo, ornamentation and

Ex. 6.3 (a) The application of Muffat's Second Rule in triple time.
(b) The use of *craquer* bowing in faster tempos.

(a)

(b)

'certain other customs of the Lullists';[63] most important to this study is his explanation of French bowing techniques, categorised in ten rules summarised below:

1. The first note of each bar, where there is no rest, should be played with a down-bow, regardless of its value.

2. In common time, notes on 'odd' beats of the bar (beats 1, 3, 5 etc.) should be played with a down-bow and those on 'even' beats should be played with an up-bow. This rule also applies in 6/8 and 12/8.

3. Rule no. 2 may also apply in triple metre (including 9/8) at slow tempos and may involve re-taking a down-bow between the end of one bar and the beginning of the next, as in Ex. 6.3a. The *craquer* bowing, involving taking two notes in the same up-bow, is preferred in faster tempos (Ex. 6.3b).

4. The hierarchy of the bar should be preserved in metres such as 6/4, 9/8 and 12/8 by using *craquer* bowing except when a rest is substituted for the first note, in which case the note following the rest is normally taken with a down-bow (Ex. 6.4).

5. When several notes, each of one bar's duration, appear in succession, each should be taken with a down-bow (Ex. 6.5).

6. Equal successive syncopated notes usually require alternate down- and up-bows (Ex. 6.6).

7. Bars of mixed note-values should be accommodated by employing *craquer* or by bowing 'as it comes' (Ex. 6.7).

Ex. 6.4 The application of Muffat's Fourth Rule when a rest is indicated on the strong beat(s).

Ex. 6.5 Muffat's Fifth Rule.

Ex. 6.6 Muffat's Sixth Rule.

Ex. 6.7 Muffat's Seventh Rule.

8. When subdivisions of the bar comprise three notes and the first of each is dotted, this first note should normally be played with a down-bow (Ex. 6.8).
9. Several successive notes, each completing the bar after a pause or rest, should be taken down-bow and up-bow alternately (Ex. 6.9).
10. Short up-beats and a short note following a dotted note, a rest or a longer syncopated note should be taken with an up-bow.

These ten rules provide useful guidelines to bowing Bach's French dance movements, but, as Muffat himself readily admits, should not be rigidly applied. It should also be borne in mind that they are intended primarily

Ex. 6.8 Muffat's Eighth Rule.

Ex. 6.9 Muffat's Ninth Rule.

Ex. 6.10 J. S. Bach: Partita no. 3 in E. Loure, bb. 1–4, bowed according to Muffat's rules.

as instruction in the performance of actual dance music rather than of the stylised dances that constitute abstract instrumental suites.

The Loure of the Third Partita embraces the first, second and particularly the fourth and eighth of Muffat's rules (Ex. 6.10), while the Gavotte en Rondeau largely follows rules 1 and 2, with rule 7 operating in b. 1, bt. 2 (Ex. 6.11) and the addition of a phrasing articulation in the middle of b. 2. The figures in bb. 26–7 and 72–3 might best be bowed out, as Muffat seems to suggest in one of his exceptions on grounds of tempo, but bb. 74–9, 86–7 and 89–91 seem to require bowing solutions beyond his guidelines for optimum results.

Menuet I complies well with Muffat's rules 1 and 2 and his separate example of French (as opposed to German and Italian) Menuet bowing (Ex. 6.12), but it is unlikely that the long tied dotted minims of Menuet II would

Ex. 6.11 J. S. Bach: Partita no. 3 in E. Gavotte en Rondeau, bb. 1–8, bowed according to Muffat's rules.

Ex. 6.12 J. S. Bach: Partita no. 3 in E. Menuet I, bb. 1–8, bowed according to Muffat's rules.

have been played literally. The solution illustrated in Ex. 6.13 would seem most sensible. Apart from bb. 3–4 and 11–12, the Bourrée complies with Muffat's rules 1 and 2. A re-taken down-bow on the last note of b. 3 and the first note of b. 4 would remedy the first problem, while bb. 9–13 should simply be bowed out, starting with a down-bow (b. 9). The final Gigue adheres largely to Muffat's fourth rule, but his seventh is brought into play in bb. 15–16, 23–4 and 31–2, and an up-bow is inevitable at the beginning of bb. 13 and 29.

Towards an interpretation: general concerns

Authentic dynamic markings are found only in the Fuga and Allegro of the Second Sonata and in the Preludio, Bourrée and Gigue of the Third Partita of Bach's autograph manuscript. Although these are confined

Ex. 6.13 J. S. Bach: Partita no. 3 in E. Menuet II, bb. 1–8, bowed according to Muffat's rules.

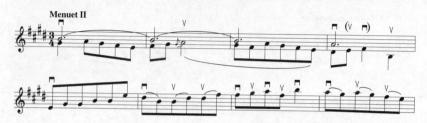

mainly to 'echo' effects, performers should cultivate a wide range of subtle nuances that fluctuate freely and continuously during a section or movement, assisting with expressive phrasing and highlighting dissonances, ornaments, chromatic notes or cadences. Closely interconnected with matters of phrasing are effective use of accentuation and, in some cases, prolongation of important notes within the phrase, the tasteful use of vibrato colouring, and the choice of rational fingering and bowing appropriate to the character of the phrase.

As we discovered in Chapter 4, much of the Baroque repertory, particularly French dance music, was executed in the fundamental hand-positions. Performers should aim to use half-position and only the first five positions inclusive in the Third Partita, employing the fourth and fifth positions only where absolutely necessary. It would be unstylish either to seek richer sonorities and more unified timbres using the higher positions or natural harmonics to avoid or facilitate shifts, and it would be inadvisable to follow blindly the recommendations of nineteenth-century virtuosi/editors. Baroque violinists tended to adopt one position to accommodate an entire phrase without shifting the hand, fingering concepts being aligned less to melody (as nowadays) than to harmony (allowing all fingers to rest on the string, and lifting them only when necessary).

As noted in Chapter 4, passages of sustained polyphony were often written in long note-values in order to clarify both the musical progression and the melodic and harmonic functions of the different voice parts. Many are impossible to execute exactly as written; thus, three- or four-note chords often had to be spread in order to sustain the principal harmonic and melodic notes where possible for their full written values and thereby bring out the melodic lines. Most importantly, there is no evidence in Bach's time of the modern practice of breaking a four-note chord upwards in twos where the higher of the two double stops is played on the beat and sustained.

No one will pretend that using a Baroque violin and bow will solve all the problems of interpreting Bach's Third Partita; but it is surprising how many problems will naturally be overcome. Nothing is gained by denying to the violin (or viola) its natural expression, but particular twentieth-century playing traits such as continuous vibrato, expressive portamenti, high position-work for timbral effect and bowings such as *spiccato* and *martelé* should be avoided. Instead, players should favour selective use of vibrato to enhance special expressive moments (on long notes in particular, often accompanied by a *messa di voce*), varying the speed of oscillation for striking effect. They should also cultivate a light, articulated style and, if using modern instruments, they might benefit from holding the bow a few inches along the stick from the frog.

Haydn: String Quartet in E flat major, Op. 33 no. 2 (Hob. III:38)

Introduction

After a gap of almost ten years in his string quartet composition, Haydn wrote to prospective subscribers about his set of six 'Russian' quartets Op. 33, claiming that they were 'written in a new and special way'.[64] These works were dedicated to the Russian Grand Duke Pavel Petrowich and were first published in Vienna by Artaria on 17 April 1782. They were highly successful and were rapidly republished in many other European capitals.

Much ink has been spilt over what Haydn meant by 'written in a new and special way'. Most scholars agree, however, that Haydn was referring neither to his remarkable 'operatic' motivic writing nor to his developing equality of the four instruments, but rather to these works' light popular style, with their folk-like tunes and remarkable wit. The most obvious humorous features are a number of jokes – hence the alternative nickname 'Gli scherzi' ('The Jokes') for the set – and in all but one the conventional Minuets are replaced by light rapid movements labelled 'Scherzo' or 'Scherzando'. The

Scherzo movement of Op. 33 no. 2, with its Trio's prescribed portamenti, is a particularly jocular case in point; but the ultimate joke occurs in its hunting-style finale, which ends with a passage in which the rondo theme dissolves into stuttering, broken phrases. Just as the audience thinks this movement, with its established symmetrical four-bar phrases, has concluded, the players add a pianissimo repeat of the opening two-bar phrase, breaking both the theme's symmetry and impetus and making the audience the butt of the humour.

Text

The traditional texts of Haydn's string quartets are largely corrupt; dynamics, articulation, ornamentation, time signatures, tempo markings, rhythmic values, part-writing, melody, harmony, and even the number of bars in certain phrases have been 'improved' by editors. Until about the 1970s ensembles had little alternative but to perform from editions which were not necessarily based on autograph or wholly reliable source materials; among such editions are the four volumes of 'Famous Quartets' in the Moser–Dechert series for Peters and the scores of Ernst Eulenberg Ltd., reincarnated under the Dover Books imprint, which are accessible and kind on the pocket, yet riddled with errors. Not even the editions published by Artaria from the beginning of its association with Haydn around 1780 until his departure for England in 1790 are models of accuracy, a fact that continually distressed the composer.

Happily, a project originally conceived by Faber Music (London) in the late 1960s and subsequently taken over by Doblinger Verlag (Vienna) has involved publication, in pocket score and sets of parts, of a complete critical edition of Haydn's Quartets based on the composer's autographs (such as are extant), the earliest and most reliable manuscript copies and the eighteenth-century printed editions. The editors of the project, Reginald Barrett-Ayres and H. C. Robbins Landon, aimed to 'reconstruct Haydn's intentions in an authentic manner and to transmit them with a minimum of editorial apparatus to the scholar and musician'.[65] Although no Haydn autograph of Op. 33 no. 2 is currently available, their edition is based on an extensive range of sources, notably an original copy of the parts by an Esterházy copyist, an original set of printed parts published by Artaria and Company (Vienna, 29 December 1781), four further copies of the instrumental parts dating from the 1780s, and various other printed editions of the parts by J. J. Hummel (Berlin/Amsterdam, 1782), Sieber (Paris, 1783) and Schmitt (Amsterdam, n.d.). Although these sources are often incomplete as regards performing directions (e.g. dynamic and articulation markings), ambiguous regarding the placement of slurs, ornaments, staccato and other such markings, and inconsistent in their annotations for parallel passages within movements, they furnish invaluable information regarding such interpretative issues as expression, articulation, phrasing, accentuation and ornamentation, thus enabling performers to convey as faithfully as possible, yet personally, the music's character and style.

Instruments

Haydn's chamber music spans that period of change in the construction of stringed instruments and bows which significantly affected their sound, idiom and playing techniques. 'Period performers' must therefore decide whether the use of short-necked instruments with lighter fittings and with pre-Tourte bows is appropriate, or whether, as is probably the case for, say, Haydn's Op. 50 quartets (1787) onwards, Tourte-model bows and even instruments designed for greater volume may best achieve their objectives. The Cramer-type bow described in Chapter 3 will probably offer the most suitable compromise here.

Tempo and rhythm

Haydn's simple descriptive words at the beginning of each movement – Allegro moderato; Scherzo:Allegro; Largo e sostenuto; and Presto – suggest broadly its mood and approximate tempo. According to Leopold Mozart, Allegro 'indicates a cheerful, though not too hurried a tempo, especially when moderated by adjectives and adverbs, such as: . . . *moderato*, which is to say that one is not to exaggerate the speed. For this a lighter and livelier, but at the same time somewhat more serious and rather broader bowing is demanded than in a quicker tempo'. Largo, on the other hand, was considered slower than Adagio ('slow'), and was 'to be performed with long strokes and much tranquillity' in keeping with its sostenuto appendage, which Leopold Mozart describes as 'drawn out, or rather held back, and the melody not exaggerated. We must therefore in such cases use a serious, long, and sustained bowing, and keep the melody flowing smoothly'. Presto simply means 'quick' and the Adagio passage near the close signals an equally simple 'slow' tempo.[66] The speed of the second movement (Scherzo: allegro) is often misrepresented in performance, its Allegro heading often being reduced to the speed of a minuet.

Bowing and articulation

Leopold Mozart considered bowing to be one of the most important aspects of violin playing, for it 'gives life to the notes' and is of paramount importance in realising the appropriate affect.[67] He consistently encourages expressive playing and the development of a 'singing' style of performance, favouring the kind of 'strong, masculine bow stroke' required to realise Haydn's cantabile and articulation annotations for the opening theme of the first movement of Op. 33 no. 2.

Haydn sources reveal an inconsistent approach to the use of articulation symbols. Dots generally indicated an on-the-string articulation somewhat greater than the fundamental non-legato stroke of 'period' bows,[68] while strokes (in print usually wedges) normally signified a lifted bowing, tempo permitting; however, this was not without exception. True legato bowing was achieved only by slurring. In this connection, it is worth noting that Classical or early Romantic music incorporates very few phrasing slurs. Few slurs even cross the bar-line in eighteenth-century texts, for when a continuous legato was required, each complete bar would be bowed with a separate slur. For this and other interpretative reasons, the addition and unification of the vast majority of bowings in the Doblinger edition has been left to the players' discretion; however, as Dene Barnett argues, Haydn's variety of bowings should not be taken as a licence to reproduce randomly non-uniform or contradictory slurs in performance.[69] However, the edition addresses the tacitly understood convention of slurring appoggiaturas and other such dissonances to their 'resolutions'.

Phrasing and accentuation

Although Haydn's balanced, complementary phrasing was rarely indicated, it was occasionally implied in the notation, sometimes by appropriate placement of the beams of notes, as, for example, at i/8 of Op. 33 no. 2. Good realisation of phrasing requires careful articulation; subtle nuances may be added to establish the general contours of phrases, as well as their expressive content, the briefest of pauses may be made on the last note of one phrase before starting anew on the first note of its successor, reducing slightly the tonal volume of the last note and re-establishing it with the first note of the next phrase or shortening the last note of one phrase when appropriate to separate it from the first note of the next.

Eighteenth-century musicians observed in their performances the three categories of accent used in everyday speech – 'grammatic', 'rhetorical' and 'pathetic'. 'Grammatic' accents, which occurred regularly at the beats of the bar were not given equal length and emphasis, the first (and strongest) accent in the bar being accommodated in string playing by the 'rule of down-bow'. 'Rhetorical' and 'pathetic' accents were distinguished from 'grammatic' accents not only by the more pronounced manner in which they were executed but also by the fact that they were not restricted to any part of the bar. A note that is longer, or markedly higher or lower than its predecessor, and dissonant notes are all common instances when emphasis through prolongation of that note beyond its written length generally provided a flexible, musicianly solution. Haydn also annotates *tenuto* on notes to be particularly sustained (for example, at i/54 bt. 1, and at the end of the first phrase of each occurrence of the principal theme of the third movement), and players should be mindful of the expressive quality of the slur, where the first notes of slurs were given prominence by being 'somewhat more strongly stressed' while the remaining notes under the slur were played 'quite smoothly and more and more quietly'.[70]

Expression

Haydn indicated dynamic markings sparingly in his early works; however, players should constantly bear in mind that his basic markings in Op. 33 no. 2, extending from *ff* to *pp*, call not for sudden changes from dynamic extremes, but for a sensitively graduated expressive approach. *Forzato* (*fz*) is a surprisingly common direction (for example, at i/7 and equivalent passages), employed either to emphasise chromatic alterations of notes, to characterise a particular movement, or instead of an accent, the symbol for which (>) is rare in Haydn's chamber music. The various pauses in the finale require careful treatment. Leopold Mozart offers some useful guidelines, explaining that such an annotation requires the relevant note to be sustained 'according to fancy, but it must be neither too short nor too long . . . the tone of the instrument must be allowed to diminish and die entirely away before beginning to play again'. In the 1787 edition he adds that a pause sign over a rest requires that rest to be 'silent for a longer space of time than the value of the bar demands', a remark particularly pertinent to the dramatic silent pauses in the finale of Op. 33 no. 2.[71] Some first violinists may see fit to add a brief ornamental flourish to the pause in b. 140, but the general consensus would seem to opt for a solution strictly faithful to the notated score.

Fingering, shifting and tone-colour

Fingering was closely related to expressive ideals, but according to Leopold Mozart, necessity, convenience and elegance were the principal reasons for using positions other than the first.[72] As indicated in Chapter 4, 'necessary' and 'convenient' shifts were generally made, until at least the end of the eighteenth century, when the music's punctuation so allowed. 'Elegant' shifts were made largely to achieve uniformity of timbre within the phrase, as indicated by Haydn's fairly common directions such as *sopra una corda, sull'istessa corda*, or *sull'una corda* (see, for example, Op. 33 no. 2, ii/50–1), his fairly long slurs (of which there are no true examples in Op. 33 no. 2) or his specific fingerings. William Drabkin claims that Haydn generally applies a verbal direction to passages which demand special attention for their own sake (as at bb. 50–4 in the second movement).[73]

In the quest for an even tone, open strings were generally avoided when stopped notes were technically viable, but they nonetheless appeared in certain scale passages, figurations and double stops, to facilitate shifting and for special effect.

A number of Haydn's recommended fingerings have come down to us in the sources used for the Doblinger edition; in the case of Op. 33 no. 2 (ii/34–68) the fingerings concerned have timbral implications and call for a specific humorous portamento effect (See Ex. 6.14). The presence at Esterháza (1780–85) of Nicolo Mestrino, who evidently implemented portamento in exaggerated fashion, may have encouraged Haydn to introduce such effects in some of his string quartets.[74] Baillot confirms that the slide effect was intended to be heard, distinguishing in the 'trio' of Op. 33 no. 2 between the 'slight sliding from one note to the next with the same finger' of

Ex. 6.14 Haydn: Quartet Op. 33 no. 2, 2nd movement, bb. 34–59.

the ascending *port de voix* and the sliding of the finger used for the lower note of the descending variety. In this latter case, the finger 'will just barely touch the semitone above'.[75]

Ornamentation

While it is impracticable to present here a definitive interpretation of so-called 'essential' ornaments indicated by symbol – the appoggiatura, acciaccatura, trill and turn in Haydn's Op. 33 no. 2 – performers should make themselves aware not only of the variety of ornaments documented in eighteenth-century treatises but also of the wide range of valid interpretations of most of those ornaments according to national theory, musical context, and even individual practice: for example, the modification of trills by the addition of preparations or terminations and by varying the number, rhythm, speed and nuances of the notes comprising the ornament. In Leopold Mozart's day, 'ornamentation was still very much more an art than a science. The speed, duration, articulation and weight of an ornament depended on the character of the music and on the precise context of the ornament itself. If the ornament sounded laboured or out of context, it quite simply was wrong'.[76] Leopold's 'rules' should thus be regarded as guidelines, and not instructions.

This only seems commonsense when addressing the interpretation of appoggiaturas in Haydn's Op. 33 no. 2. While Leopold Mozart's general instruction that appoggiaturas normally take half the value of the note against which they are placed and are always slurred to it is practicable in most cases, some violinists may prefer not to adhere to this guideline in i/11, where a quaver-length appoggiatura seems less sluggish and more characterful. The guidelines that appoggiaturas on dotted notes should take up two thirds of the value of the principal notes and that appoggiaturas against minims and longer notes may last for three quarters of their value can reasonably be applied in Op. 33 no. 2, the application of the latter guideline effecting an untraditional realisation of the second bar (and parallel places) of the recurrent principal theme of the third movement. With a 'textbook' dotted crotchet-length as opposed to the normal crotchet-length appoggiatura, less time is allowed for the execution of the ensuing trill.[77]

Leopold Mozart distinguishes three ways of beginning and three ways of ending a trill. The ornament may begin: immediately from the upper note; on a descending appoggiatura, suitably performed as described above; or with an ascending appoggiatura or other ornament from below. Possible trill endings include: the use of an anticipatory note; a turn (as in Op. 33 no. 2, iii/2 and 6 and parallel places); or 'with an embellishment'.[78] The absence of a turn sign should not necessarily prevent the ornament's inclusion if context and taste demand. The speed of oscillation of the trill depended on the character of the music. Despite their misleading notation, the realisation of Haydn's turns at bb. 20 and 77 seems straightforward enough,[79] but those at i/21–2, 46–8, 78–9 most closely approximate Leopold Mozart's *Doppelschlag* or the five-note turn of C. P. E. Bach and Türk.[80] An acciaccatura-like interpretation seems apt for the fast-moving, staccato ornament in iv/7 and parallel places.

Leopold Mozart also considered vibrato to be a branch of ornamentation and despised those who overused it. Recommending three speeds of vibrato oscillation (slow, increasing and rapid), he suggests that 'a closing note [of a passage] or any other sustained note may be decorated with a tremolo[vibrato]'.[81] Sparing, tasteful and expressive must therefore be the period performer's watchwords in vibrato application, which should also take advantage of the varied opportunities for colour offered by the 'ornament' in marrying its speed and intensity with the music's dynamic, tempo and character.

Finally, thought should be given to the appropriateness of additional extempore embellishment additions. Leopold Mozart warns against the addition of ornamentation that is insensitive to the overall affect of the movement/piece, while Charles Rosen concludes that 'the music of Haydn after 1775 cannot be ornamented':

> The idea of the recapitulation as a dramatic reinterpretation of the exposition attacks the practice of decoration at its root: the structure itself now does the work of the improvised ornaments. The ornamentation of the repeat of the exposition becomes an actual embarrassment: it implies either that the material heard in a dramatically different form in the recapitulation will be less ornamented and inevitably less elaborate than the repeat of the exposition, or that the recapitulation must also be ornamented, which can only obscure and minimize the structural changes with their radically different expressive significance.[82]

While Rosen's argument is convincing enough in respect of sonata-form movements, his blanket rejection of added embellishment in Haydn's works post 1775 is questionable. The outside possibility of a first-violin flourish at b. 139 of the finale has already been mentioned; and there are certainly opportunities for tasteful further embellishment, not least in the various repetitions of the principal melody of the third movement. Ferdinand David's addition of enterprising free ornamentation in quartet playing, even to the recapitulation sections of Haydn's sonata-form movements, was renowned, and Spohr praised the manner in which the younger Eck embellished 'the poorest spots' of a quartet by Krommer with 'the most tasteful of flourishes'. Referring to string quartet playing, he concludes, 'In passages, decidedly solo, the usual embellishments may be allowed.'[83]

Quartet placement and seating

There has never been unanimity about the placement and seating of a string quartet. Spohr, for example, is believed to have stood while his colleagues sat; Joachim preferred the cellist at his left, the second violinist opposite and the violist in between them. Evidence for the placement of the individual instruments of the quartet in Haydn's time is scarce, but the use of quartet desks in the eighteenth and nineteenth centuries (an excellent example is housed in the Haydn Museum, Eisenstadt) was doubtless an influential factor in the seating arrangement, even though the extent of their usage is not documented.

7 Historical awareness in practice 2 – three nineteenth-century case studies: Beethoven, Mendelssohn and Brahms

Beethoven: Sonata in A major for violin and piano, Op. 47 ('Kreutzer')

Introduction

Beethoven's 'Kreutzer' Sonata Op. 47 stands out from his other accompanied sonatas on account of its size, virtuoso demands, and the relationship it fosters between the violin and the piano. Its unusual subtitle, 'Sonata per il Piano-forte ed un Violino obligato, scritta in uno stile molto concertante, quasi come d'un concerto' (Sonata for piano and obbligato violin, composed in a decidedly concertante style, as though a concerto), indicates a departure from Beethoven's previous efforts in the accompanied sonata and confirms the elevation of the violinist from a subordinate participant to an equal partner, initiated in Op. 24 and the Op. 30 set. The original jocular dedication[1] was to the mulatto violinist George Polgreen Bridgetower (?1779–1860), who had met Beethoven through the good offices of Prince Lichnowsky and whose unique artistry and 'bold and extravagant style of playing' clearly inspired the sonata's concertante character.[2] The dedication was later changed in favour of Rodolphe Kreutzer (1766–1831), allegedly because of a quarrel between Beethoven and Bridgetower over a mutual female acquaintance. Beethoven considered the French violinist ideally suited to the work, but Berlioz later reported that Kreutzer 'could never bring himself to play this outrageously unintelligible composition'.[3]

The change of dedication in favour of Kreutzer may have been an attempt to facilitate Beethoven's projected move to Paris (*c.*1803). However, Beethoven is also believed to have used Kreutzer's Grande Sonate as a model for his Op. 47. Suhnne Ahn points to the common key of A minor, the similarity of the second themes of the first movements,[4] the identical tempo marking, certain parallels between the developments of each, and a peculiar

139

structural feature of 'half step motives'; furthermore, the first edition of Op. 47 includes, at the head of the violin and piano parts, the note: 'Grande Sonate'.[5]

Beethoven's Op. 47 has a rich compositional history; its movements were composed in the order third–first–second. Its last movement was originally written in 1802 as the finale of Sonata Op. 30 no. 1. Having been substituted by another finale for aesthetic reasons, it subsequently served as the compositional catalyst for Op. 47, generating motivic, structural and harmonic features in the other two movements.[6] Beethoven reportedly composed the first two movements in great haste for the premiere in Vienna's Augarten on 24 May 1803, when Bridgetower apparently played the second movement from the autograph and Beethoven performed the piano part of the first two movements mostly from memory and sketches.

Sources and editions

The principal sources for Op. 47 comprise sketches, the so-called *Vorautograph*, the *Stichvorlage* or engraver's copy, the autograph and two printed editions, Simrock's first edition of April 1805 and one by Birchall of London, based on the Simrock publication.[7] The best edition of this work currently available is by Sieghard Brandenburg, published by Henle Verlag (Munich, 1974). This takes into account the revelations of the Stichvorlage, including Beethoven's numerous corrections and additions and clues concerning the treatment of ii/196.[8]

Other sources of information about performance practice

Useful information about Beethoven's performing style and practice can be gleaned from his correspondence, from the writings of his pupils such as Carl Czerny and Ferdinand Ries, and from remarks credited to him by contemporaries such as Franz Wegeler (with Ries), and, less reliably, Anton Schindler. Czerny's legacy is arguably the most helpful; he studied many of Beethoven's piano works under the composer's supervision and did much to sustain the Beethoven tradition in his teaching, his own performances and concert arrangements and in his transcriptions of orchestral and chamber works (some of them under Beethoven's supervision), which became widely circulated in their adaptations.[9] Czerny also left memoirs and writings of his encounters with Beethoven, an edition of Beethoven's

piano sonatas and other piano pieces with metronome markings and fingerings. A chapter in vol. IV of his *School for the Piano* Op. 500 includes brief
discussion of general interpretative issues in Beethoven's works involving
the piano.

These various sources indicate Beethoven's concern for performance
issues, particularly matters of tempo, expression, and fidelity to the composer's intentions. Even though Beethoven is reported occasionally to have
recommended departures from the text, Czerny is adamant, having himself
been reprimanded by Beethoven for similar liberties, that 'the performer of
Beethoven's works (and in general those of all Classical masters) must not
tolerate any alterations of the music whatsoever, no additions, no omissions'.[10]

Editions made by violinists of the composer's era also constitute a valuable resource for rediscovery of performance traditions. Clive Brown
describes Ferdinand David's editions of Beethoven's violin sonatas, piano
trios, string quartets and other works as 'by far the most extensive body of
information about what was regarded as an appropriate style of performance for them by an important German violinist whose training was
already complete at the time of Beethoven's death'. They are the earliest
systematically bowed and fingered editions of these works.[11] While David's
manner of performing Beethoven may not have had any direct link with the
composer's conception or even with traditions of performance stemming
from Beethoven's circle, and while it cannot be assumed that Beethoven
would have been uncritical of David's technical and aesthetic approach, it is
evident that David's performing style would not have seemed alien to
Beethoven. As a pupil of Spohr, one of the first violinists outside Vienna to
champion Beethoven's Op. 18 quartets and his violin sonatas,[12] David's
approach to Beethoven performance was considerably influenced by his
mentor's style, even though it admitted 'the greater facility and piquancy of
a later school'.[13]

Joseph Joachim's editions of Beethoven's violin sonatas for Peters (pl. no.
8762), which replaced David's edition in 1901, will also inform our enquiry.
Although there are numerous differences of detail between David's and
Joachim's editions, they also have much in common.

David's editions are largely accurate as regards note-lengths and pitches –
Ex. 7.1 illustrates one discrepancy between the violin part and the correct

Ex. 7.1 Beethoven: Violin Sonata Op. 47, first movement, b. 495 (ed. David).

violin (in piano) part – but there are many places where phrasing and articulation differ from the most reliable sources. The differences sometimes occur in both the score and the separate violin part, suggesting to Clive Brown that they are not so much a deliberate departure from Beethoven's text as a misreading or an alternative interpretation of the sources; this is often simply a matter of a slur extended or shortened by a single note especially over a bar-line or on to a strong beat. These are probably modifications for technical convenience, a more idiomatic bowing or occasionally a particular effect.

Left-hand considerations (violin)

No record of Beethoven's views about portamento usage seems to have been preserved. However, Clive Brown cites two isolated fingerings, one in Beethoven's own quintet arrangement of his Piano Trio Op. 1 no. 2 and the other in his Violin Sonata Op. 96 iv/158, which suggest that the composer may sometimes have felt the effect to be appropriate,[14] and David's edition of Beethoven's Op. 47 incorporates several fingerings which imply portamento usage for expressive effect. For example, David frequently employed semitone shifts to change position, thereby often preserving tonal uniformity within a phrase and implying a possible portamento effect (Ex. 7.2). Furthermore, he normally (but not exclusively) executed each trill in a chain of consecutive trills with similar fingering, thus allowing the possibility of an intermediary portamento (Ex. 7.3).

David typically avoids the even-numbered positions, especially second position, where their use would be more logical, resulting in some unnecessarily awkward shifts. For the first movement's second subject (bb. 91–105), which is playable throughout in second position, David prescribes a fingering which requires two similar third-finger shifts with portamento from first

Ex. 7.2 Beethoven: Violin Sonata Op. 47, second movement, theme, bb. 8–13 (ed. David).

Ex. 7.3 Beethoven: Violin Sonata Op. 47, second movement, var. 4, bb. 46–51 (ed. David).

Ex. 7.4 Beethoven: Violin Sonata Op. 47, first movement, bb. 91–105 (ed. David).

to third position (Ex. 7.4).[15] In the recapitulation (bb. 412–26) the same theme lies comfortably in first position and no fingering is suggested. David also employs the characteristic nineteenth-century string technique of playing notes which lie above or below the hand's present position through finger repetition and extension/contraction (i.e., the use of 1–1 or 4–4, as in Ex. 7.5a and b), or even through shifting, either of which may sometimes have portamento implications, but often do not. Among numerous other examples of his possible portamento implications are ii/var. 2/1, and the implications of bars 10–11 and its subsequent 'slithery' octave passage.

David's use of open strings is generally compliant with that of his teacher, Spohr; but in Op. 47 it is less at odds than usual with eighteenth-century

Ex. 7.5 (a) Beethoven: Violin Sonata Op. 47, first movement, bb. 460–5 (ed. David).

(b) Beethoven: Violin Sonata Op. 47, first movement, bb. 582–5 (ed. David).

(a)

(b)

attitudes, typified by Leopold Mozart, Reichardt and many other authorities, that open strings should be avoided wherever possible, unless required for a special tonal effect or a shift, and should in any case only occur on short notes. Perhaps the most surprising example of open-string usage is Beethoven's own prescription of an open E-string at iii/335–6. David's additional open-string indications in Op. 47 are negligible in the context of his other editions, but his use of natural harmonics, sometimes in combination with open strings, is more remarkable; he often looked upon natural harmonics as convenient technical aids towards realising securely passages which might otherwise present problems of position-work or intonation (e.g. at i/116–17, i/245, ii/var. 4/18 and iii/253). Two especially interesting prescriptions for technical convenience are the harmonic d^2 in the opening bar of the sonata and the high e^4 harmonic at the end of the challenging second variation (Ex. 7.6).

In keeping with his use of harmonics and open strings David's vibrato usage was selective; he claimed that it 'must not be employed too frequently nor without sufficient reason'.[16]

Bowing considerations

Like subsequent editors, David broke up the impracticably long slurs which Beethoven seems often to have employed as an indication of legato rather than specific bowing. For example, in i/36–40 and i/303–7 he divided a lengthy Beethoven slur into three bow strokes with volume or tonal reasons in mind; and he also modifies the bowing of the opening two

Ex. 7.6 Beethoven: Violin Sonata Op. 47, second movement, var. 2, bb. 6–8 (ed. David).

Ex. 7.7 Beethoven: Violin Sonata Op. 47, first movement, bb. 210–16 (Beethoven and ed. David).

bars of the movement, slurred one bar to a bow in Beethoven's original, for greater technical and sustaining facility.

David's editing also extended to making Beethoven's music more idiomatic for the instrument; at i/210–26, for example, Beethoven's extremely awkward, if not impossible, bowing indications have been suitably modified (Ex. 7.7).

Bowings prescribed in nineteenth-century editions often cause problems for modern string players, normally because players of that era tended to use the bow very differently. For example, the predominant stroke for articulated notes in the music of Classical German composers was made with the bow on the string, as opposed to the modern player's typical use of a lifted or springing stroke in the middle or lower half. The crotchet–quaver figure of the finale's opening would probably have been taken in the middle of the bow or towards the frog, whereas many modern violinists normally opt for a sharply articulated *martelé* stroke at the point.

Clive Brown suggests that this on-the-string preference of early-nineteenth-century German violinists is indicative of a more legato, singing style; he cites as evidence Spohr's pupil Alexander Malibran's account of a conversation with his master about Haydn, Mozart and Beethoven performance in the 1840s, when springing bowings were becoming common, especially among French-trained violinists:

> To his horror he noticed how violinists played the *détachés* in a springing manner, and that they did this even in the earliest masters, who, more than all others wish to have a free, well-nourished tone. He was absolutely adamant that one should not play all composers in the same way; on the contrary, he wished the artist to adhere to the true tradition; so to say, to deny himself and reproduce the composition himself, just as it is. 'There, however', he exclaimed, 'they do not bother either about the style of the man nor about the instrument, which in the time of the composer was a wholly different one than now; they depict Frederick the Great with a haircut *à la Titus*, in a black coat and trousers!' – Only in certain passages, in certain scherzos of Beethoven, Onslow and Mendelssohn did he allow that one could let the bow spring.[17]

Joachim seems to have been among the earliest German violinists to advocate, after some soul searching,[18] various kinds of springing strokes (whose effect he described as snow, rain and hail) in Classical compositions; David, though discussing their execution briefly in his *Violinschule*, appears on the evidence of his editions largely to have eschewed them in his performances of the Classical repertory.

Some bowings in David's edition might appear 'upside-down' to modern violinists. His bowing of i/156–71, for example, works adequately until the up-bow for the slur and accompanying sforzando in bb. 159–60, where Joachim's suggestion seems preferable, (Ex. 7.8); and the down-bow start for the cantabile line commencing at the end of b. 8 of ii/var. 4 seems unorthodox nowadays. David, again recalling Spohr's practice, favoured ending scale and arpeggio passages with an up-bow, as in ii/var. 2/26–7.

Tempo and tempo rubato

Beethoven evidently attached great importance to matters of tempo.[19] Although he 'played his compositions very moodily . . . he did remain for the most part strictly in tempo, pushing the tempo only on rare

Ex. 7.8 Beethoven: Violin Sonata Op. 47, first movement, bb. 156–64 (ed. David and ed. Joachim).

occasions. Now and then he would hold the tempo back during a crescendo, creating a crescendo with ritardando, which had a very beautiful and most striking effect.'[20] Czerny also implies that steady time was generally the normal Beethoven practice, but Schindler reports that Beethoven's 'playing was free of all constraint in respect to the beat, for the spirit of his music required that freedom'.[21]

Unfortunately, Czerny left no metronome markings for Beethoven's 'Kreutzer' Sonata, but his interpretative commentary incorporates helpful ideas regarding the perceived tempo and character of individual movements or subdivisions. He suggests that the Adagio introduction should be 'performed with majesty and expression' and that the theme of the ensuing Presto should be 'very marked'.[22] The calm melody at bb. 91–116 should be 'played in time, and, from the 8 bars before the pause, *ritardando*'.[23]

For the theme of the second movement Czerny recommends the adoption of 'All that can possibly contribute to a highly melodious and expressive (but not dragging) performance . . . The chain of shakes in the second part must be strictly connected, *crescendo*, and played clearly.' The first variation should be 'rather more lively, well marked, and the triplets . . . *staccato*', while the second 'must be detached very lightly and *piano*'. Variation 3 should be 'extremely *legato*, and with earnest expression; but lively, otherwise it would appear spun out', while the fourth variation should be played 'in the time of the theme, with the most tender delicacy, and the embellishments light and rounded'.

The Presto finale is 'very quick, and as brilliant and fiery as the first movement, but much more lively. All the quavers must be played *staccato*, where the contrary is not expressly stated. The middle melody [bb. 62ff.] . . .

piquant and humorous. The subsequent passage in 2/4 [bb. 126–33] . . . must be played in the same time as the rest; so that, in it, a crotchet is of the same duration as a dotted crotchet elsewhere. The little *Adagio* at the end of the piece, which recurs twice, must by no means be performed draggingly, but as full of expression as possible. The conclusion, noisy and *prestissimo*.'

Articulation

Beethoven consistently required his pianos to be capable of 'singing', and he greatly emphasised legato qualities in his playing and teaching.[24] Czerny reports that Beethoven made him 'particularly aware of the Legato of which he had such an unrivalled command, and which all other pianists at that time considered unfeasible at the pianoforte; choppy and smartly detached playing was still in favour then (as it had been in Mozart's time)'.[25] Historical performers should naturally be mindful of this legato emphasis, wherever appropriate, but should also be aware that Viennese notational conventions at the turn of the century distinguished between two types of slur. A short slur over two or three notes required the player to shorten and detach the last note under the slur; but a long slur over several notes in a cantilena simply indicated legato, irrespective of whether it ended at the bar-line or not. Slurs should thus be interpreted with due caution, as their purpose was largely to indicate phrasing rather than bowing (although, of course, the two issues are inter-related).

Ambiguity in the writing or printing of slurs also presents problems in Beethoven sources, and performers are often required to solve such imprecisions, inconsistencies or illogicalities intelligently. Sandra Rosenblum pinpoints an interesting and subtle use of a slur over repeated notes in Op. 47 iii/206–13 (alternately by the bar in the piano and violin parts).[26] As the note over which the slur begins was normally gently stressed, the effect is to shift the emphasis to a normally weak part of the metre and to lessen the importance of the crotchet on the second beat. The slur in the initial theme of the second movement serves a similar kind of purpose in masking the squareness of the four-bar phrase.

Few pedal markings will be found in Op. 47; those that are annotated are mainly on long sustained notes/chords (for example at i/36–7, 116, 192–3, 320–3, 324–5, 437 and particularly in the Adagio passage 575–82). However, the work is notable as the first of Beethoven's in which the *Ped.* and O indications, used earlier by Dussek and Clementi, are in the composer's hand.[27] The accuracy or appropriateness of some of these pedal markings are open to question. Literal realisation of that prescribed at i/36–7 could obscure the subsequent violin entry, while the marking at i/561–74 might more logically refer to i/ 563–74 to make the minims more sustained.[28]

Instruments

By the early nineteenth century the violin and bow had each achieved essentially its modern form. Although Beethoven and most of the violinists in his circle appear to have been fully conversant both with the modifications made to the instrument and with the potentialities of the relatively new Tourte-model bow, one cannot state categorically that the 'Kreutzer' sonata was premiered using an instrument and bow of essentially modern condition. Indeed, Vienna was probably the most conservative major European city when it came to instrumental innovation and some commentators believe that 'no Tourte bow came to Vienna before 1825 or so'.[29] No evidence is provided to substantiate such a statement, but Robert Winter suggests that 'it was no accident that Leopold Mozart's *Violinschule* . . . was still popular in nineteenth-century re-printings in Vienna'; he also points out that the Viennese 'maintained a near fanatical loyalty to their simpler [piano] action well into the twentieth century', despite the significant developments in England and Paris during the first half of the nineteenth century.[30]

Viennese models by Stein and Streicher certainly influenced Beethoven's early career and, despite being given an Érard piano in 1803, his preference for Viennese instruments is well documented. The lightish action, delicate tone and transparent bass of an early-nineteenth-century Viennese piano would certainly assist in conquering the balance problems that many performers experience nowadays with the modern grand piano.

Dynamics and Expression

Beethoven prescribed expressive markings more consistently and comprehensively than most, if not all, of his predecessors, and he evidently attached great importance to his annotations.[31] His 'Kreutzer' Sonata is no exception, even incorporating a crescendo on a long held chord for the piano in 1/115 and 436. However, much has still been left for the performer to interpret regarding, for instance, the difference between *fp* and *sfp* or to realise tastefully and musically the extraordinary number of *sf* indications. Jelly d'Aranyi totalled some 262 *sf* markings in the violin part alone, not counting *fp* or *ff*, and she points out that 'beautiful as the theme of the andante is, it can be terribly disfigured (especially by the pianist) if all the *sfs* are exaggerated. Most of them ought to be treated very gently, more like >, considering there are thirty-nine of them in the theme alone.'[32]

Evidence suggests that Beethoven incorporated strong accents in his playing, both in support of and in conflict with the metre. According to Schindler, he stressed 'above all the rhythmic accent . . . most heavily . . . On the other hand, he treated the melodic accent (or grammatic, as it was generally called) mostly according to the internal requirements. He would emphasise all suspensions more than other pianists, especially that of the the diminished second in *cantabile* sections.'[33]

Ornamentation

Each question concerning trills and other specific ornamentation must be decided on its own merits, with harmony, melody, technical fluency, rhythm and voice leading being the main determinants. Broadly speaking, however, harmonic and rhythmic considerations tend to favour main-note starts, unless otherwise indicated (e.g. piano part ii/var. 4/6; iii/148), in Op. 47.[34] Kullak attaches great weight to the main-note trill start advocated by Beethoven's close friend Hummel[35] and Beethoven's stepwise chains of trills afford excellent examples that almost invariably need to be begun on their main notes, notably the passage at ii/24–5 and equivalent places.

The question of whether the turn in the violin part in i/95 and 416 should have a semitone (as the piano) or tone for the lower interval has long been argued. Sieghard Brandenburg's edition for Henle indicates a whole tone at i/95 (and in the piano at i/111) and nothing whatsoever in the later passage. Evidently, the turn added to the violin's g sharp[1] in the *Stichvorlage* at i/95 (it is missing in the autograph) has a pair of sharp signs beneath it, probably to signify an f double sharp[1]. At the equivalent place of the recapitulation the sign after the violin's c sharp[2] is written with a sharp above it, signifying a b sharp[1]. Both David and Joachim endorse the findings in the *Stichvorlage* and specify a semitone interpretation on both occasions.

That Beethoven was generally opposed to extempore additions to his music is beyond dispute; but there were certainly occasions on which he might add ornaments himself, extravagantly embellish a fermata (as occurred in a performance of his Piano and Wind Quintet Op. 16) or even applaud a performer's initiative in similar circumstances, as happened in the 'Kreutzer' Sonata with Bridgetower.[36] Bridgetower relates:

> When I accompanied him [Beethoven] in this Sonata-concertante at Wien at the repetition of the first part of the Presto [i/36], I imitated the flight at the 18th bar of the pianoforte part of this movement thus

This apparently so excited Beethoven that he jumped up, embraced me, saying, 'Noch einmal, mein lieber Bursch'['Once more, my dear fellow']. Then he held the open pedal during this flight, the chord of 6 as at the ninth bar.[37]

Mendelssohn: Violin Concerto in E minor, Op. 64

Introduction

In contrast to Beethoven's 'Kreutzer' Sonata, Ferdinand David's association with and relevance to interpretative issues of Mendelssohn's Violin Concerto in E minor require less explanation. Following his violin studies with Spohr (1823–5), David joined the Königstädter Theater orchestra in Berlin (1826); he became acquainted with Mendelssohn and often played chamber music with him and Julius and Edward Rietz. He left Berlin in 1829 to lead a quartet for Karl von Liphart in Dorpat; but when Mendelssohn became conductor of the Leipzig Gewandhaus Orchestra, he appointed David as leader (1836). David also led the Stadttheater orchestra and later became the first head of the violin faculty at the Leipzig Conservatory, founded by Mendelssohn in 1843.

It was some years after composing his early Violin Concerto in D minor (1822) that Mendelssohn wrote to David, 'I would like to compose a violin concerto for you next winter. One in E minor is forming in my mind, and its opening bars give me no rest.'[38] Work on the concerto did not begin until 1839 and it was not completed in first draft until 16 September 1844. Even though Mendelssohn was a fairly accomplished violinist, David was asked to advise on matters of technique and practicability,[39] and he eventually premiered the work at the Leipzig Gewandhaus on 13 March 1845. The premiere was so successful that David played the concerto in one of the first concerts of the following season (20 October 1845), and the work was performed again the following month in a concert organised by Robert Schumann in Dresden. As David was otherwise engaged, his fourteen-year-old pupil Joseph Joachim deputised and Ferdinand Hiller conducted.

Sources and editions

The re-emergence in 1989 of the autograph manuscript of the concerto in the Biblioteka Jagiellonska in Krakow, Poland revealed various divergences from the established version, causing some scholars to question the veracity of Breitkopf and Haertel's published score, dating from 1862.[40]

In the autograph, the first movement is characterised by the designation Allegro con fuoco rather than the published Allegro, molto appassionato;[41] furthermore, many solo violin passages appear in a higher register and various bars of the familiar version do not exist. The harmonic texture of the autograph, especially in the wind sections, seems more transparent and the rhythmic construction of some passages in the first movement of the printed version clearly shows that the melodic line became highly exaggerated with added syncopations in the violin part, which have no parallel in the manuscript. The autograph's cadenza in the first movement is shorter and very different (although it does incorporate a characteristic arpeggiando idea). The Andante includes various differences of register between autograph and printed version as well as a very different ending, while among the variants in the finale is the passage at iii/233–6,[42] set one octave above the printed version.

David evidently played the autograph version at the premiere, as the manuscript bears an inscription, signed by him: 'Zum ersten Mal ist Manuskript gespielt im letzten Abonnement-Konzert am 13 März 1845' (This manuscript was played for the first time in the last Abonnement Concert on 13 March 1845). The process by which the manuscript version evolved into the printed score has been clarified by the discovery of a second manuscript source in the same Krakow collection. This manuscript includes the score neatly written in ink with various modifications in pencil. The inked score is a copy of the final version of the autograph in a hand other than Mendelssohn's, but the numerous pencilled alterations appear to be in the composer's writing.[43] Mendelssohn's correspondence also confirms that this manuscript score served as a master-copy in the preparation of the first edition.[44]

Violinists contemplating an historically aware performance should consult all these primary sources to comprehend the thought processes behind Mendelssohn's revisions. However, their most valuable interpretative insights will be gained from Ferdinand David's edition of the revised solo part and Joachim's commentary and edition, published in his *Violinschule*. As a sixteen-year-old, Joachim was 'repeatedly accompanied in this concerto by the composer and thus became very familiar with his intentions regarding its performance'.[45] Further useful observations may be gleaned from Heinrich Dessauer's edition of the concerto, which purports to record Joachim's 'artistic conception' of the work.

Tempo

Joachim is more helpful than David with regard to Mendelssohn's tempo intentions. He suggests metronome marks for each 'movement', indicates modifications of tempo within 'movements', and, as mentioned in the section on the cadenza (below), adds the occasional bracketed Italian term with tempo implications. Minim = *c*.108 is his principal tempo for the first movement, but he suggests a slightly slower speed (minim = *c*.92) for the tranquillo second theme at b. 139, a resumption of the original tempo in the second half of b. 168, and an eventual Presto of minim = 168 at b. 493. In his commentary, Joachim expands upon these metronome markings thus:

> Six bars before the *piano tranquillo* [b. 121] the time must be gradually, but very imperceptibly, slackened, so as to let the second principal theme begin quietly and consolingly. The *tranquillo*, however, at the descending triads, must not degenerate into the strong *ritardando* with which it is unfortunately so often

burdened. Any essential change of *tempo* at the G major motive
which might spoil the *alla breve* feeling would be in direct opposi-
tion to the desire of the composer. For Mendelssohn, who so perfectly understood the elastic management of time as a subtle
means of expression, always liked to see the uniform tempo of a
movement preserved as a whole. Also, in ending the melody after
the fermata on the high harmonic A [b. 165], one must avoid a too
strongly marked *ritardando*. (A misuse of the latter often occurs by
exaggerating it until a change of rhythm sets in, and *allegro* and
adagio find themselves in close but unrelated proximity to one
another.) The solo should be brought to a close with a spirited
swing, rising to a fine climax, but with the tempo held well within
its own characteristic limits.[46]

Joachim stresses that tempo modification should be implemented only
gradually and with subtlety so that it is barely noticeable. Prior to the
cadenza he suggests that 'From *sempre pianissimo* onwards one should
imperceptibly retard the time a little.' He further proposes that 'in the excite-
ment of the *più presto* an acceleration of the tempo without undue haste
must be consciously maintained as well as a pithy volume of tone in the
extreme *presto*'.[47]

Joachim suggests a metronome marking of quaver = *c*.92 for the
Andante,[48] but he acknowledges the greater urgency of the middle section of
the 'movement' with an editorial 'un pochino più animato' at b. 51. In the
transitional bars to the reprise of the principal melody at b. 79, he proposes
'a delicately applied *diminuendo*, dying away to *pianissimo*, but not by a
ritardando; at the most an almost imperceptible protraction of the time is
permissible. It is just in this gliding into, and unexpected appearance of the
theme, that its charm lies. The hearer at such places should not have his
attention roused by a "Look out! now it's coming!"'[49]

For the Allegretto non troppo link into the finale Joachim suggests a
tempo of crotchet = *c*.96. He urges performers particularly to observe 'the
sudden, gladsome buoyancy of the *molto crescendo*, and not repeat at the
eighth bar the *fermata*, which is only in its proper place at the fourth'.[50] The
final Allegro molto vivace has a metronome marking of minim = *c*.92 in

Joachim's edition. His commentary focuses on the interaction of soloist and orchestra:

> In close connection with the charming development of the second principal theme in the orchestral accompaniment [from b. 95], the soloist must treat with metronomic precision the semiquavers which playfully encircle it, and which should be executed with the springing bow *staccato*; before the pizzicato occurs they should be worked up to brilliancy. The development then following of the principal theme, beginning in G major, with the melodic accompaniment in the orchestra, must also be characterised by unbending exactness of *tempo*, no matter how vivacious the performance. On no account let the *senza ritardare* [b. 145] be forgotten before the return of the theme in E major.[51]

Contrary to the impression given by many performers nowadays, no accelerando or più presto is indicated in the coda.

Style and expression

David himself remarked that style and expression 'cannot well be taught by printed words and music examples',[52] and his *Violinschule* is largely unhelpful regarding the style, expression and general interpretation of this concerto. Joachim, however, added various expressive indications and summarised character and affect with some flowery descriptive prose. He commented about the first movement thus:

> The first subject opens like a tender lament; it should be delivered with emotional feeling but *piano*. Obtrusive accentuation must be avoided although the strength of tone employed should vary in delicately undulating lines. If these, however, were to be indicated by signs the expression might easily lose in subtlety. The *crescendo* leads first to the fiery up-beat, placed just before the passion-swayed triplet groups; these latter, constantly rising and falling, then lead to the *fortissimo* of the principal motive which is caught up by the *tutti*. The swelling tones of the subordinate theme, proceeding from the orchestra, must be impetuously rendered, and

the rising and falling of the quaver passage (extended to three bars and repeated three times) should be played with large tone and broad bowing and without any undue haste. In all the succeeding episodes, which with continuous lively swing carry us forward to the second subject, scrupulous regard must be paid to the various marks of expression in the up and down dashing passages.[53]

Mendelssohn did not leave the cadenza to be improvised by the performer but wrote out a thirty-six–bar solo passage that dovetails into the following section with orchestra. Correspondence with David reveals that its content caused him some anguish. One letter from Frankfurt (17 December 1844) asks for David's opinion of various modifications to both the orchestral and the solo parts, including 'the altered and extended cadenza'. Mendelssohn continues: 'It pleases me much more than the original version: but is it playable and correctly no[ta]ted? I want the arpeggios to begin at once in strict time and in four parts up to the *tutti*. I hope this will not be too exacting for the performer.'[54] Three weeks before the premiere, Mendelssohn was having second thoughts:

> The bar before the cadenza I wish not to be repeated; I put there Cadenza ad libitum, by which I mean that the arpeggios can be made as long or short as you like . . . The four-part arpeggios are what I like best, with the same bowing from the beginning ff to the end pp. But if that is inconvenient, then alter them thus: (Ex. 7.10a)

(a)

> in that case, from the semiquavers onwards, by all means use a staccato bow. Please alter the end of the first movement entirely according to your wish: (Ex. 7.10b)

(b)

only, if not more difficult, I should naturally like it thus:[55] (Ex. 7.10c)

(c)

Joachim is the most helpful regarding the cadenza's execution, urging that, 'as an integral part of the movement considered as one great whole, [it] must not resolve itself into little details. The introductory *arpeggios* must be played with long bow-strokes, the broken chords which follow must strive brilliantly upwards, and must never, under any circumstances, diminish to a *piano* on the highest *fermata* note, such as we so often have to listen to. The only exception to this may be made at the pauses on the high E. From the chain of shakes then vigorously onward, especially in the bars which immediately precede the *fermata*! On this the composer laid especial weight.'[56] Interestingly, Joachim adds editorial annotations (in brackets) indicative of tempo and expression, suggesting 'largamente' for the trills at b. 307 and 'risoluto e senza ritardare' at b. 319. Contrary to Mendelssohn's wishes, expressed in a letter to David, that the *a tempo* from b. 323 should be played fairly strictly in time, Joachim suggests that the arpeggios should 'begin broadly, but are to be treated with a certain amount of extempore freedom'. He continues: 'Let the transition be accomplished from firm to springing bow, from *forte* to *piano*, and from slower movement to quicker, so that the original *tempo* of the piece is arrived at one bar before the orchestra takes up the principal theme. A difficult task, but worth the trouble!'[57]

The Andante, Joachim maintains, 'cannot be played too smoothly'. He urges careful attention to dynamic shading and states that the melody in the minor (from b. 55) 'should pursue its course undisturbed by the demi-semi-quavers in the lower part: the semiquavers occurring in the melody must be played with a beautiful, sonorous legato, and must not sound like disconnected demi-semiquavers'. He highlights the leap to the $c\#^3$ (b. 207) in the finale's coda for its climactic effect, recommending that it should be 'played with large tone and strongly sustained brilliancy'.[58]

David and Joachim are on common ground regarding vibrato usage, reflecting the influence of Spohr. Joachim was of the opinion that 'the steady tone' should predominate and that vibrato should be used 'only where the

Ex. 7.11 Mendelssohn: Violin Concerto Op. 64, Andante, bb. 99–103 (ed. David).

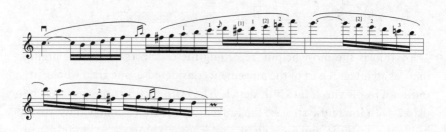

expression seems to demand it', calling performances with excess vibrato 'circus music'; David similarly maintained that vibrato 'must not be employed too frequently nor without sufficient reason'.[59] Likewise, Heinrich Dessauer recommends vibrato on 'a few and appropriate notes' of the first movement's tranquillo melody (i/139ff.), 'but without the least exaggeration; above all the tremolo upon *every* note, a fault which brings about a style of playing both affected and full of mannerism, must be positively avoided'.[60]

Given his attitude towards embellishing the recapitulations of Haydn's string quartet movements (see Chapter 6), David may well have adorned his interpretation with some extempore elaboration. One candidate for such embellishment may have been the slow movement's reprise (from b. 79), but such an interpretation would be purely hypothetical.

Left-hand considerations (violin)

Numerous fingerings in David's and Joachim's editions of the concerto imply expressive portamenti. David frequently advocates semitone shifts, thereby often preserving tonal uniformity within a phrase and implying a possible portamento effect (Ex. 7.11). He also characteristically avoids the even-numbered positions, especially second position, where their use might be more logical.

David's edition specifies the use of the same finger consecutively for some expressive passages (Ex. 7.12a), in one case for up to three successive notes (Ex. 7.12b), thus using portamento to maintain the cantabile line, and sometimes more intensely than treatises suggest. Among other remarkable

Ex. 7.12 (a) Mendelssohn: Violin Concerto Op. 64, Andante, bb. 9–17 (ed. David). (b) Mendelssohn: Violin Concerto Op. 64, Andante, bb. 35–40 (ed. David).

related fingerings are those implied in iii/25 and 29–31 (Ex. 7.13a), where Joachim utilises a more orthodox fourth finger extension from first position, and the slithery chromatic melodic passages at i/239–62 and i/363–9 (Ex. 7.13b). David also suggests playing notes which lie above or below the hand's current position by finger repetition and extension/contraction (i.e., the use of 1–1 or 4–4), possibly with a resultant sliding effect.

Joachim prescribes portamento considerably less than David, in keeping with the sentiments of his *Violinschule*, which endorses the effect as a means of expression and preserving timbral uniformity but advocates its selective introduction, lest it should 'degenerate into an unbearable whining and snivelling'. Violinists who connect a stopped note with an open string 'by a backward sweeping movement of the finger on the string' (as at * in Ex. 7.14) are cautioned against creating such an 'unpleasant effect'.[61]

David's use of open strings in this concerto is generally compliant with Spohr's instruction. However, his use of natural harmonics merits attention, particularly in melodic contexts such as the first movement's opening theme and the cantabile melody of the slow movement. Most natural harmonics seem to be introduced with greater facility, convenience and security in mind, irrespective of any consequent timbral contrast within a phrase. In

Ex. 7.13 (a) Mendelssohn: Violin Concerto Op. 64, Allegro molto vivace, bb. 22–7 (ed. David and ed. Joachim).
(b) Mendelssohn: Violin Concerto Op. 64, Allegro molto appassionato, bb. 238–55 (ed. David).

comparison, Joachim seems more concerned with uniformity of timbre, venturing high on the D string in ii/81–2 and often preferring a stopped note to an harmonic, for example for the d^2 at i/168; however, he still prescribes a fair amount of harmonic usage, much of which is in common with David's edition.

Some bowing issues

As mentioned in the Beethoven case study, the on-the-string preference of early-nineteenth-century German violinists is indicative of the

Ex. 7.14 Mendelssohn: Violin Concerto Op. 64, Andante, bb. 9–12, quoted in Joachim and Moser, *Violinschule*, III, pp. 8–9.

Spohr school's cantabile aims. It raises questions particularly about Mendelssohn's intended bow stroke for his finale (e.g. bb. 23–4 and parallel passages). Joachim implies that a light spiccato may have been intended:

> In regard to the fresh and sparkling Finale, let it at once be remarked that the author never wished the theme to be rendered with the flying staccato, but rather with a light, pointed note, sharp and piquant. The flying bow-strokes appeared to him to be too soft and flaky. . . . The third bar of the principal theme is to be treated in an especially light and playful manner every time it recurs.[62]

Nevertheless, Moser informs us that Joachim was among the earliest German violinists to employ and advocate various kinds of springing bowing in Classical compositions. He evidently sought the advice of Mendelssohn, who replied: 'Always use it, my boy, where it is suitable, or where it sounds well.' Such a response apparently helped to liberate Joachim from rigorous adherence to German bowing traditions.[63]

Although he discusses springing bowings briefly in his *Violinschule*, David appears, on the evidence of his editions, largely to have eschewed them in his performances of the Classical repertory. Of his two types of 'springing' stroke, only one involved the bow leaving the string entirely, and then 'harshness and dryness of sound' were to be avoided 'by grazing the string for a short distance'.[64]

David seems to have aimed for a smoother interpretation overall than Joachim. Where he employs 'tucked-in' bowings or even slurs, Joachim often resorts to articulating one or more notes of a phrase, with unwanted accents a possible result (especially in the down-bow); compare, for example, their annotated bowings for the first movement's opening theme (Ex. 7.15), the opening melody of the Andante (Ex. 7.16), and the Allegretto non troppo. However, David's articulations seem fussy at i/292–3 and i/419 and 423 and

Ex. 7.15 Mendelssohn: Violin Concerto Op. 64, Allegro molto appassionato, bb. 2–18 (ed. David and ed. Joachim).

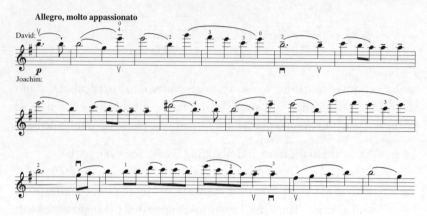

Ex. 7.16 Mendelssohn: Violin Concerto Op. 64, Andante, bb. 9–17 (ed. David and ed. Joachim).

Joachim's phrasing of i/76–80 and i/261–3 seems more logical than David's, even if his shortened harmonic e^2 in i/78 seems somewhat unusual; and it is he rather than David who resorts to bowings that overlap the strong beats at iii/66. David's overlapping bowings at iii/111–15 seem unnecessarily complex (Ex. 7.17), and his overlapping slurs involving repeated d^1s in the cadenza at i/324f., defy literal interpretation.

Various bowings in both David's and Joachim's editions may appear 'upside-down' to modern violinists. Joachim's down-bow start for the portato bowing of the tranquillo melody at i/139 is a case in point, while the two violinists' bowing prescriptions for iii/29–40 make for interesting

Ex. 7.17 Mendelssohn: Violin Concerto Op. 64, Allegro molto vivace, bb. 111–15 (ed. David).

comparisons, David's seeming the less straightforward. Both David and Joachim, recalling Spohr's practice, preferred scale and arpeggio passages to be concluded with an up-bow, as in i/40–7 and iii/163–4.

Mendelssohn's use of dots under slurs is often ambiguous, for he employs similar notation for slurred staccato and portato. David clarifies the intended portato strokes, using lines rather than dots in his edition, notably for i/139–47. Joachim and Moser recommend that the articulation of this theme 'must sound neither too sharp nor too dull . . . the violinist will do well to follow the distinct articulation used by the woodwinds, without which any repetition of the same note in succession would be quite indistinguishable on these instruments. He should also endeavour to equal them in their *gentle* separation of the notes. This will depend chiefly on the capacity of the player to lift and guide the bow so steadily, that in letting it fall again on the string, no trembling occurs, but a fleecy tone of soft roundness is produced.'[65]

Both David and Joachim prescribe some down-bow re-takes in appropriate places, notably in i/213 and 217 and i/462 and 466, and David extends such re-takes to the cadenza, but Joachim's up-bow fortissimo start at i/465 seems odd.

Finally, Alberto Bachmann informs us about two aspects of Joachim's interpretation of the first movement that are not mirrored in his edition. He reports that in performance Joachim tied the three g#[2]s at i/277–9 and mentions a 'Joachim tradition' that resulted in the interpretation of i/348ff, as in Ex. 7.18.[66]

Ex. 7.18 Mendelssohn: Violin Concerto Op. 64, Allegro molto appassionato, bb. 348ff., as Joachim reportedly executed them.

Brahms: Sonata in E flat major, Op. 120 no. 2 for piano and viola (clarinet)

Introduction

When Brahms visited Meiningen in March 1891, his attention was
drawn by Fritz Steinbach to the clarinet playing of Richard Mühlfeld, principal clarinettist of the Meiningen court. He wrote to Clara Schumann,
'Nobody can blow the clarinet more beautifully than Herr Mühlfeld', and he
dubbed Mühlfeld the 'Nightingale of the Orchestra'. Mühlfeld's playing
inspired Brahms to compose the Trio Op. 114, the Clarinet Quintet Op. 115
and the two Sonatas for piano and clarinet Op. 120.[67] The sonatas were completed in 1894, premiered publicly at the Tonkünstlerverein in Vienna on 7
January 1895 and published by N. Simrock in Berlin in the Spring of 1895.
They have achieved lasting success as works for piano and clarinet or viola,
Malcolm MacDonald actually expressing a preference for the viola 'whose
darker, huskier tone seems to suit their elusive moods even better than the
veiled and silken clarinet'.[68]

Text and editions

Brahms actively concerned himself with the entire publication
process of his music. His works are thus relatively error-free. He routinely
kept a copy of the first edition of his publications and he was rigorous at
correcting mistakes.[69] Such copies, where available, could thus be viewed as
the definitive text for Brahms's music, but Robert Pascall warns that for
many works 'no definitive text exists in a unified state'. He points to details
such as expression or articulation annotations which were purposely
revised or replaced, suffered human error (via copyist or engraver) in
transcription or were simply not rectified during the publication process.

Furthermore, one should not necessarily expect definitive texts in Brahms's autograph manuscripts, since Brahms often revised his works during publication and laid special emphasis on the proof stage as an opportunity to finalise his music. Thankfully, most (but by no means all) of Brahms's post-publication alterations were assimilated in the old Brahms Complete Edition of 1926–7.

The engraver's copies of the original version of Op. 120 no. 2 (score and clarinet part), with numerous corrections and alterations/additions in Brahms's hand, are housed in the Staats- und Universitätsbibliothek in Hamburg and have served as primary sources for the most reliable available edition, the Wiener Urtext by Hans-Christian Müller (Vienna, Schott, 1973). However, viola players may wish to review various passages of the arrangement for their instrument, which Bruno Giuranna suggests is not by Brahms and which Brahms himself evidently described in a letter to Joachim as 'ungeschickt und unerfreulich' ('unpleasant and ungrateful').[70] Giuranna particularly finds distasteful many of the sudden octave displacements and registral changes in the viola part that destroy the musical continuity of several melodic phrases (for example, at i/18) and he recommends as far as possible restoring the original notes.[71] The viola version also incorporates some passages of double stopping (for example, ii/126ff.) and extends the viola part in the second movement for three more bars than the clarinet after b. 133. There are also divergences in the articulation and phrasing of the viola part, as well as some additional appoggiature. Viola players may therefore be best advised to use Hans-Christian Müller's Wiener Urtext edition in conjunction with the IMC edition by Milton Katims, until the eventual appearance of the relevant volume of the *Neue Brahms Gesamtausgabe*.

Instruments

Apart from size and stringing, there is little controversy about the general condition of the viola and its other accessories in the 1890s; but historical performers should be mindful of the characteristics of Brahms's preferred pianos, especially the more conservative German-Austrian instruments of the Streichers and the Bösendorfers, favoured for their light, responsive key-action, striking registral variety, crisp articulation and light, clear bass sound.[72] Such models would best realise the clear textural balance of his Op. 120 sonatas, particularly their rich tenor melodies, their distinctive handling of the bass range and their incorporation of symbols and words that indicate, among other details, touch and articulation (for example, the 'sotto voce' passage in inverted canon starting at i/22 of Op. 120 no. 2).[73] Brahms's bass parts, often considered thick or muddy and problematic as regards balance on modern pianos, have remarkable clarity and lightness on an appropriate period instrument; the bass notes, though initially prominent, have a rapid rate of decay.

Tempo

Brahms presented his tempo markings either in Italian (as in Op. 120 no. 2) or in German; they were carefully considered and finely tuned through revision. Clara Schumann's pupil Fanny Davies (1861–1934), who heard Brahms perform frequently between 1884 and 1896, made some interesting comparisons between early-twentieth-century performances of Brahms and the composer's own playing. She confirmed (1905) that 'the tendency is usually to play the andantes too slowly, and the quick movements, scherzos, &c., too quickly',[74] while artists like Enescu and Casals, who all heard Brahms's playing, evidently insisted upon the very moderate speed of his allegro movements.[75]

Brahms's ideas regarding tempo evidently fluctuated regularly, as his correspondence with Alwin von Beckerath and Sir George Henschel verifies. He wrote to the former: ' I can quite easily start you on a subscription for metronome markings. You pay me a tidy sum and each week I deliver to you – different numbers; for with normal people, they cannot remain valid for more than a week.'[76] Such a view seems to give the lie to the theory that Brahms may have cultivated with any consistency proportional tempo relationships, based on the unifying principle of the *tactus* found in Renaissance music, between and within movements of his works.[77] Fanny Davies puts such matters firmly in perspective by recalling Brahms's revealing comment about the interpretation of one of his pieces: 'Machen Sie es wie Sie wollen, machen Sie es nur schön (Do it how you like, but make it beautiful).'[78]

Historical performers will do well to bear this remark in mind when contemplating appropriate tempos for Op. 120 no. 2. The Allegro amabile begs as expansive a tempo and mood as the similarly headed first movement of

the A major Violin Sonata Op. 100, while there is an ongoing debate as to
how far the tranquillo marking at i/162 and the sostenuto indication in the
middle section of the second movement, Appassionato, ma non troppo
allegro,[79] imply a slower tempo. The contrast is essentially more of character
(and tonality) than of tempo, but it seems likely that Brahms would have
favoured some tempo variation, however slight, to accommodate his ritardando un poco at the end of the first movement and his additional annotation 'forte ma dolce e ben cantando' in the central section of the second.

The Finale (Andante con moto) is a strict set of variations on a 14–bar
binary theme. Its 6/8 time signature signals a more flowing pulse than its
motivic subdivisions may imply; furthermore, its contrasts of reflective and
impassioned moods also inflect tempo considerations, particularly in
respect of the fourth variation (bb. 57ff.), whose simple syncopations seem
well suited to a slower tempo.

Tempo modification

Brahms, in common with numerous composers, performers and
theorists,[80] regarded tempo modification as an essential constituent of
expressive performance, especially the proper characterisation of extended
movements. Fanny Davies reports of occasions when Brahms 'would
lengthen infinitesimally a whole bar, or even a whole phrase, rather than
spoil its quietude by making it up into a strictly metronomic bar'. Such
'expansive elasticity', she claims, was one of the chief characteristics of his
interpretation.[81] Brahms evidently wrote tempo modifications into some of
his autographs as an aid to the first performers of the music, but he later
erased them prior to publication.[82] Since many of these erased markings are
still decipherable, they offer direct evidence of how Brahms himself considered his music should be performed with more restraint. He referred to the
tempo modifications in the Fourth Symphony in a letter to Joachim:

> I have pencilled in a few modifications of tempo into the score.
> They seem desirable, useful, even perhaps necessary, when dealing
> with a first performance. Unfortunately they then creep into print
> (with me and with others), where in the main they do not belong.
> Such exaggerations are only really necessary as long as a work is

unfamiliar to an orchestra (or virtuoso). In this case I can often
not do enough with the pushing on and holding back, so that the
expression of passion or calm comes out as I want it. But when a
work has got under the skin, my view is that there should be no
more talk of such things, and the more one departs from this, the
more artificial I find the performance.[83]

Brahms was thus not only against the cultivation of rigid, metronomic
tempos, but also against an excess of modification, as emerges from his
comment to Henschel that tempo modification was nothing new and should
be taken *con discrezione*.[84] Historical performers should thus steer a middle
course in such matters, following Joachim's view that tempo modification
should be 'effected in such a manner that no sudden shock is produced on
the listener by the change'.[85] However, it appears that Joachim was not
always that subtle in his modification of tempo; according to one of his
Quartet, his was often a spontaneous and unpredictable approach to tempo:
'To play with him is damned difficult. Always different tempi, different
accents.'[86] Joachim's recordings demonstrate his flexible approach to the
notated rhythms, especially his recording of his Romance in C.[87]

Early recordings demonstrate broadly that the main theme of a sonata
form movement, for example, has one consistent tempo, while the second
theme has yet another, and the closing theme, if substantially different from
the other two, yet a third steady pulse. When the various themes are reprised
in the recapitulation, they are similarly differentiated by their individual
tempos, and the transitional passages between them prepare the way gradually for the appropriate pulse. In this way, stable tempos were matched to
stable thematic and harmonic areas in a movement, while tonally unstable
areas were marked by changing tempos. Large unstable areas, like the development and coda often featured accelerating tempos to heighten tension
and drama when appropriate.

Articulation, phrasing and expression

Brahms's penchant for composing continually developing variations is made more intelligible by phrasing which clearly separates the
melodic and motivic units from each other. Fanny Davies explains that

Brahms 'belonged to that racial school of playing which begins its phrases well, ends them well, leaves plenty of space between the end of one and the beginning of another, and yet joins them without any hiatus'.[88] Brahms clarified his intentions, using three main indicators of touch – legato, leggiero and marcato – and two kinds of articulation – slurs and staccatos. Violists should also be mindful of the common nineteenth-century articulation practice of shortening the second note of a pair of slurred notes, as, for example, in Op. 120 no. 2, i/7 and ii/48–59. Florence May's claim that Brahms made much of this effect and that pairs of slurs have a special significance in his music is corroborated in correspondence between Brahms and Joachim, although the practice was probably not rigorously applied in especially long phrases.[89]

The introduction of expressive rubato often had implications for articulation. Analysing the Flonzaley Quartet's performance of the scherzo of Brahms's Piano Quintet, Jon Finson concludes that rubato 'is not only an expressive device meant to intensify the drive of this pressing scherzo but also an articulatory strategy which highlights the repetition of motivic ideas. The modern performer's stereotype of Brahms's music, that it consists of long uninterrupted phrases, runs totally contrary to the practice of performers trained during his lifetime. In the surviving recordings these contemporary musicians use every expressive means at their command to separate melodic and motivic units from one another in Brahms's music, revealing his penchant for composing continually developing variations.'[90]

Brahms was very explicit about his dynamic markings, often making much out of contrast. 'Like Beethoven', writes Fanny Davies, 'he was most particular that his marks of expression (always as few as possible) should be the means of conveying the inner musical meaning. The sign <>, as used by Brahms, often occurs when he wishes to express great sincerity and warmth (for example Op. 120 no. 2 i/8, 11–12, 47, ii/16–20), applied not only to tone but to rhythm also. He would linger not on one note alone, but on a whole idea, as if unable to tear himself away from its beauty. . . . His touch could be warm, deep, full, and broad in *fortes*, and not hard even in the *fortissimos*; and his *pianos*, always of carrying power, could be as round and transparent as a dewdrop. He had a wonderful legato.'[91]

'Dolce' is a common expressive marking in this sonata and Brahms also specifies 'sotto voce' to good effect. His use of the diminuendo hairpin requires thoughtful interpretation, Paul Mies claiming that it was sometimes used to indicate that the note (or phrase) concerned should begin with an accent and then diminish in volume.[92] The theme of the central section of the second movement (bb. 81, 85, 95 and 99) illustrates Mies's theory well. However, a particularly remarkable example occurs at ii/60–3, where repeated diminuendo hairpins in the piano part are combined with a crescendo marking. Here, Brahms probably intended a diminuendo within each bar, combined with a crescendo over the four-bar phrase. Among other subtleties about Brahms's dynamic prescriptions, Imogen Fellinger points out that 'p espressivo' in one instrument indicates that it requires slightly more emphasis than a simple accompanying 'p'; and pianists should also note that Brahms's friend Eugen d'Albert observed that: 'the Master wished that the use of the pedal be left to the player's taste'.[93]

Portamento

Portamento and vibrato also served to shape the melodic line in Brahms performance. Portamento achieved this by emphasising structurally important pitches such as the peaks of phrases or suspensions and cadences. Joachim emphasised its vocal heritage and admits its good effect when used tastefully and in moderation,[94] as illustrated in his recording of his transcription of Brahms's Hungarian Dance No. 1. Performers might contemplate a similar use of the device, with lightened bow and the relevant notes unstressed, at i/69 of Op. 120 no. 2, but they should heed Joachim's and Moser's warning against the 'constant use of wrongly executed portamenti [whereby] . . . the performance of a piece can become so disfigured as to result in a mere caricature . . . [one should use] taste and judgement'.[95]

Vibrato

As noted in Chapter 5, the use of vibrato was limited in Brahms's day. Joachim and Moser cite Spohr regarding its basic principles and warn against its 'habitual use, especially in the wrong place. A violinist whose taste is refined and healthy will always recognise the steady tone as the ruling one, and will use vibrato only where the expression seems to demand it.'[96]

In Brahms's Op. 120 no. 2, the violist (or violinist) should thus use vibrato sparingly as a melodic ornament to highlight important notes in phrases (for example, long or accentuated notes such as those in i/51–2, 149–50 and ii/28 and the *messe di voce* effects in ii/17–20, 156–60 and 206–7). One late-nineteenth-century writer sees its role as providing 'an emotional thrill'; for, as soon as vibrato 'degenerates into a mannerism, its effect is either painful, ridiculous, or nauseous, entirely opposed to good taste and common sense'.[97]

8 Related family members

The *violino piccolo* and other small violins with four strings tuned in fifths at the interval of a third, fourth or even a fifth higher than the standard violin, were fairly common in the early seventeenth century. Michael Praetorius calls the instrument a 'klein discant Geig' (small treble fiddle) and several 'claine discant' violins are included in an inventory (1596) of the collection in Schloss Ambras in Austria.[1] These violins produced a clear, bright sound at their higher tunings – the most common was c^1–g^1–d^2–a^2 – and were probably used not only to fulfil the tonal requirements of a higher voice range than the standard-size violin, but also to allow for comfortable playing in higher registers; with them, players could retain a lower left-hand position with limited shifting at a time when such shifts were rarely executed. Leopold Mozart confirms that 'Some years ago one even played concertos on this little violin (called by the Italians *Violino Piccolo*) and, as it was capable of being tuned to a much higher pitch than other violins it was often to be heard in company with a transverse flute, a harp, or other similar instruments. The little fiddle is no longer needed, and everything is played on the ordinary violin in the upper registers.'[2] That the *violino piccolo* was used well into the third quarter of the eighteenth century suggests that many performers accepted or gained proficiency in the art of shifting only very slowly; ironically, eventual mastery of the technique led to the instrument's demise.

Small-pattern violins appear to have been made in at least three distinct body lengths during the sixteenth, seventeenth and eighteenth centuries, ranging from the smallest of *c.*23–7cm body length through instruments of *c.*30–1cm to the largest of *c.*34cm (only *c.*1.5cm shorter than the standard full-size instrument).[3] Available evidence suggests that the term *violino piccolo* was commonly applied to the variety with a body length of *c.*27cm, as corroborated by Praetorius,[4] an excellent example of which, by the brothers Amati (1613), is illustrated in Fig. 8.1.

Monteverdi's requirement of 'violini piccoli alla francese' in *Orfeo* (1607),

Fig. 8.1 (*left to right*) Violino piccolo (75%) by Antonio and Girolamo
Amati (1613); kit (dancing master's fiddle) attributed to Richard Tobin,
London, early nineteenth century; standard size violin by Nicolo Amati
(1628). (America's Shrine to Music Museum, University of South Dakota,
Vermillion)

the earliest-known prescription for the *violino piccolo*, probably refers to an
instrument of *c.*27cm in length as opposed to the *pochette*[5] or the standard-
size violin.[6] Moser and Bessaraboff support this view, but suggest that the
instrument was tuned in fourths.[7] Three major works by J. S. Bach call for
violino piccolo, tuned in fifths a minor third higher than the normal standard-size violin tuning: Cantatas 96 (*Herr Christ, der einge Gottessohn*) and
140 (*Wachet auf, ruft uns die Stimme*)[8] and the Brandenburg Concerto No. 1
(BWV1046). Dittersdorf, Doles, Erlebach, Foerster, Fux, Harrer, Janitsch,
Krause, Pfeiffer and Rosetti, among others, wrote significant works for the
instrument.

The rebec, a bowed string instrument distinguished by its vaulted one-piece back and no clear demarcation between its body and neck (see Fig. 3.1.1), was known in Europe from the tenth century, when it appeared in various shapes and under several different names. Two early types are broadly distinguishable: the completely wooden pear-shaped variety terminating in a flat peg-holder; and a skin-bellied, narrower instrument with right-angled pegbox. However, its size and features of its design and accessories varied according to its intended function – any number of strings from one to five (or sometimes more) was possible, for example, with tuning generally in fifths;[9] but the traditional European model of the late thirteenth century was pear-shaped with a wooden soundboard and sickle-shaped pegbox. Much of the nomenclature used to describe it – notably 'lyra', 'lira', 'rubeba' – reflects its Byzantine and Arab origins, but this also varied considerably (the generic term 'fiddle' was often used) and involved terms used also for other medieval instruments. Virdung and Agricola described rebecs as 'clein Geigen' and Praetorius used the diminutive 'Rebecchino' for a violin.[10] From the sixteenth century onwards, the rebec was often called by the various names of its offshoot, the kit. Iconographical evidence suggests that the instrument was used in art music principally during the Middle Ages and Renaissance. It was commonly played by professional minstrels, who entertained in royal courts or were attached to a town or noble household, or by rustic musicians in processions, feasts, dances or other celebrations. It was held either down in the lap, with the bow gripped from below (particularly in southern Europe and northern Africa), or, more commonly, at the shoulder (as in northern Europe). Little specific repertory has survived for the instrument.

The design of the medieval fiddle also varied according to its function. Generally of wood – although southern and eastern European instruments often had a skin belly – most fiddles were oval, elliptical or rectangular in shape, often with a flat or nearly flat back and generally with incurved sides for ease of bowing. C-shaped soundholes were the most common of various designs employed and many instruments were decorated with elaborate carving or inlay. The bridge was often uncurved and fingerboards (some fretted) supporting between two to six or more (but commonly five) strings (one often being a lateral drone), though not universal, were common. Sometimes four strings appear to be arranged in two courses, or six in three;

the inclusion of a soundpost was probable but cannot be confirmed. No universal tuning was used, this being determined by the music to be played, and bows for the instrument seem to have resembled those for the rebec, crowd (crwth) or medieval viol. Very little medieval music was composed for specific instruments, and performers tended to play repertory that was suitable for the occasion, whether for feast, dancing or for general entertainment, solo or in consort.

The *lira da braccio* (sometimes called 'lira' or 'viola') of Renaissance Italy derived from the fiddle of the Middle Ages. Played especially by courtly Italian poet-musicians of the fifteenth and sixteenth centuries to accompany their improvised recitations of poetry, but also in various ensembles, its violin-like shape gradually evolved through three principal stages: a relatively long, thin body with a gently incurved waist without corners, and with a variety of possible soundhole shapes; a body divided into two parts, a relatively narrow upper and a shorter, broader lower section, almost invariably with C-holes; and the fully developed violin shape with three bouts, corners and f-holes, but also with a wide fingerboard, a relatively flat bridge, seven strings tuned $d/d^1–g/g^1–d^1–a^1–e^2$ (the ds were drones) and a leaf-shaped pegbox with frontal pegs.[11] It was supported against the left shoulder, but generally held with the pegbox considerably lower than the body of the instrument. Its bass equivalent, the *lirone*, gained some popularity in the sixteenth century, but both instruments became obsolete early in the seventeenth century.

Little is known about the early history of the crowd. Of Asian origin, it had become, by the eighteenth century, a bowed fingerboard lyre with three octave-tuned double courses of strings and a bridge with the right foot long enough to pass through the right soundhole and rest on the flat back of the body. The most common tuning was: $g–g^1–c^2–c^1–d^1–d^2$, g and g^1 being off the fingerboard and plucked with the thumb.

The small, unfretted, violin-shaped kit (also known as *pochette*, *canino*, *Taschengeige* and by many other names), or dancing master's fiddle (see Figs. 3.1.1, 3.1.2, and 8.1) was in common usage between the sixteenth and nineteenth centuries, but it was especially popular during the eighteenth century. Little music was composed specifically for it, so performers generally played pieces for violin, dances or popular tunes. Though made in a variety of shapes, two main types of kit are broadly distinguishable: a pear-shaped model or one resembling a narrow boat, with a distinctly vaulted back like a rebec; or a miniature viol, violin or guitar with a slightly arched back and a long neck. Most kits comprised four strings tuned generally in fifths, sometimes at the pitch of the standard violin, but more often a fourth or fifth and occasionally (especially with three-stringed models) an octave higher. The instrument's diminutive resonating body produces only a small sound, especially those models without soundpost and bass-bar. Surviving kits range from simple rustic instruments to those made by distinguished makers such as Joachim Tielke and Antonio Stradivari. The latter's working patterns for various kits have survived, including those of the elongated violin and boat-shaped *canino* models. The influence of the *viola d'amore* prompted the occasional addition of sympathetic strings, resulting in the so-called *pochette d'amour*.

Vivaldi's three concertos 'per violino in Tromba' have caused some confusion as to their intended instrumentation. However, it would appear from the chains of thirds and brilliant trumpet-like writing that these are violin concertos in which the soloist is intended simply to imitate a trumpet. Similarly, the prescription of 'violini in tromba marina' in his Concerto in C (RV558) is generally thought to indicate the use of two violins playing in the style of a *tromba marina*.[12]

Mention should also be made of the Norwegian Hardanger fiddle, a folk instrument with a narrower body than the standard violin, as well as generally deeper ribs and a more pronounced arching of the belly and back; it was also distinguished by its short neck, flat fingerboard, only slightly curved bridge, four playing stringings and four or five sympathetic strings. The earliest known example (with six strings only) dates from the mid seventeenth century, but the instrument achieved its greatest popularity in the eighteenth and nineteenth centuries. Originally held at the chest but latterly bowed at the shoulder, the instrument is still used nowadays. Its repertory, which exploits a wide range of scordatura tunings (most commonly a–d^1–a^1–e^2 for the playing strings and d^1–e^1–$f\sharp^1$–a^1 for the sympathetic strings), comprises largely folksongs, dances and bridal marches.

Viola da braccio was a sixteenth- and seventeenth-century term for any member of the violin family, or, more accurately, a generic term for any bowed string instrument played on the arm (It. *braccio*), as opposed to one played on or between the knees (differentiated by the Italian *gamba*). It could thus refer to almost any variety of early violin or viola. However, the term 'viola' was also associated with a number of instruments which were not violas at all: *viola da gamba* was the Italian term for the viol; *viola bastarda* referred to a small bass viol prevalent in sixteenth- and early-seventeenth-century Italy; *viola di bordone* was the Italian nomenclature for the baryton; and the *viola da spalla* was actually a small cello with four to six strings and held across the player's chest by a strap over the shoulder (It. *spalla*).

Michel Woldemar's *violon-alto* was an interesting compromise between the violin and viola, designed (*c*.1788) to alleviate the dearth of good violists. It involved the addition of a fifth (c) string to, basically, a violin body and was championed by Chrétien Urhan, who gave performances of Woldemar's own Concerto in C with great success. Other compromises between the violin and viola were the *viola alta* (see below) and the *violalin*, this latter a five-string viola designed by Friedrich Hillmer (Leipzig) towards the end of the eighteenth century. The *quinton*, a five-stringed compromise between the violin and the viol, achieved some degree of popularity during the eighteenth century. It had frets and sloping shoulders but its body otherwise resembled that of the violin.

Alternative nomenclature for the viola ranged from the German *Bratsche* (a corruption of *braccio*) to the Italian *violetta*[13] and the French *taille, tenor, quinte, alto-viola,* and *violette*. Other related instruments include the *viola d'amore* (discussed below), the *viola di fagotto*, a viola with the tuning range of a cello but played on the arm,[14] and the *viola pomposa*, a five-stringed instrument used *c*.1725–70 and tuned either $c–g–d^1–a^1–e^2$ or possibly $d–g–d^1–g^1–c^2$, as Galpin suggested.[15] Sometimes called the *violino pomposo*, this latter instrument has little repertory other than some duets (with flute) by Telemann (from *Der getreue Music-Meister*), a double concerto by J. G. Graun, and a continuo sonata by Christian Joseph Lidarti.

Many instruments were designed during the nineteenth century in attempts to resolve the problems of viola sonority. Scientists such as Félix Savart were adamant that the body of the instrument was much too small in relation to its intended tonal range. Subsequent experiments spawned Dubois' *violon-tenor* and Charles Henry's *baryton* (both tuned an octave lower than the violin and played cello-fashion), Jean-Baptiste Vuillaume's *contralto*, and, most significantly Hermann Ritter's *viola alta*. Ritter commissioned (*c*.1875) Würzburg luthier Karl Hörlein to build an instrument to his specifications with a body length of *c*.48cm and ribs of 4.3cm.[16] This was an exact enlargement of a violin based on the same acoustical properties and, from 1898, incorporated a fifth string tuned to e^2. Its larger size afforded improved resonance and greater brilliance and its increased range proved 'very advantageous for modern orchestral works'.[17] Hanslick also wrote favourably about the instrument,[18] which was evidently used in the Meiningen Orchestra *c*.1884 and by the Ritter Quartet, adopted by Wagner for a brief period in the Bayreuth orchestra (from *c*.1876) and admired by Liszt, Rubinstein, Hans von Bülow, Felix Weingartner and others. However, its unwieldiness and its requirement of 'greater physical power' from the player were evidently the principal reasons for its limited use.[19] Its companion instruments, the *viola tenore* (body length: 72cm) and the *viola bassa* (body length: 96cm), both played between the knees, cello-fashion, were adopted for a short time by some players and conductors, most notable being Leopold Stokowski's short-term preference for the *viola tenore* in the New York Philharmonic Orchestra. Among other designers of large violas were Heinrich Dessauer, John Reiter, Eugen Sprenger (*Tenorgeige*) and Eugen Vitachek, and the problems of the optimum viola size have persisted, having been only partially addressed by the so-called Tertis model instrument (first constructed by Arthur Richardson), Carleen Hutchins's new family of violins, and the work of luthiers such as Hans Olaf Hanson (*Violino grande*) and Hans Weisshaar (*Tenor violin*). Otto Erdesz's viola design with an indented upper bout, has afforded the left hand greater facility of execution in the higher positions.

The *viola d'amore* gained some popularity during the late seventeenth and eighteenth centuries. Of roughly viola size, it usually had a flat viol-like back, wide ribs, sloping shoulders, soundholes in the shape of a 'flaming sword' (symbolic of Islam and its Middle Eastern origins) and a carved head instead of a scroll. Eighteenth-century models normally (though not exclusively) had seven principal and seven sympathetic strings, these latter running through the bridge and under the unfretted fingerboard into separate pegs in the pegbox.[20] Played at the arm like a viola, the instrument was in great demand in eighteenth-century Austria, Germany, Czechoslovakia and

Italy. A variety of scordatura tunings was used, but a tuning of A–d–a–d^1–$f\sharp^1$–a^1–d^2 eventually became fairly standard in the late eighteenth century, the sympathetic strings being tuned in unison with the playing strings or an octave higher.

The *viola d'amore*'s early repertory was fairly extensive, ranging from its original prominence in opera and passions (e.g. Fux's *Gli ossequi della notte*, 1709; or Telemann's *Der sterbende Jesus*, 1716), to effective use in various cantatas by J. S. Bach (notably BWV36, 152 and 205), as well as in his St. John Passion, and numerous works by Telemann, Graupner, Vivaldi, Ariosti, Carl Stamitz, Hoffmeister, Rust, Haydn, Locatelli and others,[21] composers using a variety of notation systems to indicate their intentions. Although its popularity declined somewhat in the nineteenth century, the instrument was exploited effectively by Meyerbeer (*Les Huguenots*), Massenet (*Le jongleur de Notre-Dame*) and others, and interest in its special colours was later revived by composers as wide-ranging in style as Hindemith, Henri Cassadesus, Frank Martin, York Bowen, Ginastera and Janáček.

Closely related to the *viola d'amore* was the *violetta marina*, named by Leopold Mozart 'the English Violet'.[22] This was a larger variety of viola with seven principal and fourteen sympathetic strings and was the brainchild of Pietro Castrucci, the leader of Handel's opera orchestra in London for over twenty years. Handel included a pair of obbligato parts for 'violette marine per gli Signori Castrucci' in the hero's sleep aria in *Orlando*; a part for one *violetta marina* is also featured in Handel's *Sosarme*, and the same instrument may have been the violetta used in *Deborah* and *Ezio*.

Notes

Preface

1 Johann Mattheson, *Der vollkommene Capellmeister* (Hamburg, 1739), p. 484.
2 Francesco Geminiani, *A Treatise of Good Taste in the Art of Musick* (London, 1749), p. 4.

1 Historical performance in context

1 In Clive Brown, *Classical and Romantic Performing Practice 1750–1900* (Oxford, 1999), Preface, p. vii. For a philosophical discussion of the relevance of composers' intentions to performance, see Randall R. Dipert, 'The composer's intentions: an examination of their relevance for performance', *Musical Quarterly* 66 (1980), pp. 205–18.
2 See Harry Haskell, *The Early Music Revival: a History* (London, 1988); Colin Lawson and Robin Stowell, *The Historical Performance of Music: An Introduction* (Cambridge, 1999), pp. 1–11.
3 Joseph Joachim and Andreas Moser, *Violinschule* (3 vols., Berlin 1902–5), Eng. trans. Alfred Moffat (London, 1905), III, p. 5.
4 See Robert Donington, *The Work and Ideas of Arnold Dolmetsch* (Haslemere, 1932); Margaret Campbell, *Dolmetsch: the Man and his Work* (London, 1975).
5 Both scholars published influential studies about early music performance; see Robert Haas, *Aufführungspraxis der Musik* (Wildpark-Potsdam, 1931), and Arnold Schering, *Aufführungspraxis alter Musik* (Leipzig, 1931).
6 Notably *A Performer's Guide to Baroque Music* (London, 1973), *String Playing in Baroque Music* (London, 1977) and *Baroque Music: Style and Performance* (London, 1982).
7 In Dominic Gill (ed.), *The Book of the Violin* (Oxford, 1984), p. 154.
8 D. K. Nelson, 'An interview with Pinchas Zukerman', *Fanfare* 13 (March/April 1990), p. 38.
9 Edward Heron-Allen's *De Fidiculis Bibliographia* (2 vols., London, 1890–4) was one of the first major bibliographies of the violin family. The most recent parallel

publication is: Roberto Regazzi (rev. Jane H. Johnson), *The Complete Luthier's Library* (Bologna, 1990).

10 George Dubourg, *The Violin* (London, 1836, 5/1878); Wilhelm J. von Wasielewski, *Die Violine und ihre Meister* (Leipzig, 1869, 8/1927); Andreas Moser, *Geschichte des Violinspiels* (Leipzig, 1923, rev., enlarged 2/1966–7); Arnaldo Bonaventura, *Storia del violino, dei violinisti e della musica per violino* (Milan, 1925).

11 This has appeared more recently as *The Amadeus Book of the Violin*, trans. and ed. Reinhard G. Pauly (Portland, Oregon, 1993).

12 For example, R. Larry Todd and Peter Williams (eds.), *Perspectives on Mozart Performance* (Cambridge, 1991); or Robin Stowell (ed.), *Performing Beethoven* (Cambridge, 1994).

13 Duncan Druce, 'Historical approaches to violin playing', in John Paynter, Tim Howell, Stephen Orton and Peter Seymour (eds.), *Companion to Contemporary Musical Thought*, (2 vols., London, 1992), II, pp. 993–1019; Robert Philip, *Early Recordings and Musical Style: Changing Tastes in Instrumental Performance, 1900–1950* (Cambridge, 1992).

14 Important articles naturally also appear from time to time in other music journals, as the select bibliography clearly demonstrates. Among the published bibliographies on performance practice, the reader is referred to: Mary Vinquist and Neal Zaslaw, *Performance Practice: a Bibliography* (New York, 1971); Roland Jackson, *Performance Practice, Medieval to Contemporary: a Bibliographic Guide* (New York and London, 1988).

15 See Joanna Pieters, 'Editorial', *The Strad* 111 (2000), p. 589; 'Sense and sensibility', *The Strad* 111 (2000), p. 606.

16 See Lawson and Stowell, *Historical Performance*, ch. 1. It is largely the ethos rather than the detailed practicalities of period performance which has been debated in the work of Harnoncourt (*Baroque Music Today; Music as Speech* (London, 1988)), Dreyfus ('Early music defended . . ., *Musical Quarterly 49* (1983), pp. 297–322); Kerman (*Musicology* (London, 1985)); Kenyon ((ed.) *Authenticity and Early Music* (Oxford, 1988)); Brown and Sadie ((eds.) *Performance Practice: Music after 1600* (2 vols., London, 1989)); Kivy *Authenticities* (Ithaca and London, 1995)); Taruskin (*Text and Act* (Oxford, 1995)); and Sherman ((ed.), *Inside Early Music: Conversations with Performers* (Oxford, 1997)).

17 See Lawson and Stowell, *Historical Performance*, pp. 11–12.

18 In Gill (ed.), *The Book*, p. 157.

19 Joseph Szigeti, *A Violinist's Notebook* (London, 1969), p. 134.

20 See Philip, *Early Recordings*.

21 Peter Williams, 'Performance practice studies: some current approaches to the early music phenomenon', in Paynter, Howell, Orton, and Seymour (eds.), *Companion to Contemporary Musical Thought* (2 vols., London and New York, 1992), II, p. 946.

2 The repertory and principal sources

1 Willi Apel (ed. Thomas Binkley), *Italian Violin Music of the Seventeenth Century* (Bloomington and Indianapolis, 1990), p. 238.

2 For more information about the Italian music mentioned in this section, its sources, and various available modern editions, see Apel (ed. Binkley), *Italian Violin Music*.

3 Cited in the dedication to the posthumous (1641) sonata publication and quoted in Apel (ed. Binkley), *Italian Violin Music*, p. 42.

4 Another volume of sonatas was published in Rome in 1669.

5 John Evelyn, *Diary*, ed. E. S. de Beer (4 vols., Oxford, 1955), IV, p. 177 (17 November 1674).

6 William S. Newman, *The Sonata in the Baroque era*, (4th edn New York, 1983), p. 234.

7 Sébastien de Brossard, *Dictionnaire de musique* (Paris, 1703/R1964).

8 The sonatas of 1713 use the viol to telling effect as a duet partner to the violin.

9 See Terence Best, 'Handel's solo sonatas', *Music & Letters* 58 (1977), pp. 430–8.

10 A few brief sections remain where the harpsichordist is required to realise the figured harmonies.

11 The second concerto is lost.

12 See Robin Stowell, *Beethoven: Violin Concerto* (Cambridge, 1998).

13 The variation form had remained a favourite type of display piece from Marini's variations on the romanesca (Op. 3) through Corelli's 'Follia' variations (Op. 5 no. 12) and Tartini's *L'arte del arco* to works by Rode, Kreutzer and many others.

14 Maurice Riley, *The History of the Viola* (2 vols., Ypsilanti, Mich., 1980, 1991) I, p. 71. See Franz Zeyringer, *Literature für Viola* (Hartberg, 1985), Michael D. Williams, *Music for Viola* (Detroit, 1979) and Margaret K. Farisch, *String Music in Print* (2nd edn, New York and London, 1973) for extensive catalogues of the viola repertory.

15 In H. M. Brown and S. Sadie (eds.), *Performance Practice: Music after 1600* (2 vols., London, 1989), II, p. 61.

16 Notably in the string quartet and string quintet repertory and in the violin/viola

duos of Mozart, Spohr and others. See Rebecca Clarke, 'The history of the viola in quartet writing', *Music and Letters* 4 (1923), pp. 6–17.

17 Riley (*The history*, I, pp. 194, 196) mentions an early sonata (1823–4) by Mendelssohn and sonatas by Georges Onslow (*c.*1820), Anton Rubinstein (1855), Carl Reinecke and Friedrich Kiel.

18 See Philip, *Early Recordings.* José Bowen ('Why should performers study performance? Performance practice vs. performance analysis', *Performance Practice Review* 9 (1996), p. 17) is more sceptical about the relevance of early recordings to nineteenth-century performance.

19 See Malcolm Boyd and John Rayson, 'The gentleman's diversion, John Lenton and the first violin tutor', *Early Music* 10 (1982), pp. 329–32.

20 David Boyden (*The History of Violin Playing*, p. 358) states that at least thirty works devoted to amateur violin instruction were printed in England alone between 1658 and 1731, these works apparently being read also in other countries.

21 John Wilson (ed.), *Roger North on Music* (London, 1959), p. 194.

22 If sixteenth-century treatises devoted any space at all to instruments, it was generally at the end almost as an afterthought. Jambe de Fer's disdain for the violin (*Epitome musical des tons sons et accordz, es voix homaines, fleustes d'Alleman, fleustes à neuf trous, violes, & violons*, Lyons, 1556) was typical of the period.

23 Michel Montéclair: *Méthode facile pour aprendre [sic] à jouer du violon* (Paris, [1711–12]); Pierre Dupont, *Principes de Violon* (Paris, 1718); Michel Corrette, *L'école d'Orphée* (Paris, 1738).

24 For a comprehensive list of these pirated adaptations of Geminiani's work, see Boyden's facsimile edition [1952] of Geminiani's *The Art of Playing on the Violin* (London, 1751), pp. x–xi.

25 For example, Robert Bremner's *The Compleat Tutor for the Violin* (London, *c.*1750), Stephen Philpot's *An Introduction to the Art of Playing on the Violin* (London, 1767?), and the anonymous *An Abstract of Geminiani's Art of Playing on the Violin* (Boston, 1769); and numerous English publishers used Geminiani's name on posthumous publications, very little of whose content was his.

26 The original date of this treatise is subject to disagreement, but it was in preparation, at the very least, during the 1790s. See Montanari, *Bartolomeo Campagnoli, violinistica compositore (1751–1827)* (n.p., 1969) and S. Sadie (ed.), *The New Grove Dictionary of Music and Musicians* (20 vols., London, 1980), art. 'Campagnoli, Bartolomeo'.

27 L. Mozart, *Versuch einer gründlichen Violinschule* (Augsburg, 1756; Eng. trans. Editha Knocker as *A Treatise on the Fundamental Principles of Violin Playing*, London, 1948), Author's preface.

28 Charles Auguste de Bériot, *Méthode de violon* Op. 102 (Paris, 1858, Eng. trans. Westbrook and Phipson, London, 1876), preface.

29 Carl Guhr, *Ueber Paganinis Kunst die Violine zu spielen* (Mainz, [1829]), preface, p. 2.

30 Johann Joachim Quantz, *Versuch einer Anweisung die Flöte traversiere zu spielen* (Berlin, 1752, 3/1789/R1952; Eng. trans. E. R. Reilly as *On Playing the Flute*, London, 1966), p. 237; Hector Berlioz, *Mémoires de Hector Berlioz* (Paris, 1870; ed. and Eng. trans. David Cairns, 1969, rev.3/1987), p. 341.

31 Carl Philipp Emanuel Bach, *Versuch über die wahre Art das Clavier zu spielen* (2 vols., Berlin, 1753 and 1762/R1957; Eng. trans. W. J. Mitchell as *Essay on the True Art of Playing Keyboard Instruments*, New York, 1949); Daniel Gottlob Türk, *Clavierschule, oder Anweisung zum Clavierspielen* (Leipzig and Halle, 1789, enlarged 2/1802/R1967; Eng. trans. Raymond Haggh, Lincoln, Nebraska, 1982); Johann Georg Tromlitz, *Ausführlicher und gründlicher Unterricht die Flöte zu spielen* (Leipzig, 1791; Eng. trans. and ed. Ardall Powell as *The Virtuoso Flute-player*, Cambridge, 1991).

32 Mathis Lussy, *Traité de l'expression musicale: Accents, nuances et mouvements dans la musique vocale et instrumentale* (Paris, 1874; Eng. trans. M. E. von Glehn, London, c.1885); *Le Rhythme musical, son origine, sa fonction et son accentuation* (Paris, 1883).

33 Notably by Kastner (1837, 1839), Berlioz (1843) and later Strauss (1905) and Rimsky-Korsakov (1913).

34 By, among others, Berlioz (1856), Wagner (1869) and Weingartner (1895).

35 For more detailed information about relevant stringed instrument collections, see James Coover, *Musical Instrument Collections: Catalogues and Cognate Literature* (Detroit, 1981) and Sadie (ed.), *New Grove*, vol. IX, pp. 245–54, art., 'Instruments, collections of'.

36 Thomas Heck's *Picturing Performance: the Iconography of the Performing Arts* (Rochester, NY, 2000) reviews the theoretical and practical problems associated with traditional depictions of performers. See also Lawson and Stowell, *Historical Performance*, pp. 20–1 for discussion of other pitfalls associated with iconographical sources.

3 Equipment

1 See Laurence Libin, 'Early violins: problems and issues', *Early Music* 19 (1991), pp. 5–6.

2 See François Lesure, '*L'Épitome musical* de Philibert Jambe de Fer (1556)', *Annales Musicologiques* 6 (1958–63), pp. 341–86.

3 See Boyden, *The History*, frontispiece and plate 2; E. Winternitz, 'Early violins in paintings by Gaudenzio Ferrari and his school', in *Musical Instruments and their Symbolism in Western Art* (London, 1967), pp. 99–109.

4 See Holman, *Four and Twenty Fiddlers*, pp. 1–31.

5 Boyden (*New Grove Violin Family* (London, 1989), p. 21) states that Andrea Amati made 38 violins for the King, comprising 12 'large' and 12 'small' violins (both sizes were smaller than today's models), 6 violas and 8 cellos.

6 The authenticity of 'Le Messie' has been doubted, but current opinion, strengthened by recent dendrochronological surveys by John Topham and Derek McCormick, suggests that Stradivari was its maker.

7 Vincetto Lancetti, *Biographical Notices* (Milan, 1823), cited in George Hart, *The Violin: its Famous Makers and their Imitators* (London, 1875), p. 151.

8 See 'Noch etwas über der Bau der Geige', *Allgemeine musikalische Zeitung* (24 October 1804), col. 50.

9 See Edward Heron-Allen, *Violin Making as it was and is* (London, 1884) pp. 104–21; Jane Dorner, 'Fiddlers' fancy', *The Strad*, 94 (1983), pp. 180–5, 243–6.

10 The naming of the viola parts in Louis XIII's *24 Violons du Roi* as *haute-contre*, or *haute-contre taille, taille,* and *quinte* or *cinquiesme* also verifies such conclusions.

11 Antonio Stradivari's enormous 1690 'Medici' instrument (48.3cm long) contrasts with his smaller contralto models (41.3cm long), while Jacob Stainer's Cremonese models between 1649 and 1670 varied between 40cm and 46.3cm in length. See John Dilworth, 'Unfinished journey', *The Strad* 107 (1996), p. 484.

12 Dilworth (*Ibid.*, p. 487) confirms that the success of smaller violas made in England, the Netherlands and elsewhere from the early 1700s influenced Italian makers such as Guadagnini, Storioni and Bellosio to produced violas of a length of 40.6cm or less.

13 For example, Hermann Ritter's championing of Hörlein's *viola alta*. See Chapter 8.

14 High twist is a term coined by Ephraim Segerman (no such term is found in available primary sources) for a length of gut (treated, twisted and polished intestines of sheep, rams or wethers) which is given as much twist as possible when wet and subjected to further twisting while it dries or slims. Such a string is more flexible, but weaker than plain gut. Catline strings (variously called 'Katlyns', 'Cattelins', 'Catlings' or 'Catlins') were made by twisting together two or more wet high-twist strings in a rope construction. They are thicker but more flexible than plain gut. See Djilda Abbot and Ephraim Segerman, 'Gut strings', *Early Music* 4 (1976), pp. 430–7; Ephraim Segerman, 'Strings through the ages', *The Strad* 99 (1988), p. 52. For a contrary view re 'catline' strings, see Stephen Bonta, 'Catline strings revisited', *Journal of the American Musical Instrument Society* 14 (1988), p. 38.

15 In Brown and Sadie (eds.), *Performance Practice*, II, p. 48.

16 *Ibid.*

17 L. Mozart, *A Treatise*, p. 23; Joseph Friedrich Majer, *Neu-eröffneter theoretisch-und praktischer Music-Saal* (Nuremberg, 1741), p. 95.

18 Open-wound strings involved the gut core being wound, covered or overspun with tensioned metal (traditionally brass or silver) wire. If the core were visible between the windings, the strings were variously called 'open wound' or half-wound' ('half-covered' or 'half-overspun' were further alternatives), but when the winding was applied tightly and close together, 'close wound' was the usual description. See Segerman, 'Strings through the ages', p. 52.

19 Boyden, *The History*, p. 321.

20 Georg Löhlein (*Anweisung zum Violinspielen* (Leipzig and Züllichau, 1774), p. 9) states that the g string was wound with silver. Pierre Baillot (*L'art du violon: nou-velle méthode* (Paris, 1835), p. 247) later cites either brass or silver, and Louis Spohr (*Violinschule* (Vienna, 1832), pp. 12–13) stipulates either plated copper or solid silver wire.

21 Alberto Bachmann, *An Encyclopedia of the Violin*, (New York, 1925/R1966), p. 150.

22 Segerman, ('Strings through the ages', pp. 195–201) has calculated string diameters and tensions, making reasonable assumptions as necessary from information (or lack of it) provided in a variety of sources from the early seventeenth century to the present.

23 Boyden, *The History*, pp. 321–2.

24 Brossard, *Fragments*, p. 12.

25 Quantz, *On Playing*, p. 215; Leopold Mozart, *A Treatise*, p. 16. See also Johann Reichardt, *Ueber die Pflichten des Ripien-Violinisten* (Berlin and Leipzig, 1776), p. 86.

26 François-Joseph Fétis, *Antoine Stradivari, luthier célèbre* (Paris, 1856; Eng. trans. John Bishop, London, 1864/R1964), p. 74, and Carl Guhr, *Ueber Paganinis Kunst die Violine zu spielen* (Mainz, [1829]), sec. 1, p. 5; Spohr, *Violinschule*, p. 13.

27 Segerman ('Strings through the ages', p. 198) considers that the most likely unit is the gauge system known as 'grades of millimeters' commonly employed in the nineteenth century and still used in Pirastro's string gauges (called PM or Pirastro Measure). In this system a mm is divided equally into 20 grades, each grade therefore measuring 0.05mm.

28 Spohr, *Violinschule*, pp. 8–9.

29 Quantz, *On Playing*, pp. 233–4.

30 See Heron-Allen, *Violin Making*, p. 194, and Baillot, *L'art*, p. 223.

31 Baillot, *L'art*, p. 16.

32 Brown and Sadie (eds.), *Performance Practice*, II, p. 49.

33 The Vega (or 'Bach') bow, promoted by Emil Telmányi in the 1950s to facilitate smooth sustained performances of polyphonic violin music, is not a reproduction of a baroque model and enjoyed limited success.

34 Hawkins, *A General History of the Science and Practice of Music* (5 vols., London, 1776), II, p. 782.

35 Carel van Leeuwen Boomkamp and John Henry van der Meer, *The Carel van Leeuwen Boomkamp Collection of Musical Instruments* (Amsterdam, 1971), pp. 57–8.

36 Boyden, *The History*, p. 209 and plate 29d.

37 In his 'edition' of Leopold Mozart's violin treatise (1801), Woldemar illustrates one further type, used by Mestrino, which is similar to, though a little longer than, the Cramer model.

38 Fétis, *Antoine Stradivari*, Eng. trans., p. 124.

39 David Boyden, 'The violin bow in the eighteenth century', *Early Music* 8 (1980), p. 206.

40 Woldemar, *Grande méthode*, p. 3.

41 François-Joseph Fétis, *Biographie universelle des musiciens et bibliographie générale de la musique* (Brussels 1835–44, 2/1860–5/R1963), VII, p. 246. Boyden ('The violin bow in the eighteenth century', p. 210) verifies that the measurement given conforms to that of Baillot's own Tourte bow preserved in the Library of Congress in Washington.

42 Fétis, *Antoine Stradivari*, Eng. trans., p. 117.

43 Franz Farga, *Violins and violinists*, Eng. trans. E. Larsen (2nd rev. and enl. edn London, 1969), p. 92.

44 Fétis, *Antoine Stradivari*, Eng. trans., p. 124. Such a curve has the general equation of $y = a + b \log. x$ and empirically $y = 3.11 + 2.571 \log. x$.

45 Spohr, *Violinschule*, p. 18.

46 Joseph Roda, *Bows for Musical Instruments of the Violin Family* (Chicago, 1959), p. 65.

47 L. Mozart, *A Treatise*, p. 97.

48 M. Woldemar, *Méthode de violon par L. Mozart rédigée par Woldemar* (Paris, 1801), p. 5.

49 A review in *Les tablettes de Polymnie* (April, 1810, pp. 3–4) of the Paris Conservatoire Concerts highlights one particular attempt at achieving some uniformity in the bows employed.

50 Spohr, *Violinschule*, p. 17.

51 Roda, *Bows*, p. 53.

52 See Roger Millant, *J. B. Vuillaume: sa vie et son oeuvre*, Eng. trans. (London, 1972), p. 108; Mark Reindorf, 'Authentic authorship', *The Strad* 101 (1990), p. 548.

53 Octagonal sticks were largely favoured by Tourte.

54 Charles Beare (in Sadie (ed.), *New Grove*, art. 'Dodd') suggests that the improvements in bow construction implemented in France before 1800 came to England much later, perhaps only after 1815.

55 Charles Beare, in Sadie (ed.), *New Grove*, art. 'Dodd'.

56 Contact details and addresses of makers and suppliers are provided in several publications, of which the following will be particularly useful: *The Strad*, published monthly by Orpheus Publications Ltd.; *The Early Music Yearbook*, published annually by The National Early Music Association; and *The British and International Music Yearbook*, published annually by Rhinegold Publishing Ltd. Orpheus Publications have also published *A Guide to British Lutherie* (London, 1996) and *The Strad Directory 2001* (London, 2000) and specialist violin, viola and stringed instrument web-sites include links to leading craftsmen.

57 There is a fine example of a violin bow from *c*.1700 with a clip-in frog in the Ashmolean Museum, Oxford.

58 See n56 for contact links with makers.

4 Technique

1 Löhlein's instructions (*Anweisung zum Violinspielen* (Leipzig and Züllichau, 1774), pp. 12–15; see Stowell, *Violin Technique and Performance Practice in the Late Eighteenth and Nineteenth Centuries* (Cambridge, 1985), pp. 32–4) are consistent with most of those of his successors.

2 L. Mozart, *A Treatise*, p. 57.

3 L'abbé *le fils*, *Principes du Violon*, p. 1; François Cupis, *Méthode d'Alto* (Paris, 1803), p. 10; Johann Jacob Prinner's *Musicalischer Schlissl* (MS, 1677) is well in advance of its time in suggesting a chin-braced grip.

4 Cupis, *Méthode*, p. 10.

5 Baillot, *L'art*, p. 16.

6 See n2.

7 L'abbé *le fils*, *Principes*, p. 1.

8 L. Mozart, *A Treatise*, p. 57.

9 *Ibid.*, pp. 57–8.

10 *Ibid.*, p. 148.

11 Spohr, *Violinschule*, p. 108.

12 Geminiani, *The Art*, p. 5.

13 For example, Bartolomeo Campagnoli, *Metodo della mecanica progressive per violino* (?Milan, 1797?), Eng. trans., pt. iii, no. 188.

14 For example, Reichardt, *Ueber die Pflichten*, p. 35; Burney, *A General History,* 1776–89, IV, p. 643.

15 Baillot, *L'art,* pp. 146–9.

16 Spohr, *Violinschule,* pp. 120–1.

17 *Ibid.,* p. 196; Baillot, *L'art,* pp. 152–5; François Habeneck, *Méthode théorique et pratique de violon* (Paris, c.1835), p. 103.

18 Bériot, *Méthode,* p. 237.

19 Carl Flesch, *Die Kunst des Violinspiels* (2 vols., Berlin, 1923 and 1928; Eng. trans. Frederick H. Martens, as *The Art of Violin Playing,* London, 1924 and 1930), I, p. 29.

20 Early recordings confirm some of Flesch's concerns, as exemplified in CDs such as 'Great Violinists' (Symposium 1071), 'Great Virtuosi of the Golden Age' (Pearl GEMM CD 9101) and '20 Great Violinists play 20 Masterpieces' (Pearl GEMM CD 9125).

21 Carl Flesch, *Violin Fingering, its Theory and Practice* (London, 1966), p. 365.

22 Hermann Schröder (*Die Kunst des Violinspiels* (Cologne, 1887), p. 33) implies that the 'L' portamento was implemented mostly by members of the French school.

23 Brown and Sadie (eds.), *Performance Practice,* II, p. 463.

24 Spohr, *Violinschule,* pp. 54ff.; Baillot, *L'art,* p. 152.

25 Peter Walls, 'Violin fingering in the 18th century', *Early Music* 12 (1984), p. 307. See also 'Tuning systems and scordatura' (below).

26 Habeneck, *Méthode,* pp. 103–6; Baillot, *L'art,* pp. 140–4.

27 Galeazzi, *Elementi,* 'Dell'Eguaglianza', I, pp. 122–9; Spohr, *Violinschule,* p. 195.

28 Sometimes described ambiguously as *tremolo, Bebung,* close shake or by other terminology with various meanings.

29 Thomas Mace, *Musick's Monument* (London, 1676), cited in Werner Hauck, *Das Vibrato auf der Violine* (Cologne, 1971; Eng. trans. Kitty Rokos as *Vibrato on the Violin,* London, 1975), p. 4. Geminiani, *The Art,* p. 8.

30 See Roger Hickman, 'The censored publications of *The art of playing on the violin* or Geminiani unshaken', *Early Music* 11 (1983), pp. 71–6.

31 Robert Bremner, 'Some thoughts on the performance of concert music', in J. G. C. Schetky, *Six Quartettos Op. 6* (London, 1777), p. i. See, for example, L. Mozart, *A Treatise,* p. 203.

32 Spohr (*Violinschule,* p. 175) is among many who associate its use with accented notes 'marked *fz* or >', and theorists also commonly link vibrato usage with the *messa di voce* effect.

33 Tartini's trill-cum-vibrato with two fingers was an unusual expressive effect especially suited to 'con affetto' movements. See Tartini, *Traité des agrémens*, Eng. trans., p. 78.

34 L. Mozart, *A Treatise*, p. 204; Spohr, *Violinschule*, pp. 175–6.

35 Baillot, *L'art*, pp. 137–9.

36 Bériot, *Méthode*, Eng. trans., p. 242; David, *Violinschule*, p. 43; Joachim and Moser, *Violinschule*, Eng. trans., II, p. 96; Leopold Auer, *Violin Playing as I Teach It* (New York, 1921), pp. 147–51. Flesch's view (*The Art*, I, p. 40) that Joachim's vibrato was 'very close and quick', while Sarasate 'started to use broader oscillations', is verified by early recordings, which also confirm these violinists' discreet and selective use of the device.

37 Flesch, *The Art*, I, p. 40. Flesch here claims that it was customary in the early twentieth century to distinguish between expressive themes, which might be given a little vibrato, and 'unexpressive neutral passages', which would not. See Brown and Sadie (eds.), *Performance Practice*, II, p. 461.

38 Cited in Louis Paul Lochner, *Fritz Kreisler* (London, 1951), p. 19.

39 See, for example, Mondonville's set of sonatas *Les sons harmoniques* Op. 4 (Paris and Lille, 1738).

40 See L. Mozart, *A Treatise*, p. 101.

41 L'abbé *le fils*, *Principes*, p. 73.

42 *The Harmonicon* (1833), p. 130; L. Mozart, *A Treatise*, p. 101.

43 Hector Berlioz, *Grand traité de l'instrumentation et d'orchestration modernes* Op. 10 (Paris, 1843), Eng. trans. M. C. Clarke (London, 1858), p. 21.

44 Quantz, *On Playing*, pp. 267–9. For further information on pitch, see Arthur Mendel, 'Pitch in Western music since 1500, a re-examination', *Acta Musicologica* 1 (1978), pp. 1–93.

45 Among specialist writings on the subject, see those of Mark Lindley in Sadie (ed.), *New Grove*, art. 'Temperaments', and in Brown and Sadie (eds.), *Performance Practice*, II, pp. 169–85; also Owen H. Jorgensen, *Tuning: Containing the Perfection of Eighteenth-Century Temperament, the Lost Art of Nineteenth-Century Temperament, and the Science of Equal Temperament* (East Lansing, Michigan, 1991).

46 See Lawson and Stowell, *Historical Performance*, pp. 87–9.

47 Johann Kirnberger, *Die Kunst des reinen Satzes in der Musik* (Berlin and Königsberg, 1776–9); Pietro Lichtenthal, *Dizionario e bibliografia della Musica* (Milan, 1826). For further information on issues of key colour see Rita Steblin, *A History of Key Characteristics in the Eighteenth and Early Nineteenth Centuries* (Ann Arbor, 1983).

48 Bruce Haynes, 'Beyond temperament: non-keyboard intonation in the 17th and

18th centuries', *Early Music* 19 (1991), p. 359. See also Patrizio Barbieri, 'Violin intonation: a historical survey', *Early Music* 19 (1991), pp. 69–72; David Boyden, 'Prelleur, Geminiani and just intonation', *Journal of the American Musicological Society* 4 (1951), pp. 202–19.

49 Tosi, *Observations on the Florid Song* (London, 1742, trans. and ed., Galliard), pp. 19–21; See also Quantz, *On Playing*, pp. 31, 43, 46–7. One result of this system was the appearance of keyboard instruments with split keys, offering a choice of, say, D sharp or E flat.

50 Geminiani, *The Art*, p. 3.

51 Haynes, 'Beyond temperament', p. 359. The comma referred to here is different to that described by Tosi, which is close to the 'syntonic comma' at just under 22 cents wide.

52 In Wilson (ed.), *Roger North on Music*, p. 234.

53 Galeazzi, *Elementi* (1791), I, pp. 118–19.

54 Quantz, *On Playing*, p. 267.

55 Barbieri, 'Violin intonation', p. 87; See also Boyden, *The History*, pp. 186, 370–1. Campagnoli's method (?1797) is generally accepted as the first violin tutor to advocate the Pythagorean-type system, while Galeazzi's syntonic fingering charts in different keys up to four sharps or flats (*Elementi*, I, pp. 100–22, reproduced on p. 70 of Barbieri's article) require remarkably precise finger-placement.

56 Rameau, *Génération harmonique* (Paris, 1737), quoted in Sadie (ed.), *New Grove*, art. 'Temperaments'.

57 See, for example, F. W. Marpurg, *Principes du clavecin* (1756) and *Versuch über die musikalische Temperatur* (1776); Türk, *Clavierschule* (2nd enlarged edition, 1802); Johann Nepomuk Hummel, *Ausführlich theoretisch-practische Anweisung zum Piano-Forte Spiel* (3 vols., Vienna, 1828/R1929).

58 Spohr, *Violinschule*, Eng. trans. (Marshall), Preface for parents and teachers, p. 3n.

59 John Fuller-Maitland, *Joseph Joachim* (London, 1905), pp. 32–4.

60 John H. Chesnut, 'Mozart's teaching of intonation', *Journal of the American Musicological Society* 30 (1977), pp. 270–1.

61 The fingerboard chart in Prelleur's *The Art of Playing on the Violin* (London, 1731) provides a good illustration of unequal semitones.

62 Mattheson, *Der vollkommene Capellmeister*, Eng. trans., p. 168.

63 Johann G. Walther, *Hortulus Chelicus* (Mainz, 1688), preface.

64 See Theodore Russell, 'The violin scordatura', *Musical Quarterly* 24 (1938), pp. 84–96.

65 L'abbé *le fils*, *Principes*, p. 1; this phrase is used by many writers on the violin from Bismantova (1677) to those of the current century.

66 José Herrando, *Arte y puntual explicación del modo de tocar el violín* (Paris, 1756), p. 2.

67 Not until Corrette's *L'école d'Orphée* (1738) is the thumb-on-stick grip offered as an alternative in French tutors, and, even then, it is identified as an Italian practice.

68 L'abbé *le fils, Principes*, p. 1; Cupis, *Méthode*, p. 10. Cupis directs readers to grip the bow 'as near to the end as possible', with the little finger 'an inch (*pouce*) from the screw'.

69 Baillot, *L'art*, p. 12.

70 L'abbé *le fils, Principes*, p. 1.

71 See, for example, Jean Baptiste Cartier, *L'art du violon* (Paris, 1798), p. 1, and Baillot, *L'art*, p. 12.

72 For example, Baillot, *L'art*, p. 15; Jacques-Féréol Mazas, *Méthode de violon* (Paris, 1830), p. 6.

73 Advocated especially by L'abbé *le fils, Principes*, p. 1.

74 L. Mozart, *A Treatise*, pp. 98–9.

75 Ferdinand David (*Violinschule* (Leipzig, 1863)) is one of the first German theorists to include *sautillé* and *sauté* bowing.

76 See, for example, Reichardt, *Ueber die Pflichten*, pp. 9–10; exceptionally Hiller uses this expression to indicate slurred staccato (*Anweisung*, p. 41).

77 Joachim and Moser, *Violinschule*, Eng. trans., III, p. 12.

78 *Ibid.*, p. 12.

79 See Clive Brown, 'Ferdinand David's editions of Beethoven', in Stowell (ed.), *Performing Beethoven*, pp. 117–49.

80 In Brown and Sadie (eds.), *Performance Practice*, II, p. 55.

81 Spohr, *Violinschule*, p. 147.

5 The language of musical style

1 English and other national practices largely comprised a synthesis of Italian, Spanish, Dutch, German and French customs, the English most closely approximating the Italians for sheer impulsiveness, expressive freedom and richness of fantasy.

2 See Lawson and Stowell, *Historical Performance*, pp. 42–7.

3 For example, François Raguenet, 'Parallèle des Italiens et des Français en ce qui regarde la musique et les opéras' (1702), in Oliver Strunk, *Source Readings in Music History* (New York, 1950/R1965), pp. 473–88; Jean Laurent le Cerf de Viéville, 'From the "Comparaison de la musique italienne et de la musique française"' (1704), in Strunk, *Source Readings*, pp. 489–507. See also Kenneth

Cooper and Julius Zsako, 'Georg Muffat's observations on the Lully style of per-formance', *Musical Quarterly* 53 (1967), pp. 220–45.

4 Quantz, *On Playing*, pp. 338, 342.

5 Baillot, *L'art*, Eng. trans., pp. 477, 479.

6 Spohr, *Violinschule*, p. 195.

7 Parallels between instrumental playing and singing are common in theoretical material of our core period, C. P. E. Bach recommending (*Versuch*, Eng. trans., pp. 151–2) as good practice the singing of instrumental melodies 'in order to reach an understanding of their correct performance'. Tartini also believed that 'to play well one must sing well'; but Bériot arguably draws the closest compari-sons between violin playing and singing, claiming that the playing of those who cannot reproduce the accents of song is likely to be 'pale and colourless' (*Méthode*, Eng. trans., pp. 219–20).

8 Joachim and Moser, *Violinschule*, Eng. trans., III, pp. 34, 35, 5.

9 *Ibid.*, p. 5.

10 See Lawson and Stowell, *Historical Performance*, pp. 67–75. For detailed surveys of eighteenth-century ornaments, the reader is referred to Frederick Neumann, *Ornamentation in Baroque and post-Baroque Music with Special Emphasis on J. S. Bach* (Princeton, 1978); and *Ornamentation and Improvisation in Mozart* (Princeton, 1986).

11 Many French composers published tables of ornaments in which the signs were realised in conventional notation. See, for example, Mondonville's Sonata Op. 3 no. 1, where the violinist is instructed to imitate the specific ornaments anno-tated in the keyboard part. A + or x was used in French music to indicate the inci-dence of an ornament, the exact detail of which was sometimes undefined and left to the performer.

12 See, for example, the Bach case study in Chapter 6.

13 See, for example, the opening movement of J. S. Bach's Sonata in G minor (BWV1001).

14 Such divisions were not as clear-cut as may be implied; Austro-German orna-mental practice, for example, was itself a hybrid of national customs, some areas (e.g. Celle) being primarily French-influenced, and others (e.g. Salzburg) Italian-influenced.

15 Türk, *Clavierschule*, Eng. trans., pp. 213–21.

16 Baillot, *L'art*, Eng. trans., p. 132.

17 See, for example, J. P. Milchmeyer, *Die wahre Art das Pianoforte zu spielen* (Dresden, 1797), p. 37.

18 Türk, *Clavierschule*, Eng. trans., pp. 310–11, 313.

19 Reported by Reinecke, as quoted in Haas, *Aufführungspraxis*, p. 259. In answer to

his sister's complaint about the sketchy form of the slow movement of his Piano Concerto K.451, Mozart sent her an ornamented variant, implying that he expected the soloist to add extempore embellishment.

20 See Beethoven's letter of 12 February 1816, in which he states that he would rather have heard the work performed 'exactly as written'; in E. Anderson (ed. and trans.), *The Letters of Beethoven* (3 vols., London, 1961), II, p. 560. Schindler explains that Czerny, aspiring towards a new school of keyboard virtuosity, introduced all kinds of elaborations into his performances and thus did not always practise what he preached. See Anton Schindler, *Biographie von Ludwig Beethoven* (Münster, 1840; rev. 3rd edn, Münster, 1860; Eng. trans. Constance Jolly as *Beethoven as I Knew Him*, ed. Donald MacArdle, London, 1966), pp. 415–16, 447; Carl Czerny, *Vollständige theoretisch-practische Pianoforte-Schule* Op. 500 (Vienna, 1839; Eng. trans., London [1839]; vol. IV [chs. 2 and 4], *Über den richtigen Vortrag der sämtlichen Beethoven'schen Klavierwerke*, ed. Paul Badura-Skoda, Vienna, 1963; Eng. trans., Vienna, 1970), p. 26.

21 A cadenza may also be indicated by words such as 'solo', 'tenuto' or 'ad arbitrio' and will normally be implied when two movements of a work are separated only by two chords, usually constituting a Phrygian cadence, as in Bach's Third Brandenburg Concerto.

22 *Cadenza* is Italian for 'cadence'. Some of Haydn's early keyboard sonatas, for example, admit a cadenza opportunity, while Mozart's Piano Sonata K.333/315c and Violin Sonata K.306/300l include fully written-out cadenzas. For a detailed discussion of the cadenza, see Philip Whitmore, *Unpremeditated Art – The Cadenza in the Classical Keyboard Concerto* (Oxford, 1991); Neumann, *Ornamentation*, pp. 257–63; Eva and Paul Badura-Skoda, *Mozart-Interpretation* (Vienna and Stuttgart, 1957), Eng. trans. Leo Black as *Interpreting Mozart on the Keyboard* (London, 1962), pp. 214–34.

23 Quantz, *On Playing*, pp. 179–95; Türk, *Clavierschule*, ch. 5, section 2.

24 See Brown and Sadie (eds.), *Performance Practice*, II, p. 280.

25 Türk, *Clavierschule*, Eng. trans., pp. 297–301; See also Lawson and Stowell, *Historical Performance*, p. 77 for the format of piano concerto cadenzas, and Brown and Sadie (eds.), *Performance Practice*, II, pp. 280–3 for a comparison of Mozart's cadenza for K.453 with Türk's theories.

26 Violinists' searches for authentic material, together with the novelty value of introducing an 'accompanied' cadenza, have prompted some to adapt for violin Beethoven's piano cadenzas for Op. 61a, but with very mixed results.

27 C. P. E. Bach, *Essay*, pp. 143–6; Türk, *Clavierschule*, Eng. trans., pp. 289–96. Good examples also occur in the finale of Mozart's Piano Sonata K.333/315c.

28 Johann Friedrich Agricola, *Anleitung zur Singkunst* (Berlin, 1757), pp. 133–4; C.

P. E. Bach, *Essay*, pp. 157–8; L. Mozart, *A Treatise*, pp. 41–2. See also Quantz, *On Playing*, p. 67.

29 See Frederick Neumann, 'The dotted note and the so-called French style', *Early Music* 5 (1977), pp. 310–24; David Fuller, 'Dotting, the "French Style" and Frederick Neumann's Counter-Reformation', *Early Music* 5 (1977), pp. 517–43. See also Frederick Neumann, *Essays in Performance Practice* (Ann Arbor, 1982); R. Donington, 'What *is* rhythmic alteration?', *Early Music* 5 (1977), pp. 543–4; John O'Donnell, 'The French style and the overtures of Bach', *Early Music* 7 (1979), pp. 190–6, 336–45; Graham Pont, 'Rhythmic alteration and the majestic', *Studies in Music* 12 (1978), pp. 68–100; and 'French overtures at the keyboard: "how Handel rendered the playing of them"', *Musicology* 6 (1980), pp. 29–50.

30 There are numerous examples of this in the first movement, particularly in the flute and first violin parts, of Bach's orchestral Suite No. 2 (BWV1067).

31 See Michael Collins, 'The performance of triplets in the 17th and 18th centuries', *Journal of the American Musicological Society* 19 (1966), pp. 281–328.

32 Quantz, *On Playing*, p. 68; see Lawson and Stowell, *Historical Performance*, pp. 65–6.

33 See David Fuller, in Sadie (ed.), *New Grove*, vol. XIII, pp. 420–7, art. 'Notes iné-gales', and its bibliography; also Stephen Hefling, *Rhythmic Alteration in Seventeenth- and Eighteenth-Century Music* (New York, 1993) and the various articles mentioned in the endnotes. There are good cases for employing *notes inégales* in some seventeenth- and early-eighteenth-century English music (e.g. by Purcell, Locke and others) and possibly even in German and Italian music in a French style.

34 See Lawson and Stowell, *Historical Performance*, p. 66.

35 Johann David Heinichen, *Der General-Bass in der Composition* (Dresden, 1728), p. 24.

36 Quantz, *On Playing*, p. 119.

37 The principal classical texts on oratory included Cicero's *De Oratore* and *De Inventione*, Quintilian's *Institutio Oratoria* and Aristotle's *The 'Art' of Rhetoric*. See Lawson and Stowell, *Historical Performance*, pp. 28–33.

38 Quantz, *On Playing*, pp. 125–6.

39 The colours and characters of keys were emphasised by methods of unequal temperament, which affected the relative sizes of the semitones for each key. See Steblin, *A History of Key Characteristics*.

40 Quantz, *On Playing*, pp. 125–6. For more detail on the emotions expressed by intervals and other affects, see F. T. Wessel, 'The Affektenlehre in the eighteenth century (diss., Indiana University, 1955).

41 *Ibid.*, pp. 124–5, 163, 231.

42 See Türk, *Clavierschule*, Eng. trans., pp. 358ff.; Geminiani, *The Art*, p. 7. See Lawson and Stowell, *Historical Performance*, pp. 28–33.

43 J. A. P. Schulz, in J. G. Sulzer (ed.), *Allgemeine Theorie der schönen Künste* (4 vols., Leipzig, 1771–4), art. 'Vortrag', IV, 700; Türk, *Clavierschule*, ch. 6.

44 Baillot, *L'art*, p. 163; Joachim and Moser, *Violinschule*, III, p. 13; Bériot, *Méthode*, Eng. trans., pp. 226, 219, 220.

45 François Couperin often used a slanting stroke or strokes to indicate those notes to be grouped closely together, while Mattheson (*Der vollkommene Capellmeister*, Eng. trans., pp. 451–2) employs a system of punctuation markings to articulate musical phrases. The practice of connecting notes with beams (or not, as the case may be) also provided clues to phrasing and articulation.

46 Quantz, *On Playing*, p. 122.

47 See Tartini, *Traité des agréments*, Eng. trans., p. 55.

48 C. P. E. Bach, *Essay*, pp. 154–6; Quantz, *On Playing*, pp. 216–20, 230–2.

49 Quantz, *On Playing*, pp. 223, 232; L. Mozart, *A Treatise*, p. 45; Türk, *Clavierschule*, Eng. trans., p. 342. Repeated notes under a slur with or without dots normally indicated the slurred tremolo, sometimes called 'bow vibrato'.

50 See, for example, F. W. Marpurg, *Anleitung zum Clavierspielen* (Berlin, 1755); Türk, *Clavierschule*.

51 L. Mozart, *A Treatise*, p. 97. See Chapter 3, pp. 46–7.

52 Called *détaché* by many French writers, but this should not be confused with the use of the same term, from the early nineteenth century onwards, to describe a smooth, separate on-the-string stroke.

53 Giuseppe Tartini, *A Letter from the Late Signor Tartini (Padua, 5 March 1760) to Signora Maddalena Sirmen*, Eng. trans. Charles Burney (London, 1771).

54 Joachim and Moser, *Violinschule*, Eng. trans., III, pp. 59, 7.

55 Türk, *Clavierschule*, Eng. trans., p. 328.

56 See Stowell, *Violin Technique*, pp. 302–4.

57 See J.-B. Lully, *Oeuvres complètes*, ed. H. Prunières (Paris, 1930–9), 'Les Ballets' vol. I (*Ballet de l'amour malade*), pp. xxvii-xliii for Muffat's bowing rules based on Lully's practice. Relevant English translations appear in Cooper and Zsako, 'Georg Muffat's Observations', pp. 222–30.

58 Spohr, *Violinschule*, Eng. trans. (Rudolphus), p. 229.

59 Geminiani, *The Art*, Example VIII, text p. 4 and Example XXIV; see also Quantz, *On Playing*, p. 223, Reichardt, *Ueber die Pflichten*, p. 28.

60 See David Boyden, 'Dynamics in seventeenth- and eighteenth-century music', in *Essays on Music in Honor of Archibald T. Davison by His Associates*, (Cambridge, Mass., 1957), pp. 185–93. W. A. Mozart, for example, indicated dynamic markings sparingly in his early works. Only rarely were the extreme dynamics *pianis-*

simo and *fortissimo* and such gradations as *mezzo-forte* or *mezzo-piano* prescribed.

61 Sometimes dynamics appeared in movement headings; for example, the third
movement of Handel's *Concerto Grosso* Op. 6 no. 2 is headed 'Larghetto andante,
e piano' with no dynamics placed under the notes.

62 Piani's twelve *Sonate a violino solo è violoncello col cimbalo,* Op. 1 (Paris, 1712)
and Veracini's *Sonate accademiche a violino solo,* Op. 2 (London and Florence,
1744) incorporate unusually thorough expressive and other interpretative markings for their time.

63 See John Robison, 'The *messa di voce* as an instrumental ornament in the seventeenth and eighteenth centuries', *Music Review* 43 (1982), pp. 1–14.

64 Geminiani, *The Art.,* Ex. XVIII; L. Mozart, *A Treatise,* pp. 130, 131, 218.

65 L. Mozart, *A Treatise,* pp. 97–100. Bériot, *Méthode,* Eng. trans., p. 124.

66 Baillot, *L'art,* p. 265.

67 Bériot, *Méthode,* Eng. trans., pp. 232, 219–21; Spohr, *Violinschule,* Eng. trans.
(Rudolphus), p. 229.

68 L. Mozart, *A Treatise,* pp. 49–53.

69 See Lawson and Stowell, *Historical Performance,* p. 60.

70 Quantz, *On Playing,* pp. 283–94. Quantz's system is a late version of the old fixed-
tactus theory; see Neal Zaslaw, 'Mozart's tempo conventions', in H. Glahn, S.
Sørensen, P. Ryan (eds.), *International Musicological Society: Report of the
Eleventh Congress, Copenhagen 1972* (Copenhagen, 1974), II, pp. 720–33.

71 All six words were qualified as required, Vivaldi being especially prolific in the
variety and detail of his descriptions.

72 L. Mozart, *A Treatise,* p. 33.

73 Galeazzi, *Elementi,* I, p. 36; Cartier, *L'art,* p. 17; Türk, *Clavierschule,* Eng. trans.,
p. 106; Clementi, *Introduction to the Art,* p. 13; Johann Nepomuk Hummel,
Ausführlich theoretisch-practische Anweisung zum Piano-Forte Spiel (Vienna,
1828), III, p. 66.

74 Kirnberger, *Die Kunst,* Eng. trans., ch. 4. The alteration of Mozart's alla breve
markings (even in several andante and larghetto movements) in the old
Breitkopf Mozart edition – notably in the overture to *Don Giovanni* and in the
opening of Symphony no. 39 – affect adversely the intended accentuation and
could result in the adoption of a slower tempo than the composer intended.

75 For example, the first movement of his Piano Sonata Op. 101 is marked *Allegretto
ma non troppo, Etwas lebhaft und mit der innigsten Empfindung.*

76 See Robert Münster, 'Authentische Tempi zu den sechs letzten Sinfonien W. A.
Mozarts?', *Mozart-Jahrbuch* (1962–3), pp. 185–99; see also Walter Malloch, 'Carl
Czerny's metronome marks for Haydn and Mozart symphonies', *Early Music* 16

198 NOTES TO PAGES 99–104

(1988), pp. 72–82. For Mozart's tempos in general, see further N. Zaslaw, 'Mozart's tempo conventions'; J.-P. Marty, *The Tempo Indications of Mozart* (New Haven, 1988), and 'Mozart's tempo indications and the problems of interpretation', in Todd and Williams (eds.), *Perspectives on Mozart Performance*, pp. 55–73.

77 See Peter Stadlen, 'Beethoven and the Metronome', *Music and Letters* 48 (1967), pp. 330–49.

78 See George Henschel, *Personal Recollections of Johannes Brahms* (Boston, Mass., 1907), pp. 78f.

79 See Robert Philip, 'The recordings of Edward Elgar (1857–1934)', *Early Music* 12 (1984), pp. 481–9.

80 For a comprehensive survey of tempo rubato, see Richard Hudson, *Stolen Time: The History of Tempo Rubato* (Oxford, 1994).

81 See, for example, Tosi, *Observations*, VIII 5, 17; IX 41, 42, 63; X 23; C. P. E. Bach, *Essay*, pp. 150–1; L. Mozart, *A Treatise*, p. 224; Türk, *Clavierschule*, Eng. trans., pp. 363–4; Spohr, *Violinschule*, pp. 199, 202.

82 See Türk, *Clavierschule*, Eng. trans., pp. 364–5.

83 C. P. E. Bach, *Essay*, pp. 160–1.

84 See H. C. Koch, 'Ueber den technischen Ausdruck Tempo rubato', *Allgemeine musikalische Zeitung*, 10/33 (1808), col. 518.

85 See S. Gerlach, 'Gedanken zu den "Veränderten" Violinstimmen der Solosonaten von Franz Benda in der Staatsbibliothek Preussischer Kulturbesitz, Berlin', in M. Bente (ed.), *Musik Edition Interpretation* (Munich, 1980), pp. 199–212; Hudson, *Stolen Time*, pp. 90–8.

86 Tosi, *Observations*, Eng. trans. (Galliard), p. 156; Burney, *A General History of Music*, 2nd edn, IV, p. 641.

87 L. Mozart, *A Treatise*, p. 224.

88 Hudson, *Stolen Time*, p. 99; Schumann, in Joachim and Moser, *Violinschule*, Eng. trans., III, p. 16.

89 Czerny, *Vollständige theoretisch-practische Pianoforte-Schule*, Eng. trans., III, pp. 31–8.

90 Baillot, *L'art*, pp. 136–7.

91 Spohr, *Violinschule*, Eng. trans. (Marshall), p. 178, 181.

92 Joachim and Moser, *Violinschule*, Eng. trans., III, p. 16.

93 R. Wagner, *Über das Dirigieren* (Leipzig, 1969), Eng. trans., 1887/R1976, p. 43.

94 In Philip, *Early Recordings*, p. 26.

95 Spohr, *Violinschule*, Eng. trans. (Marshall), pp. 178–9. See Baillot's views on genius of execution, cited earlier in this chapter. See also Geminiani, *The Art*, p. 6; Johann Mattheson, *Die neueste Untersuchung der Singspiele, nebst beygefügter musikalischen Geschmacksprobe* (Hamburg, 1744), p. 123; François Couperin,

preface to the *Pièces de clavecin: troisième livre* (Paris, 1722); Quantz, *On Playing*, pp. 22–3.

96 Mattheson, *Der vollkommene Capellmeister*, Foreword.

97 Joachim and Moser, *Violinschule*, Eng. trans., II, p. 95.

6 Historical awareness in practice 1 – three eighteenth-century case studies: Corelli, Bach and Haydn

Corelli: Sonata in A Op. 5 no. 9

1 See Burney, *A General History*, III, p. 556.

2 The editions are listed in Marc Pincherle, *Corelli et son temps* (Paris, 1954), Eng. trans. (New York, 1956), pp. 209–10.

3 Burney, *A General History*, II, p. 442; A. Cavicchi, 'Contributo alla bibliografia di Arcangelo Corelli: L'edizione del 1700 dell'opera "Quinta" e la ristampa del 1711', *Ferrara: Rivista del Comune* 2 (1961), p. 7.

4 Facsimiles of the editions of Rome (1700) and Amsterdam (1710) are found in *Archivum Musicum: Collana di testi rari* (Florence, 1979) vol. 21; other facsimiles of the Rome edition appear in J. Adas (ed.), *Corelli and his Contemporaries: the Eighteenth-Century Continuo Sonata*, i (New York, 1991) and in a separate publication by Schott (London, 1987).

5 Wilson (ed.), *Roger North on Music*, p. 161.

6 Marc Pincherle, 'On the rights of the Interpreter in the performance of seventeenth- and eighteenth-century music', *Musical Quarterly* 44 (1958), pp. 159–60.

7 See John Holloway, 'Corelli's op. 5: text, act and reaction', *Early Music* 24 (1996), pp. 635–40; Niels Martin Jensen, 'The performance of Corelli's chamber music reconsidered: some characteristics of structure and performance in Italian sonatas for one, two and three voices in the decades preceding Corelli', *Nuovissimi studi Corelliani* (1978), pp. 241–9; Peter Allsop, *The Italian 'Trio' Sonata from its Origins until Corelli* (Oxford, 1992), ch. 2.

8 See Tharald Borgir, *The Performance of the Basso Continuo in Italian Baroque Music* (Ann Arbor, Michigan, 1987), pp. 5–9; S. Mangsen, 'The trio sonata in pre-Corellian prints: when does 3 = 4?' *Performance Practice Review* 3 (1990), pp. 138–64; and Allsop, *The Italian 'Trio' Sonata*, pp. 39ff..

9 Peter Allsop, *Arcangelo Corelli* (Oxford, 1999), p. 121.

10 Borgir, *The Performance of the Basso Continuo*, p. 57. Interestingly, the 1711 Walsh edition specifies 'a Bass Violin or Harpsichord'.

11 F. T. Arnold, *The Art of Accompaniment from a Thorough-Bass as Practised in the Seventeenth and Eighteenth Centuries* (London, 1931/R1965), p. 329.

12 See Tomaso Pegolotti's instructions in his twelve *Trattenimenti armonici da camera, a' violino solo, e violoncello* (Modena, 1698).

13 See David Watkin, 'Corelli's Op. 5 sonatas: "violino e violone *o* cimbalo"?', *Early Music* 24 (1996), pp. 645–63.

14 Arnold, *The Art of Accompaniment*, p. 329; cited in L. Malusi, 'Il violone e il suo impiego nei secoli passati', *Nuova rivista musicale Italiana* 13 (1979), pp. 606–7; Tharald Borgir, 'The performance of the basso continuo in seventeenth-century Italian music' (Ph.D. diss., University of California, 1971), p. 57.

15 Allsop, *The Italian 'Trio' Sonata*, p. 36; see also Bonta, 'From violone to violoncello: a question of strings?', *Journal of the American Musical Instrument Society* 3 (1977), pp. 64–99; and 'Terminology for the bass violin in seventeenth-century Italy', *Journal of the American Musical Instrument Society* 4 (1978), pp. 5–42.

16 Heinichen, *Der General-Bass*, pp. 128ff. See also George J. Buelow, *Thorough-Bass Accompaniment According to Johann David Heinichen* (Berkeley and Los Angeles, 1966).

17 See Peter Williams, *Figured Bass Accompaniment* (2 vols., Edinburgh, 1970), II, p. 77.

18 See Lawson and Stowell, *Historical Performance*, pp. 42–7.

19 See François Raguenet, 'Parallèle des Italiens et des Français', in Strunk, *Source Readings*, p. 486.

20 Readers should note, however, that Italian attitudes to extempore embellishment were by no means as unequivocal as is often supposed; several seventeenth-century composers from Cima to G. M. Bononcini disapproved of the practice.

21 Most of the surviving manuscript and printed sets of ornaments are listed in Hans Joachim Marx, *Die Überlieferung der Werke Arcangelo Corellis. = Arcangelo Corelli: Historisch-kritische Gesamtausgabe der musikalischen Werke, Supplementband* (Cologne, 1980), pp. 176–7, 322–3. A few additional recent discoveries are described by Neal Zaslaw and Harry D. Johnstone in *Early Music* 24 (1996), pp. 95–115, 623–33.

22 Robert Seletsky, '18th-century variations for Corelli's sonatas, Op. 5', *Early Music* 24 (1996), p. 121.

23 Wilson (ed.), *Roger North on Music*, p. 162; Quantz, *On Playing*, pp. 179–80.

24 I must acknowledge here my indebtedness to Neal Zaslaw's table of all known extant sets of ornaments with their sources, excluding wholesale recompositions of Op. 5 (e.g. Geminiani's arrangements of the sonatas as concerti grossi and Veracini's *Dissertazioni sopra l'Opera Quinta del Corelli*) and those sets reported, but apparently lost. See Zaslaw, 'Ornaments for Corelli's violin sonatas, Op. 5', *Early Music* 24 (1996), pp. 97–8.

25　See Hawkins, *A General History,* II, pp. 904–7; Hans-Peter Schmitz (*Die Kunst der Verzierung im 18. Jahrhundert* (Kassel and Basel, 1955), pp. 62–9) also includes Geminiani's version of Op. 5 no. 9.

26　Hans Joachim Marx has observed that Geminiani's approach resembles that illustrated in the graces for the first movement of the manuscript housed in the Cambridge University Library (Add. MS 7059). See Marx, 'Some unknown embellishments of Corelli's violin sonatas', *Musical Quarterly* 61 (1975), p. 74.

27　See David Boyden, 'Corelli's violin solos graced by Dubourg', in N. Schiørring and H. Glann (eds.), *Festskrift Jens Peter Larsen* (Copenhagen, 1972), pp. 113–25.

28　In Rosamond Harding, *The Piano-forte: its History Traced to the Great Exhibition of 1851* (Cambridge, 1933, rev. 2/1978), p. 5.

29　See le Huray (*Authenticity in Performance*, pp. 36–7) regarding the relationship of adagio to largo.

30　See, for example, Johann Mattheson, *Kern melodischer Wissenschaft* (Hamburg, 1737/R1976), p. 115.

31　See C. P. E. Bach, *Essay*, p. 151.

32　Georg Muffat, *Florilegium Secundum* (Passau, 1698), preface.

J. S. Bach: Partita No. 3 in E major, BWV 1006

33　C. P. E. Bach reported that his father continued to play the violin 'cleanly and penetratingly . . . until the approach of old age'. See Hans T. David and Arthur Mendel, *The Bach Reader* (New York, 1945), p. 277.

34　See David and Mendel, *The Bach Reader*, pp. 277, 346, 447.

35　For a succinct summary of the arguments see Boyden, *The History,* pp. 431–5 and plate 40a; David Boyden, 'The violin and its technique: new horizons in research', in *Bericht über den siebenten Internationalen Musikwissenschaftlichen Kongress Köln 1958* (Kassel, 1959), pp. 29ff.

36　The Joachim/Moser edition (1908) was the first based on Bach's autograph, which had then only recently come to light. For a summary of the merits of the various editions, see Robin Stowell, 'Building a library: Bach's violin sonatas and partitas', *Musical Times* 128 (1987), pp. 250–6.

37　Available in an edition published by Bärenreiter. This is based on the autograph, a copy in the hand of Anna Magdalena Bach, and a copy in an unknown hand. Full details appear in the *Kritischer Bericht*.

38　Among extant facsimile editions are: *Sei Solo á Violino senza Basso accompagnato. Libro Primo. da Joh. Seb. Bach. Faksimile*, ed. Bernhard Sprengel, with notes by Wilhelm Martin Luther, 2nd edn (Kassel, Bärenreiter, 1958); *Johann Sebastian Bach. Sonaten und Partiten für Violine allein*, with notes by Yehudi Menuhin and

Günter Hausswald (Leipzig, Insel-Verlag, 1962); *Bach, 6 Sonatas and Partitas, for Violin Solo*, ed. Ivan Galamian, with facsimile of the autograph manuscript (New York, International Music, 1971); *Sei Solo á Violino senza Basso accompagnato: BWV1001–1006, Johann Sebastian Bach*, ed. Georg von Dadelsen (Kassel, Bärenreiter, 1988). Additionally a facsimile of the MS can be found in Günter Hausswald, ed: *Johann Sebastian Bach: Sonaten und Partiten für Violine allein* (Frankfurt, 1962; New York, R1982, with Eng. trans. of foreword by K. Marie Stolba).

39 Johann Sebastian Bach, *Neue Ausgabe Sämtliche Werke; Serie VI/1, Werke für Violine. Drei Sonaten und Drei Partiten für Violine Solo*, BWV 1001–1006, ed. G. Hausswald (Bärenreiter, 1958), pp. 54–62; pp. 7–117 of corresponding volume in Kritischer Bericht. See also Frederick Neumann, 'Some performance problems of Bach's unaccompanied violin and cello works', in M. A. Parker (ed.), *Eighteenth-Century Music in Theory and Practice* (New York, 1994), pp. 19–48.

40 See Meredith Little and Natalie Jenne, *Dance and the Music of J. S. Bach* (Bloomington, 1991).

41 Quantz, *On Playing*, p. 283; Quantz (pp. 288–9) establishes eighty pulse beats per minute as the norm. On the relationship between Quantz's suggested dance tempos and those of other writers, see Ralph Kirkpatrick, 'Eighteenth-century metronomic indications', *Papers of the American Musicological Society* (1938), pp. 45–6; Donington, *The Interpretation*, pp. 326–8.

42 Donington, *The Interpretation*, p. 326.

43 The minuet's development from 'a very lively dance' (Brossard, 1703) to 'rather moderate than quick' (Rousseau, 1751–65) is a case in point.

44 See Neal Zaslaw, 'Materials for the life and works of Jean-Marie Leclair l'aîné' (Ph.D. diss., Columbia University, 1970).

45 Quantz, *On Playing*, pp. 290, 230.

46 For example, Charles Masson, *Nouveau traité des règles pour la composition de la musique* (Paris, 1697; 2nd edn, 1699. Facsimile reprint, ed. Imogene Horsley, New York, 1967), p. 8; Pierre Dupont, *Principes de musique par demandes et réponce* (Paris, 1713), p. 43.

47 Mattheson, *Der vollkommene Capellmeister*, p. 228; J. G. Walther, *Musicalisches Lexicon* (Leipzig, 1732), art. 'Loure'.

48 Brossard, *Dictionnaire de musique*, art. 'Loure'; Quantz, *On Playing*, pp. 290–1.

49 Bénigne de Bacilly, *Remarques curieuses sur l'art de bien chanter* (Paris, 1668), Eng. trans., p. 106; Pierre Dupont, *Principes de violon par demandes et réponce* (Paris, 1718), p. 39; Mattheson, *Der vollkommene Capellmeister*, Eng. trans., p. 225; J. P. Freillon-Poncein, *La véritable manière d'apprendre à jouer en perfection du Hautbois, de la flûte et du flageolet . . .* (Paris, 1700), p. 57; James Grassineau, *A Musical Dictionary* (London, 1740), p. 84.

50 Jean-Jacques Rousseau, *Dictionnaire de musique* (Paris, 1768), art. 'Gavotte'.

51 Donington, *The Interpretation*, p. 337; Kirkpatrick, 'Eighteenth-century metronomic indications', pp. 45–6; Rebecca Harris-Warrick, 'The tempo of French baroque dances: evidence from 18th-century metronome devices', *Proceedings of the 1982 Meeting of the Dance History Scholars* (Cambridge, Mass., 1982), pp. 18–27.

52 Rousseau (in his article in the Diderot and d'Alembert *Encyclopédie*), in Little and Jenne, *Dance and the Music of J. S. Bach*, p. 63.

53 Quantz, *On Playing*, p. 291.

54 Harris-Warwick's chart of dance tempos from seven different sources dating between 1705–63 gives dotted minim = *c.* 42–77. See n51.

55 For example, Rousseau, *Dictionnaire*, art. 'Bourrée', and Quantz, *On Playing*, p. 291. Mattheson, *Der vollkommene Capellmeister*, pp. 225–6.

56 Quantz, *On Playing*, p. 291.

57 Mattheson, *Der vollkommene Capellmeister*, p. 457; Quantz, *On Playing*, p. 29.

58 Frederick Neumann, *Ornamentation in Baroque and Post-Baroque Music*, ch. 29.

59 Frederick Neumann ('Some performance problems of Bach's unaccompanied violin and cello works', p. 28) favours 'an unaccented brief inflection, preferably before the beat' for these examples.

60 See Georg von Dadelsen, 'Die Crux der Nebensache; Editorische und praktische Bemerkungen zu Bachs Artikulation', *Bach-Jahrbuch* 64 (1978), pp. 95–112, and 'Zur Geltung der Legatobögen bei Bach: Eine Studie für Artikulationsfanatiker und Editoren', in Gerhard Allroggen and Detlet Altenburg (eds.) *Festschrift Arno Forchert zum 60. Geburtstag am 29 Dezember 1985* (Kassel, 1986), pp. 114–22.

61 See *Kritischer Bericht*, p. 66. NBA bowings for the E major Partita which do not follow the autograph and are not mentioned in the *Kritischer Bericht* include: Loure b. 13, bts. 4 and 5. Slur 1+3 in Autograph, slur 4 in NBA; Gavotte en rondeau b. 33, bts. 1 and 2. Slur 3+1 in Autograph, slur 4 in NBA; b. 38, bts. 3 and 4. Slur 3+1 in Autograph, slur 2+2 in NBA; b. 76, bts. 3 and 4. Slur 3+1 in Autograph, slur 2+2 in NBA.

62 For an English translation of Muffat's treatise see Cooper and Zsako, 'Georg Muffat's observations', pp. 220–45. Muffat's preface appears in English translation in Strunk (ed.), *Source Readings*, pp. 445–7.

63 These include practices concerned with repetitions, interpretation of certain notes, stylistic propriety and dance character.

Haydn: String Quartet in E flat major, Op. 33 no. 2

64 Haydn, letter of 3 December 1781, in Rosemary Hughes, *Haydn: String Quartets* (London, 1966), p. 28.

65 H. C. Robbins Landon and Reginald Barrett-Ayres, Preface to edition of Op. 33 no. 2 (Vienna, Doblinger Verlag, 1988).

66 L. Mozart, *A Treatise*, pp. 50–1.

67 *Ibid.*, p. 114.

68 This applies particularly to the two passages indicated to be played staccato in the finale (bb. 59–63 and 120–32). Leopold Mozart (*A Treatise*, p. 51) states that 'staccato' indicates 'that the notes are to be well separated from each other, with short strokes, and without dragging the bow'.

69 See Dene Barnett, 'Non-uniform slurring in 18th-century music: accident or design?', *Haydn Jahrbuch* 10 (1978), pp. 179–99.

70 L. Mozart, *A Treatise*, pp. 123–4.

71 *Ibid.*, pp. 46–7, 47n.

72 *Ibid.*, p. 132.

73 William Drabkin, 'Fingering in Haydn's string quartets', *Early Music* 16 (1988), 51–2.

74 The so-called Couler à Mestrino, evidently adopted by the Italian violinist in most slow movements (See Stowell, *Violin Technique*, p. 99), is a striking adaptation of the portamento for expressive effect.

75 Baillot, *L'art*, pp. 76–8.

76 Le Huray, *Authenticity in Performance*, p. 139.

77 L. Mozart, *A Treatise*, pp. 167, 168–9.

78 *Ibid.*, pp. 186–202.

79 Haydn frequently used what we now know as a sign for an inverted (lower) turn to indicate quite the opposite, i.e., an upper turn!

80 L. Mozart, *A Treatise*, pp. 184–5; C. P. E. Bach, *Essay*, p. 126; Türk, *Klavierschule*, Eng. trans., pp. 271ff.

81 L. Mozart, *A Treatise*, p. 204.

82 *Ibid.*, p. 252; Charles Rosen, *The Classical Style* (London, 1971), pp. 100–1.

83 Louis Spohr, *Autobiography*, Eng. trans., I, p. 31; *Violinschule*, p. 246.

7 Historical awareness in practice 2 – three nineteenth-century case studies: Beethoven, Mendelssohn and Brahms

Beethoven: Sonata in A, Op. 47 ('Kreutzer')

1 Found on the first part of the MS in the Beethoven Archives, this reads: 'Sonata mulattica composta per il mulatto Brischdauer, gran pazzo e compositore mulattico'.

2 Carl Czerny, *On the Proper Performance of all Beethoven's Works for the Piano*,

(from the *Complete Theoretical and Practical Pianoforte School* Op. 500), ed. Paul Badura Skoda (Vienna, 1970), p. 73. For further information on Bridgetower see F. G. Edwards, 'George P. Bridgetower and the Kreutzer Sonata', *Musical Times* 49 (1908), pp. 302–8; Betty Matthews, 'George Polgreen Bridgetower', *Music Review* 29 (1968), pp. 22–6; Elliott Forbes (ed.), *Thayer's Life of Beethoven* (Princeton, 1964, 2/1967), pp. 331ff.

3 See Beethoven's letter of 4 October 1804, in Emily Anderson (ed.), *The Letters of Beethoven* (London, 1961), I, p. 120; Hector Berlioz, *Voyage musical en Allemagne et Italie I* (Paris, 1844), p. 261.

4 Czerny (*On the Proper Performance*, ed. Badura-Skoda, p. 15) reports that Beethoven may have derived the theme at i/144ff. from a published work by Kreutzer. See also Forbes (ed.), *Thayer's Life of Beethoven*, p. 112.

5 See Suhnne Ahn, 'Genre, style and compositional procedure in Beethoven's "Kreutzer" Sonata, Opus 47', (Ph.D. diss., Harvard University, 1997).

6 See, for example, Rudolph Réti, 'The thematic pitch of the Kreutzer Sonata', in *Thematic Patterns in Sonatas of Beethoven* (New York, 1967), pp. 145–65; Hans Hollander, 'Das Finale-Problem in Beethovens "Kreutzersonata"', *Neue Zeitschrift für Musik* 130 (1969), pp. 182–4.

7 See Sieghard Brandenburg, 'Zur Textgeschichte von Beethovens Violin Sonate, Opus 47', in *Musik-Edition Interpretation Gedenkschrift Günther Henle*, ed. Martin Bente (Munich, 1980), pp. 111–24. Alan Tyson ('Notes on five of Beethoven's copyists', *Journal of the American Musicological Society* 23 (1970), pp. 439–71) identified four copyists who participated in making this copy.

8 The chief divergences are the positions of the pause-signs in the violin part, which differ from the usual notation, and the omission of the slurs in the arpeggiated seventh chord in the upper stave of the piano.

9 Czerny adapted Beethoven's 'Kreutzer' Sonata for piano, two and four hands, during Beethoven's lifetime.

10 In William S. Newman, *Performance Practices in Beethoven's Sonatas: an Introduction* (New York, 1971), pp. 14–15.

11 Clive Brown, 'Ferdinand David's editions of Beethoven', in Stowell (ed.), *Performing Beethoven*, p. 120. David's edition of the violin sonatas (Peters, pl. no. 4899) is listed in the catalogue of Hoffmeister and Whistling (1868–73). According to Brown, a later edition of the violin sonatas by Peters with the plate number 6531, though re-engraved, is textually identical except for a few amplifications of fingering in parallel passages where the earlier edition seems to have omitted them in error.

12 See Clive Brown, *Louis Spohr: a Critical Biography* (Cambridge, 1984), pp. 11, 20–2, 30–1.

13 In G. Grove (ed.), *Dictionary of Music and Musicians*, (London 1879–89), art. 'David, Ferdinand'.

14 In Stowell (ed.), *Performing Beethoven*, p. 132.

15 Joachim specifies second position for this passage.

16 Ferdinand David, *Violinschule*, pt 2, p. 43.

17 In Stowell (ed.), *Performing Beethoven*, p. 144.

18 See Andreas Moser, *Joseph Joachim*, Eng. trans. Lilla Durham (London, 1902), p. 46.

19 Anton Schindler, ed. D. MacArdle, *Beethoven as I Knew Him*, p. 423n.

20 Ferdinand Ries and Franz Gerhard Wegeler, *Biographische Notizen über Ludwig van Beethoven* (Koblenz, 1838), p. 106.

21 Czerny, *On the Proper Performance*, ed. Badura-Skoda, p. 30; Schindler, ed. MacArdle, *Beethoven as I Knew Him*, p. 412; see also pp. 409–12 and 417–20.

22 All references to Czerny's view on the interpretation of this sonata are quoted from his *On the Proper Performance*, ed. Badura-Skoda, pp. 72–4.

23 This melody has traditionally been taken more slowly. See Philip, *Early Recordings*, p. 18.

24 See Beethoven's letters in late 1796 to J. A. Streicher, in Anderson (ed.), *The Letters of Beethoven*, I, pp. 24–6; Czerny, 'Erinnerungen aus meinem Leben', Eng. trans. Ernest Saunders, *Musical Quarterly*, 42 (1956), p. 307; Franz Kullak, *Beethoven's Piano Playing*, Eng. trans. T. Baker (New York, 1901), pp. 10, 13.

25 Czerny, *On the Proper Performance*, ed. Badura-Skoda, p. 5.

26 Sandra Rosenblum, *Performance Practices in Classic Piano Music* (Bloomington and Indianapolis, 1988), p. 162.

27 *Ibid.*, p. 118.

28 See Paul Badura-Skoda, 'Fehler – Fehler! Einige Anmerkungen zu weitverbreiteten Fehlern in klassischen Notenausgaben', *Österreichische Musikzeitschrift* (Feb.–March 1987), pp. 92–8.

29 Eva Badura-Skoda, 'Historical problems in Beethoven Performance', in *Beethoven, Performers, and Critics*, ed. R. Winter and B. Carr (Detroit, 1980), p. 43.

30 In Robert Winter and Robert Martin (eds.), *The Beethoven Quartet Companion* (California, 1994), pp. 32–3.

31 See his letter to Friedrich Mayr of 8 April 1806, in Anderson (ed.), *The Letters of Beethoven*, I, p. 149.

32 Jelly d'Aranyi, 'The Violin Sonatas', *Music and Letters* 8 (1927), p. 192.

33 Schindler, ed. MacArdle, *Beethoven as I Knew Him*, p. 416.

34 Robert Winter ('Second thoughts on the performance of Beethoven's trills', *Musical Quarterly* 63 (1977), pp. 483–504) believes anyway that the issue re trills

is not so much one of main-versus upper-note starts as of strong-beat dissonance.

35 Kullak, *Beethoven's Piano Playing*, pp. 66–87.

36 Edwards, 'George P. Bridgetower', p. 302.

37 *Ibid.*, p. 305; Forbes (ed.), *Thayer's Life of Beethoven*, p. 333.

Mendelssohn: Violin Concerto, Op. 64

38 Letter of 30 July 1838, in George Grove, 'Mendelssohn's Violin Concerto', *Musical Times* 47 (1906), p. 611. Among useful articles about Mendelssohn's compositional approach to the concerto are: Reinhard Gerlach, 'Mendelssohns Kompositionweise, Vergleich zwischen Skizzen und Letztfassung des Violinkonzerts opus 64', *Archiv für Musikwissenschaft* 28/2 (1971), pp. 119–33; Hans Christoph Worbs, 'Die Entwurfe zu Mendelssohns Violinkonzert e-moll', *Die Musikforschung* 12 (1959), pp. 79–81.

39 Mendelssohn also valued the observations of Ferdinand Hiller and Ignaz and Charlotte Moscheles during the composition process. See Ferdinand Hiller, *Felix Mendelssohn-Bartholdy, Briefe und Erinnerungen* (Cologne, 1878), pp. 132–3, 141; F. Moscheles, *Briefe von Felix Mendelssohn-Bartholdy an Ignaz und Charlotte Moscheles* (Leipzig, 1888; Eng. trans., 1888/R1970).

40 Although it was advertised around 1858. See Peter Krause, 'Autographen, Erstausgaben und Frühdrucke der Werke von Felix MendelssohnBartholdy', in *Leipziger Bibliotheken und Archiven* (Leipzig, 1972), p. 63. The orchestra parts were probably published in June, 1845, and the violin/piano version was first published in May, 1845, to be re-issued around 1860 with a new title page. Correspondence between Mendelssohn and Breitkopf and Haertel (9 June 1845) is cited as the evidence for establishing the initial issue date of the violin-piano version.

41 Mendelssohn's original autograph score with a foreword by H. C. Robbins Landon and an introduction by Luigi Alberto Bianchi and Franco Sciannameo was published by Garland Publishing (New York, 1991).

42 For the purposes of bar numbering, the Allegretto non troppo linking the slow movement and finale has been considered as an introduction to the finale and identified as iii/1–14. The Allegro molto vivace thus begins at iii/15.

43 See Tyrone Greive, 'The Mendelssohn Violin Concerto in E minor: a second manuscript score', *The Violexchange* 6 nos. 2/3 (1992), pp. 97–108.

44 See R. Elvers (ed.), *Felix Mendelssohn, Briefe, 1. Briefe an deutsche Verleger* (Berlin, 1968).

45 Joachim and Moser, *Violinschule*, Eng. trans., III, p. 228.

46 *Ibid.*, pp. 228–9.

47 *Ibid.*, pp. 17, 229.

48 Bachmann (*An Encyclopedia of the Violin* (New York, 1925/R1966), p. 243) warns that the melody can sound trivial at a speed greater than crotchet = 96, and he reports that Sarasate's interpretation sounded like 'a slow waltz'.

49 Joachim and Moser, *Violinschule*, Eng. trans., III, p. 230.

50 *Ibid.*, p. 230.

51 *Ibid.*, pp. 230–1.

52 David, *Violinschule*, Preface.

53 Joachim and Moser, *Violinschule*, Eng. trans., III, p. 228.

54 Mendelssohn, letter to David (Frankfurt, 17 December 1844), in Grove, 'Mendelssohn's Violin Concerto', p. 614.

55 Mendelssohn, letter to David (Frankfurt, 19 February 1845), *ibid.*, p. 615.

56 Joachim and Moser, *Violinschule*, Eng. trans., III, p. 229.

57 *Ibid.*, p. 229.

58 *Ibid.*, pp. 229, 231.

59 *Ibid.*, II, p. 94; J. MacLeod, *The Sisters d'Aranyi* (London, 1969), p. 48; David, *Violinschule*, pt II, p. 43.

60 Dessauer edition, solo violin part, p. 5.

61 Joachim and Moser, *Violinschule*, Eng. trans., III, pp. 8–9.

62 *Ibid.*, p. 230.

63 Moser, *Joseph Joachim*, Eng. trans., p. 46; Joachim and Moser, *Violinschule*, Eng. trans., III, p. 12.

64 David, *Violinschule*, p. 38.

65 Joachim and Moser, *Violinschule*, Eng. trans., III, p. 14.

66 Bachmann, *An Encyclopedia*, p. 242.

Brahms: Sonata, Op. 120 no. 2

67 In Colin Lawson, *Brahms: Clarinet Quintet* (Cambridge, 1998), p. 32. Lawson also provides useful background material about Mühlfeld and his role in the genesis of the Sonatas Op. 120.

68 There are also violin–piano arrangements of the Op. 120 sonatas, incorporating alterations as appropriate in the piano part. See Malcolm MacDonald, *Brahms* (London, 1990), p. 369.

69 See Robert Pascall, 'Brahms and the definitive text', in Robert Pascall (ed.), *Brahms, Biographical, Documentary and Analytical Studies* (Cambridge, 1983), pp. 59–75, and 'The editor's Brahms', in Michael Musgrave (ed.), *The Cambridge*

Companion to Brahms, pp. 250–67; G. S. Bozarth, 'Editing Brahms's music', in D. Brodbeck (ed.), *Brahms Studies* (Lincoln and London, 1998), II, pp. 1–30.

70 Bruno Giuranna, 'Masterclass: Brahms' "Viola" Sonata in E flat', *The Strad* 104 (1993), p. 552.

71 However, he adopts the changes made in the viola part at, for example, i/58.

72 See Max Kalbeck, *Johannes Brahms* (4 vols., Berlin, 1904–14), III, p. 493. The three main registers – bass, middle and treble – demonstrate clear differences of sound quality and timbre. See Camilla Cai, 'Brahms's pianos and the performance of his late piano works', *Performance Practice Review* 2 (1989), p. 60.

73 These tenor melodies generally circle around c^1 or fall within the distinctive mellow yet prominent c^1 to c^2 octave and often lie between the pianist's two hands, requiring considerable control to bring out the melody notes effectively.

74 Fanny Davies, 'Some personal recollections of Brahms as pianist and interpreter', in *Cobbett's Cyclopedic Survey of Chamber Music* (London, 1929), p. 184.

75 Paul Rolland, in Max Rostal, *Beethoven: the Sonatas for Piano and Violin* (London, 1985), p. 212. This trend is also confirmed by Walter Blume (*Brahms in der Meininger Tradition* (Stuttgart, 1933), pp. 5–6) and later by Max Rudolf (*The Grammar of Conducting* (New York, 2/1980), p. 359).

76 Cited in Bernard D. Sherman, 'Tempo and proportions in Brahms: period evidence', *Early Music* 25 (1997), p. 469. See also 'George Henschel', *Musical Times* 41 (1900), p. 158.

77 See David Epstein, 'Brahms and the mechanisms of motion: the composition of performance', in G. Bozarth (ed.), *Brahms Studies* (Oxford, 1990), pp. 191–226; B. Jacobson, *The Music of Johannes Brahms* (London, 1977), pp. 51–2 (re Brahms's Second Piano Concerto). Allen Forte and Werner Schulze have also proposed proportional tempos in a few specific works by Brahms. See Allen Forte, 'The structural origin of exact tempi in the Brahms-Haydn Variations', *Music Review* 18 (1957), pp. 138–49.

78 Davies, 'Some personal recollections', p. 184.

79 Some editions give Allegro appassionato.

80 For example, Adolph Kullak, *The Aesthetics of Pianoforte-Playing* (Berlin, 1861, Eng. trans. New York, 1893/rev., 1972, pp. 280–94; Mathis Lussy, *Traité de l'expression musicale* (Paris, 1874, Eng. trans. London, 1885), pp. 162–96; Adolph Christiani, *The Principles of Expression in Pianoforte Playing* (New York, 1885/rev., 1974), pp. 264–96.

81 Davies, 'Some personal recollections', p. 184.

82 See Musgrave (ed.), *The Cambridge Companion to Brahms*, p. 265.

83 *Ibid.*, p. 266.

84 George Henschel, *Musings and Memories of a Musician*, (London, 1918), p. 314.

85 Joachim and Moser, *Violinschule*, Eng. trans., III, p. 17.

86 J. Levin in *Die Musik* (1926), cited in Joseph Szigeti, *Szigeti on the Violin* (London, 1969), p. 176.

87 See Clive Brown's analysis in his *Classical and Romantic Performing Practice 1750–1900*, pp. 449–54.

88 Davies, 'Some personal recollections', p. 182.

89 Florence May, *The Life of Brahms*, 2nd edn (2 vols., London, 1948), I, p. 19.

90 Jon Finson, 'Performing practice in the late nineteenth century, with special reference to the music of Brahms', *Musical Quarterly* 70 (1984), p. 473.

91 Davies, 'Some personal recollections', p. 182.

92 See Paul Mies, 'Über ein besonderes Akzentzeichen bei Johannes Brahms', in Reichert, Georg, and Just, Martin (eds.), *Bericht über den internationalen musikwissenschaftlichen Kongress Kassel 1962* (Kassel, 1963), pp. 215–17.

93 Imogen Fellinger, *Über die Dynamik in der Musik von Johannes Brahms* (Berlin, 1961); in Robert Pascall, *Playing Brahms: a Study in 19th-century Performance Practice* (Nottingham, 1991), p. 10.

94 Joachim and Moser, *Violinschule*, Eng. trans., II, p. 92.

95 *Ibid.*, II, pp. 92, 95.

96 *Ibid.*, p. 96.

97 Grove I (1879–89).

8 Related family members

1 See Michael Praetorius, *Syntagma Musicum*, II: *De Organographia*, p. 48; Julius von Schlosser, *Die Sammlung alter Musikinstrumente* (Vienna, 1920), p. 12.

2 L. Mozart, *A Treatise*, p. 10. However, Leopold Mozart acknowledges the value of the *violino piccolo* in the teaching of very small children.

3 See Banks, 'The violino piccolo and other small violins', p. 589.

4 As proved by Nicholas Bessaraboff, *Ancient European Musical Instruments* (Boston, Mass., 1941), p. 301 and Appendix A, 'Scaling of Praetorius' drawings', pp. 353–6.

5 A small boat-shaped violin tuned an octave above the ordinary violin, as proposed by Julius Ruhlmann (*Zur Geschichte der Bogeninstrumente* (Brunswick, 1882), p. 65) and Boyden (*The History*, pp. 118–19). See also David Boyden, 'Monteverdi's *violini piccoli alla francese* and *viole da brazzo*', *Annales Musicologiques* 6 (1958–63), pp. 387–401.

6 As proposed by Curt Sachs in his *The History of Musical Instruments* (New York, 1940), p. 358.

7 Andreas Moser 'Der Violino piccolo', *Zeitschrift für Musikwissenschaft* (1919), pp. 377–80; Bessaraboff, *Ancient European Musical Instruments*, pp. 299–300.

8 The instrument is also sometimes used as a substitute for the transverse flute in Cantata 102.

9 As recommended by Hans Gerle (*Musica teusch* (Nuremberg, 1532, rev. 3/1546/R1977)) and in most of Agricola's prescribed tunings: discant g–d¹–a¹, alto and tenor c–g–d¹, bass F–G–d–a (in *Musica instrumentalis deudsch*, Wittenberg, 1529/R1969, enlarged 5/1545).

10 Sebastian Virdung, *Musica getutscht* (Basle, 1511/R1970); Agricola, *Musica instrumentalis deudsch* (Wittenberg, 1529/R1969); Praetorius, *Syntagma Musicum*, II.

11 See Emanuel Winternitz, *Die Musik in Geschichte und Gegenwart*, art. 'Lira da braccio'.

12 The tromba marina was a bowed monochord. It comprised a tapering three-sided body and was in use from the fifteenth until the mid eighteenth century (see Fig. 3.1.7).

13 This could also mean viol or violin, but most commonly denoted the viola in the seventeenth and eighteenth centuries.

14 See Daniel Speer, *Grundrichtiger . . . Unterricht der musicalischen Kunst* (Ulm, 1687); Daniel Merck, *Compendium musicae instrumentalis chelicae* (Augsburg, 1688); Joseph Majer, *Museum musicum* (Schwäbisch Hall, 1732); and L. Mozart, *A Treatise*.

15 Francis W. Galpin, 'Viola pomposa and Violoncello piccolo', *Music and Letters* 12 (1931), pp. 354–64. See also H. Husmann, 'Die Viola pomposa', *Bach-Jahrbuch* 33 (1936), pp. 90–100.

16 See H. Ritter, *Die Geschichte der Viola alta und die Grundsätze ihres Baues* (Leipzig, 1877/RWiesbaden, 1969); G. Adema, *Hermann Ritter und seine Viola alta* (Würzburg, 1881, 2/1890).

17 Berlioz-Strauss, *Instrumentationslehre*, Eng. trans., p. 74. Otto Sand made his 'E-viola' (1961) and H. Hanson his *violino grande* (1963–6) with the similar aim of expanding the sonority and range of the viola by adding a fifth string.

18 See Eduard Hanslick, *Concerte, Componisten und Virtuosen der letzten fünfzehn Jahre: 1870–1885* (Berlin, 1886), trans. and ed. H. Pleasants (New York, 1950), p. 272.

19 Berlioz-Strauss, *Instrumentationslehre*, Eng. trans., p. 74.

20 Sympathetic strings were first mentioned in Joseph Majer's *Museum musicum* (1732). The earlier, shallower seventeenth-century models, for example, were generally equipped with metal playing strings but no sympathetic strings.

Leopold Mozart (*A Treatise*, p. 12) describes a viola d'amore 'with six gut strings of which the lower ones are covered' and six steel sympathetic strings.

21 For more detail about the history and repertory of the viola d'amore, see Harry Danks, *The Viola d'amore* (Halesowen, 1976, rev. 2/1979); Myron Rosenblum's article in Sadie (ed.), *New Grove Dictionary*, vol. XIX, pp. 814–18; and W. Schrammek, 'Die Viola d'amore zur Zeit J. S. Bach', in *Bach-Studien* 9 (Leipzig, 1986), pp. 55–66.

22 L. Mozart, *A Treatise*, p. 12.

Select bibliography

Pre-1900

Abbé le fils, L', *Principes du violon pour apprendre le doigté de cet instrument, et les différens agrémens dont il est susceptible* (Paris, 1761, 1772/R1976)

Agricola, Johann Friedrich, *Anleitung zur Singkunst* (Berlin, 1757)

Agricola, Martin, *Musica instrumentalis deudsch* (Wittemberg, 1529/R1969; Eng. trans. William Herrick, Cambridge, 1994)

Bach, Carl Philipp Emanuel, *Versuch über die wahre Art das Clavier zu spielen*, vol. I (Berlin, 1753, rev. 2nd edn, 1787), vol. II (Berlin, 1762, rev. 2nd edn, 1797); Eng. trans. and ed. William J. Mitchell as *Essay on the True Art of Playing Keyboard Instruments* (New York, 1949)

Baillot, Pierre Marie François de Sales, *L'art du violon: nouvelle méthode* (Paris, 1835; Eng. trans. Louise Goldberg, Illinois, 1991)

Baillot, Pierre Marie François de Sales, Rode, Pierre, and Kreutzer, Rodolphe, *Méthode de violon* (Paris, 1803/R1974)

Bériot, Charles Auguste de, *Méthode de violon* Op. 102 (Paris, [1858]; Eng. trans. Westbrook and Phipson, London, 1876)

Berlioz, L. Hector, *Grand traité d'instrumentation et d'orchestration modernes* Op. 10 (Paris, 1843; Eng. trans. Mary C. Clarke, London, 1858)

Brossard, Sébastien de, *Dictionnaire de musique* (Paris, 1703/R1964)
  Fragments d'une méthode de violon, MS in the Bibliothèque Nationale, Paris, c.1712

Bruni, Antonio Bartolomeo, *Méthode pour l'alto-viola* (Paris, c.1820)

Burney, Charles, *A General History of Music from the Earliest Ages to the Present Period* (4 vols., London, 1776–89; ed. F. Mercer, London, 1935)

Campagnoli, Bartolomeo, *Metodo della mecanica progressive per violino* (?Milan, 1797?; Eng. trans. John Bishop (London, 1856)

Cartier, Jean Baptiste, *L'art du violon* (Paris, 1798, enlarged 3/c.1803/R1973)

Corrette, Michel, *L'école d'Orphée: méthode pour apprendre facilement à jouer du violon dans le goût françois et italien. L'art de se perfectionner dans le violon* (Paris, 1738 and 1782/R1972)

213

Méthodes pour apprendre à jouer de la contre-basse à 3, à 4, et à 5 cordes, de la quinte ou alto et de la viole d'Orphée . . . avec des leçons et des sonates pour ces trois instruments (Paris, 1773/R1977)

Cupis, François, *Méthode d'alto* (Paris, 1803)

Czerny, Carl, *Vollständige theoretisch-practische Pianoforte-Schule* Op. 500 (Vienna, 1839; Eng. trans. London, [1839]; chs. 2 and 4 of vol. IV ed. P. Badura-Skoda, Vienna, 1963, Eng. trans. Vienna, 1970)

David, Ferdinand, *Violinschule* (Leipzig, 1863)

Fétis, François-Joseph, *Biographie universelle des musiciens et bibliographie générale de la musique* (8 vols., Paris, 1835–44, 2/1860–5/R1963)

   Antoine Stradivari, luthier célèbre (Paris, 1856; Eng. trans. John Bishop, London, 1864/R1964)

Galeazzi, Francesco, *Elementi teorico-pratici di musica, con un saggio sopra l'arte di suonare il violino annalizzata, ed a dimostrabili principi ridotta. . . .* (2 vols., Rome, 1791–6)

Gebauer, Michel Joseph, *Méthode d'alto* (Paris, c.1800)

Geminiani, Francesco, *Rules for playing in a true taste* (London, 1748)

   A Treatise of Good Taste in the Art of Musick (London, 1749/R1969)

   The Art of Playing on the Violin (London, 1751/R[1952])

Gerle, Hans, *Musica teusch* (Nuremberg, 1532, rev. 3/1546/R1977)

Guhr, Carl, *Ueber Paganinis Kunst die Violine zu spielen* (Mainz, [1829])

Habeneck, François, *Méthode théorique et pratique de violon* (Paris, c.1835)

Hawkins, Sir John, *A General History of the Science and Practice of Music* (5 vols., London, 1776)

Heinichen, Johann David, *Der General-Bass in der Composition* (Dresden, 1728)

Herrando, J., *Arte y puntual explicación del modo de tocar el violin* (Paris, 1756)

Hiller, Johann Adam, *Anweisung zum Violinspielen* (Leipzig, 1792)

Hummel, Johann Nepomuk, *Ausführlich theoretisch-practische Anweisung zum Piano-Forte Spiel*, 3 vols. (Vienna, 1828/R1929; Anon. Eng. trans. as *A Complete Theoretical and Practical Course of Instructions on the Art of Playing the Pianoforte*, London, [1828])

Jambe de Fer, Philibert, *Epitome musical* (Lyons, 1556), repr. in F. Lesure (1958–63)

Kirnberger, Johann Philipp, *Die Kunst des reinen Satzes in der Musik*, I (Berlin and Königsberg, 1771/R1968), II (Berlin and Königsberg, 1776–9/R1968); Eng. trans. David Beach and Jurgen Thym as *The Art of Strict Musical Composition* (New Haven and London, 1982)

Kreutzer, Rodolphe, *see* Baillot, Pierre Marie François de Sales

Löhlein, Georg Simon, *Anweisung zum Violinspielen* (Leipzig and Züllichau, 1774)

Lussy, Matthis, *Le Rhythme musical, son origine, sa fonction et son accentuation* (Paris, 1883)

Traité de l'expression musicale: Accents, nuances et mouvements dans la musique vocale et instrumentale (Paris, 1874; Eng. trans. M. E. von Glehn, London, 1885)

Mace, Thomas, *Musick's Monument* (London, 1676/R1977)

Marpurg, Friedrich Wilhelm, *Anleitung zum Clavierspielen* (Berlin, 1755)

Martinn, Jacob J. B., *Nouvelle méthode d'alto* (Paris, c.1830)

Mattheson, Johann, *Der vollkommene Capellmeister* (Hamburg, 1739/R1954; Eng. trans. and ed. Ernest C. Harriss, Ann Arbor, 1981)

Mazas, Jacques-Féréol, *Méthode de violon* (Paris, 1830)

Mersenne, Marin, *Harmonie Universelle* (3 vols., Paris, 1636–7/R1963)

Milchmeyer, J. P., *Die wahre Art das Pianoforte zu spielen* (Dresden, 1797)

Montéclair, Michel, *Méthode facile pour aprende [sic] à jouer du violon* (Paris, [1711–12])

Mozart, Leopold, *Versuch einer gründlichen Violinschule* (Augsburg, 1756/R1976; 3rd edn, Augsburg, 1787; Eng. trans. Editha Knocker as *A Treatise on the Fundamental Principles of Violin Playing*, London, 1948, 2/1951)

Muffat, Georg, *Florilegium Secundum* (Passau, 1698)

Praetorius, Michael, *Syntagma Musicum*, vol. I (Wittenberg and Wolfenbüttel, 1614–15/R1959, 1968); vol. II (Wolfenbüttel, 1618; 2nd edn, 1619/R1958, 1980; Eng. trans. 1962, 1986); vol. III (Wolfenbüttel, 1618; 2nd edn, 1619/R1958, 1976)

Prelleur, Peter, *The Art of Playing on the Violin* (London, 1731)

Quantz, Johann Joachim, *Versuch einer Anweisung die Flöte traversiere zu spielen* (Berlin, 1752; 3rd edn, 1789/R1952; Eng. trans. Edward R. Reilly as *On Playing the Flute*, London and New York, 1966)

Reichardt, Johann Friedrich, *Ueber die Pflichten des Ripien-Violinisten* (Berlin and Leipzig, 1776)

Ries, Ferdinand, *see* Wegeler, Franz Gerhardt

Ritter, Hermann, *Die Geschichte der Viola alta und die Grundsätze ihres Baues* (Leipzig, 1876, 2/1877/R1969, 3/1885)

Rode, Pierre, *see* Baillot, Pierre Marie François de Sales

Rousseau, Jean-Jacques, *Dictionnaire de musique* (Paris, 1768/R1969), Eng. trans. W. Waring (London, 1779/R1975)

Schindler, Anton Felix, *Biographie von Ludwig Beethoven* (Münster, 1840; rev. 3rd edn, Münster, 1860; Eng. trans. Constance Jolly as *Beethoven as I Knew Him*, ed. Donald MacArdle, London, 1966)

Schröder, Hermann, *Die Kunst des Violinspiels* (Cologne, 1887)

Spohr, Louis, *Violinschule* (Vienna, 1832/R1960; Eng. trans. C. Rudolphus, London, [1833]; Eng. trans. Florence Marshall, London, 1843)

Sulzer, Johann Georg (ed.), *Allgemeine Theorie der schönen Künste*, (4 vols., Leipzig, 1771–4)

Tartini, Giuseppe, *Traité des agréments de la musique*, (Paris, 1771; Eng. trans. Cuthbert Girdlestone ed. Erwin R. Jacobi, Celle and New York, 1961)

Tosi, Pier Francesco, *Opinioni de' cantori antici e moderni, o sieno osservazioni sopra il canto figurato* (Bologna, 1723; Eng. trans. and ed. J. E. Galliard as *Observations on the Florid Song*, London, 1742; Eng. trans. and ed. M. Pilkington (London, 1987)

Türk, Daniel Gottlob, *Clavierschule, oder Anweisung zum Clavierspielen* (Leipzig and Halle, 1789, enlarged 2/1802/R1967; Eng. trans. Raymond Haggh as *School of Clavier Playing*, Lincoln, Nebraska, 1982)

Virdung, Sebastian, *Musica getutscht* (Basle, 1511/R1970)

Wagner, Richard, *Über das Dirigieren* (Leipzig, 1869; Eng. trans., 1887/R1976)

Walther, Johann Gottfried, *Musicalisches Lexicon* (Leipzig, 1732/R1953)

Wegeler, Franz Gerhardt, and Ries, Ferdinand, *Biographische Notizen über Ludwig van Beethoven* (Koblenz, 1838)

Woldemar, Michel, *Grande méthode ou étude élémentaire pour le violon* (Paris *c*.1800) *Méthode d'alto* (Paris, *c*.1800)

Post-1900

Abbot, Djilda and Segerman, Ephraim, 'Gut strings', *Early Music* 4 (1976), pp. 430–7

Almond, C., 'The developing violin', *Early Music* 7 (1979), pp. 155–65

Apel, Willi (ed.), Thomas Binkley, *Italian Violin Music of the Seventeenth Century* (Bloomington and Indianapolis, 1990)

Arnold, Frank T., *The Art of Accompaniment from a Thorough-Bass as Practised in the Seventeenth and Eighteenth Centuries* (London, 1931/R1965)

Bachmann, Alberto, *An Encyclopedia of the Violin* (New York, 1925/R1966)

Banks, Margaret Downie, 'The violino piccolo and other small violins', *Early Music* 18 (1990), pp. 588–96

Barbieri, Patrizio, 'Violin intonation: a historical survey', *Early Music* 19 (1991), pp. 69–88

Barbour, J. Murray, 'Violin intonation in the eighteenth century', *Journal of the American Musicological Society* 5 (1952), pp. 224–34

Barnett, Dene, 'Non-uniform slurring in 18th-century music: accident or design?', *Haydn Yearbook* 10 (1978), pp. 179–99

Bessaraboff, Nicholas, *Ancient European Musical Instruments* (Boston, Mass., 1941)

Boomkamp, Carel van Leeuwen, and Meer, John Henry van der, *The Carel van Leeuwen Boomkamp Collection of Musical Instruments* (Amsterdam, 1971)

Borgir, Tharald, *The Performance of the Basso Continuo in Italian Baroque Music* (Ann Arbor, Michigan, 1987)

Boyden, David D., 'The violin and its technique in the eighteenth century', *Musical Quarterly* 36 (1950), pp. 9–38

'Prelleur, Geminiani and just intonation', *Journal of the American Musicological Society* 4 (1951), pp. 202–19

'Dynamics in seventeenth- and eighteenth-century music', *Essays on Music in Honor of Archibald Thompson Davison by His Associates* (Cambridge Mass., 1957), pp. 185–93

'Geminiani and the first violin tutor', *Acta Musicologica* 31 (1959), pp. 161–70

'Monteverdi's *violini piccoli alla francese* and *viole da brazzo*', *Annales Musicologiques* 6 (1959), pp. 387–401

'A postscript to "Geminiani and the first violin tutor"', *Acta Musicologica* 32 (1960), pp. 40–7

'The missing Italian manuscript of Tartini's Traité des agrémens', *Musical Quarterly* 46 (1960), pp. 315–28

The History of Violin Playing from its Origins to 1761 (Oxford, 1965)

Catalogue of the Hill Collection of Musical Instruments in the Ashmolean Museum, Oxford (London, 1969)

'Corelli's violin solos graced by Dubourg', in N. Schiørring and H. Glann (eds.), *Festskrift Jens Peter Larsen* (Copenhagen, 1972), pp. 113–25

'The violin bow in the eighteenth century', *Early Music* 8 (1980), pp. 199–212

Brown, Clive, 'Bowing styles, vibrato and portamento in nineteenth-century violin playing', *Journal of the Royal Musical Association* 113 (1988), pp. 97–128

'Ferdinand David's editions of Beethoven', in Robin Stowell (ed.), *Performing Beethoven*, pp. 117–49

Classical and Romantic Performing Practice 1750–1900 (Oxford, 1999)

Brown, Howard Mayer, and Sadie, Stanley (eds.), *Performance Practice: Music after 1600* (2 vols., London, 1989)

Buelow, George J., *Thorough-Bass Accompaniment According to Johann David Heinichen* (Berkeley and Los Angeles, 1966)

'The "loci topici" and affect in late baroque music: Heinichen's practical demonstration', *Music Review* 27 (1966), pp. 161–76

Chesnut, John H., 'Mozart's teaching of intonation', *Journal of the American Musicological Society* 30 (1977), pp. 254–71

Collins, Michael, 'The performance of triplets in the 17th and 18th centuries', *Journal of the American Musicological Society* 19 (1966), pp. 281–328

Cooper, Kenneth, and Zsako, Julius, 'Georg Muffat's Observations on the Lully style of performance', *Musical Quarterly* 53 (1967), pp. 220–45

Coover, James, *Musical Instrument Collections: Catalogues and Cognate Literature* (Detroit, 1981)

Cyr, Mary, 'Violin playing in late seventeenth-century England: Baltzar, Matteis, and Purcell', *Performance Practice Review* 8 (1995), pp. 54–66

Dart, R. Thurston, *The Interpretation of Music* (London, 1954)

Dolmetsch, Arnold, *The Interpretation of the Music of the Seventeenth and Eighteenth Centuries* (London, 1915; 2nd edn, London 1946/R1969)

Donington, Robert, *The Interpretation of Early Music* (London, 1963; 3rd rev. edn, London, 1974)

   String Playing in Baroque Music (London, 1977)

   Baroque Music: Style and Performance (London, 1982)

Drabkin, William, 'Fingering in Haydn's string quartets', *Early Music* 16 (1988), pp. 50–7

Dreyfus, Laurence, 'Early music defended against its devotees: a theory of historical performance in the twentieth century', *Musical Quarterly* 49 (1983), pp. 297–322

Erfrati, Richard R., *Treatise on the Execution and Interpretation of the Sonatas and Partitas for Solo Violin and the Suites for Solo Cello by Johann Sebastian Bach* (Zurich, 1979)

Finson, Jon W., 'Performing practice in the late nineteenth century, with special reference to the music of Brahms' *Musical Quarterly* 70 (1984), pp. 457–75

Flesch, Carl, *Die Kunst des Violinspiels*, I (Berlin, 1923, 2/1929; Eng. trans. Frederick H. Martens, as *The Art of Violin Playing*, London, 1924); II (Berlin, 1928; Eng. trans., London, 1930)

Forbes, Elliott (ed.), *Thayer's Life of Beethoven* (2 vols., Princeton, 1964)

Fuller, David, 'Dotting, the "French Style" and Frederick Neumann's Counter-Reformation', *Early Music* 5 (1977), pp. 517–43

Gill, Dominic (ed.), *The Book of the Violin* (Oxford, 1984)

Harnoncourt, Nikolaus, *Baroque Music Today; Music as Speech* (London, 1988)

Harris-Warrick, Rebecca, 'The tempo of French baroque dances: evidence from 18th-century metronome devices', *Proceedings of the 1982 Meeting of the Dance History Scholars* (Cambridge, Mass., 1982), pp. 18–27

Haskell, Harry, *The Early Music Revival: a History* (London, 1988)

Hauck, Werner, *Das Vibrato auf der Violine* (Cologne, 1971), Eng. trans., Kitty Rokos as *Vibrato on the Violin* (London, 1975)

Haynes, Bruce, 'Beyond temperament: non-keyboard intonation in the 17th and 18th centuries', *Early Music* 19 (1991), pp. 356–81

Hefling, Stephen E., *Rhythmic Alteration in Seventeenth- and Eighteenth-Century Music* (New York, 1993)

Heron-Allen, Edward, *Violin Making as it Was and Is* (London, 1884, 2/1885/R1984) *De Fidiculis Bibliographia* (2 vols., London, 1890–4)

Hickman, Roger, 'The Censored publications of *The Art of Playing on the Violin* or Geminiani Unshaken', *Early Music* 11 (1983), pp. 71–6

Hill, W. Henry, Alfred E. and Arthur F., *Antonio Stradivari: his Life and Work* (London, 1902; 2nd edn, 1909/R1963)

Hogwood, Christopher, *see* Schröder, Jaap

Holloway, John, 'Corelli's Op.5: text, act . . . and reaction', *Early Music* 24 (1996), pp. 635–43

Holman, Peter, *Four and Twenty Fiddlers; the Violin at the English Court 1540–1690* (Oxford, 1993)

Houle, George, *Meter in Music 1600–1800* (Bloomington and Indianapolis, 1987)

Hudson, Richard, *Stolen Time. The History of Tempo Rubato* (Oxford, 1994)

Jenne, Natalie, *see* Little, Meredith

Joachim, Joseph, and Moser, Andreas, *Violinschule* (3 vols., Berlin, 1902–5; Eng. trans. Alfred Moffat, London, 1905)

Johnstone, Harry Diacke, 'Yet more ornaments for Corelli's violin sonatas, Op. 5', *Early Music* 24 (1996), pp. 623–33

Keller, Hermann, *Phrasing and Articulation* (London, 1965)

Kenyon, Nicholas (ed.), *Authenticity and Early Music* (Oxford, 1988)

Kerman, Joseph, *Musicology* (London, 1985)

Kirkpatrick, Ralph, 'Eighteenth-century metronomic indications', *Papers of the American Musicological Society* (1938), pp. 30–50

Kivy, Peter, *Authenticities* (Ithaca and London, 1995)

Kolneder, Walter, *Georg Muffat zur Aufführungspraxis* (Strasbourg, 1970) *Das Buch der Violine* (Zurich, 1972, 3/1984; Eng. trans. and ed. Reinhard G. Pauly as *The Amadeus Book of the Violin*, Portland, Oregon, 1998)

Kullak, Franz, *Beethoven's Piano Playing: with an Essay on the Execution of the Trill*, Eng. trans., Theodore Baker (New York, 1901)

Laurencie, Lionel de la, *L'école française de violon de Lully à Viotti* (3 vols., Paris, 1922–4/R1971)

Lawson, Colin, and Stowell, Robin, *The Historical Performance of Music: An Introduction* (Cambridge, 1999)

Lee, Douglas, 'Some embellished versions of sonatas by Franz Benda, *Musical Quarterly* 62 (1976), pp. 58–71

le Huray, Peter G., *Authenticity in Performance: Eighteenth-Century Case Studies* (Cambridge, 1990)

Lesure, François, 'L'*Epitome musical* de Philibert Jambe de Fer (1556)', *Annales Musicologiques* 6 (1958–63), pp. 341–86

Little, Meredith, and Jenne, Natalie, *Dance and the Music of J. S. Bach* (Indiana, 1991)

Marty, Jean-Pierre, *The Tempo Indications of Mozart* (New Haven and London, 1988)

Marx, Hans-Joachim, 'Some unknown embellishments of Corelli's violin sonatas', *Musical Quarterly* 61 (1975), pp. 65–76

Mendel, Arthur, 'Pitch in Western music since 1500, a re-examination', *Acta Musicologica* 1 (1978), pp. 1–93

Menuhin, Yehudi, and Primrose, William, *Violin and Viola* (London, 1976)

Moens-Haenen, Greta, *Das Vibrato in der Musik des Barock* (Graz, 1988)

Monosoff, Sonya, 'Violin fingering', *Early Music* 13 (1985), pp. 76–9

Moser, Andreas, 'Der Violino piccolo', *Zeitschrift für Musikwissenschaft* 1 (1919), pp. 377–80

   Geschichte des Violinspiels (2 vols., Berlin, 1923; 2nd rev. edn, Tutzing, 1966–7)

   see also Joachim, Joseph

Neumann, Frederick, 'The use of Baroque treatises on musical performance', *Music and Letters* 48 (1967), pp. 315–24

   'The dotted note and the so-called French style', *Early Music* 5 (1977), pp. 310–24

   Ornamentation in Baroque and Post-Baroque Music, with Special Emphasis on J. S. Bach (Princeton, 1978)

   Essays in Performance Practice (Ann Arbor, 1982)

   Ornamentation and Improvisation in Mozart (Princeton, 1986)

   New Essays on Performance Practice (Ann Arbor, 1989)

   'The vibrato controversy', *Performance Practice Review* 4 (1991), pp. 14–27

   'Dots and strokes in Mozart', *Early Music* 21 (1993), pp. 429–35

   Performance Practices of the Seventeenth and Eighteenth Centuries (New York, 1993)

   'Some performance problems of Bach's unaccompanied violin and cello works', in M. A. Parker (ed.), *Eighteenth-Century Music in Theory and Practice. Essays in Honor of Alfred Mann* (New York, 1994), pp. 19–48

Newman, William S., 'Beethoven's pianos versus his piano ideals', *Journal of the American Musicological Society* 23/3 (1970), pp. 484–504

   Performance Practices in Beethoven's Sonatas: an Introduction (New York, 1971)

   Beethoven on Beethoven: Playing his Piano Music his Way (New York, 1988)

Philip, Robert, *Early Recordings and Musical Style: Changing Tastes in Instrumental Performance 1900–1950* (Cambridge, 1992)

Pincherle, Marc, 'On the rights of the interpreter in the performance of seventeenth-
    and eighteenth-century music', *Musical Quarterly* 44 (1958), pp. 145–66
Primrose, William, see Menuhin, Yehudi
Pulver, Jeffrey, 'Violin methods old and new', *Proceedings of the Royal Musical
    Association* 50 (1923–4), pp. 101–27
Regazzi, Roberto, *The Complete Luthier's Library*, rev. Jane H. Johnson (Bologna, 1990)
Reilly, Edward R., 'Quantz on national styles in music', *Musical Quarterly* 49 (1963),
    pp. 163–87
Retford, William C., *Bows and Bow Makers* (London, 1964)
Riley, Maurice W., *The History of the Viola* (2 vols., I, Ypsilanti, Michigan, 1980; II,
    Ann Arbor, Michigan, 1983)
Robison, John, 'The *messa di voce* as an instrumental ornament in the seventeenth
    and eighteenth centuries', *Music Review* 43 (1982), pp. 1–14
Roda, Joseph, *Bows for Musical Instruments of the Violin Family* (Chicago, 1959)
Rosenblum, Sandra, *Performance Practices in Classic Piano Music: their Principles
    and Applications* (Bloomington and Indianapolis, 1988)
Rothschild, Fritz, *The Lost Tradition: Musical Performance in the Time of Mozart and
    Beethoven* (London, 1961)
Russell, Theodore, 'The violin scordatura', *Musical Quarterly* 24 (1938), pp. 84–96
Sadie, Stanley (ed.), *The New Grove Dictionary of Music and Musicians* (20 vols.
    London, 1980)
    see also Brown, Howard Mayer, and Sadie, Stanley (eds.)
Schröder, Jaap, and Hogwood, Christopher, 'The developing violin', *Early Music* 7
    (1979), pp. 155–65
Schwarz, Boris, 'Beethoven and the French violin school', *Musical Quarterly* 44
    (1958), pp. 431–47
    Great Masters of the Violin (London, 1984)
Segerman, Ephraim, 'Strings through the ages', *The Strad* 99 (1988), pp. 52–5,
    195–201, 295–9
    see also Abbott, Djilda
Seletsky, Robert, '18th-century variations for Corelli's Sonatas, Op. 5', *Early Music*
    24 (1996), pp. 119–31
Sherman, Bernard D., 'Tempo and proportions in Brahms: period evidence', *Early
    Music* 25 (1997), pp. 463–77
    (ed.), *Inside Early Music: Conversations with Performers* (Oxford, 1997)
Smiles, Joan E., 'Directions for improvised ornamentation in Italian method books
    of the late eighteenth century', *Journal of the American Musicological Society* 31
    (1978), pp. 459–509

Steblin, Rita, *A History of Key Characteristics in the Eighteenth and Early Nineteenth Centuries* (Ann Arbor, 1983)

Stowell, Robin, *Violin Technique and Performance Practice in the Late Eighteenth and Early Nineteenth Centuries* (Cambridge, 1985)

  'Building a library: Bach's violin sonatas and partitas', *Musical Times* 128 (1987), pp. 250–6

  see also Lawson, Colin

  (ed.), *The Cambridge Companion to the Violin* (Cambridge, 1992)

  Performing Beethoven (Cambridge, 1994)

Straeten, Edmund S. J. van der, *The Romance of the Fiddle* (London, 1911)

  The History of the Violin (2 vols., London, 1933/R New York, 1968)

Strunk, Oliver, *Source Readings in Music History* (New York, 1950/R1965)

Taruskin, Richard, *Text and Act* (Oxford, 1995)

The New Grove Violin Family (London, 1989)

Toskey, Burnett R., *Concertos for Violin and Viola: a Comprehensive Encyclopedia* (Seattle, 1983)

Vannes, René, *Dictionnaire universel des luthiers* (2nd edn, 2 vols., Brussels, 1951–9/R1972)

Vatelot, Etienne, *Les archets français* (Nancy, 1976)

Vidal, Louis Antoine, *Les instruments à archet, les faiseurs, les joueurs d'instruments, leur histoire* (Paris, 1876–8/R1961)

Violinspiel und Violinmusik in Geschichte und Gegenwart: Internationaler Kongress am Institut für Aufführungspraxis der Hochschule für Musik und darstellende Kunst: Graz 1972 (Vienna, 1975)

Walls, Peter, 'Violin fingering in the 18th century', *Early Music* 12 (1984), pp. 300–15

  '"Ill-compliments and arbitrary taste"? Geminiani's directions for performers', *Early Music* 14 (1986), pp. 221–35

  '"Mozart and the violin", performing Mozart's music II', *Early Music* 20 (1992), pp. 7–29

  'Performing Corelli's Violin Sonatas, Op.5', *Early Music* 24 (1996), pp. 133–42

Wasielewski, Wilhelm Joseph von, *Die Violine und ihre Meister* (8th edn, Leipzig, 1927)

Watkin, David, 'Corelli's Op. 5 sonatas: "violino e violone O cimbalo"?', *Early Music* 24 (1996), pp. 645–63

Webster, James, 'The significance of Haydn's String Quartet Autographs for performance practice', in *Isham Library Papers III* (Harvard, 1980), pp. 62–98

Wessel, F. T., 'The Affektenlehre in the eighteenth century', (Ph.D. diss., Indiana University, 1955)

Whitmore, Philip, *Unpremeditated Art – The Cadenza in the Classical Keyboard Concerto* (Oxford, 1991)

Williams, Michael D., *Music for Viola* (Detroit, 1979)

Williams, Peter, *Figured Bass Accompaniment* (2 vols., Edinburgh, 1970)

Wilson, John (ed.), *Roger North on Music* (London, 1959)

Winter, Robert, 'Second thoughts on the performance of Beethoven's trills', *Musical Quarterly* 63 (1977), pp. 483–504

Winternitz, Emanuel, *Gaudenzio Ferrari, his School and the Early History of the Violin* (Milan, 1967)

'Early violins in paintings by Gaudenzio Ferrari and his school', in *Musical Instruments and their Symbolism in Western Art* (London, 1967), pp. 99–109

Zaslaw, Neal, 'Mozart's tempo conventions', in H. Glahn, S. Sørensen, P. Ryan (eds.), *International Musicological Society: Report of the Eleventh Congress, Copenhagen 1972* (Copenhagen, 1974), II, pp. 720–33

'The Italian Violin School in the 17th century', *Early Music* 18 (1990), pp. 515–18

'Ornaments for Corelli's Violin Sonatas, Op. 5', *Early Music* 24 (1996), pp. 95–115

Zeyringer, Franz, *Literatur für Viola* (Hartberg, 1985)

Zsako, Julius, *see* Cooper, Kenneth

Index

224